A PLACE WE USED TO CALL HOME

Shiraz Nomad

UK BookPublishing.com

Editing, design, typesetting and publishing by UK Book Publishing

www.ukbookpublishing.com

ISBN: 978-1-918077-20-9

A PLACE WE USED TO CALL HOME

DEDICATION

To Faraj – For your courage, your friendship, and the brotherhood we forged in silence and struggle.

Some bonds survive every border.

* * *

FOREWORD

For the last thirty years, I have carried this book inside me. So many times I have tried to sit down and write it – tried to remember what had happened, to put it into words. But the memories were not kind. Some were buried too deep, and others returned like open wounds. Often, I would get a few lines down and then stop, unable to go further. There were moments I told myself it was better to forget. And for a long time, I tried. But forgetting doesn't erase anything. The memories still came – late at night, while walking, sometimes in the middle of work – uninvited, sharp, and unresolved.

For years, I asked my daughters to help. I gave them fragments, pieces of the past, and asked them to write what I could not. But it wasn't easy for them. These were not just stories – they were wounds passed down. Sometimes I saw the pain in their faces as they listened. Sometimes we cried together. And after each telling, the memories would follow me for days, refusing to leave me in peace.

Eventually, I realised the only way to find peace was to tell the whole truth. To finish what I had started – not just for myself, but for my daughters, and for anyone who needs to understand what power in the wrong hands can do. What people are capable of when they wrap cruelty in the name of faith.

There is one memory that would never let go of me.

She was a young girl. A prisoner. A virgin. And in the twisted beliefs of those who held her, that was a problem. They said that if a virgin was executed, she would go to paradise. So, they made sure she wouldn't. The night before her execution, they raped her. Not in secrecy, but as part of an unholy system – where even so-called men of God were ordered to participate. The next morning, she was hanged. They wanted to kill her body, but they also wanted to kill her soul. To take away even the hope of peace in the afterlife. That was the logic of the regime: not just to silence you, but to erase your humanity altogether.

This book is filled with stories like hers – stories that are hard to read because they were harder to live. But I write them now because they must be known. I write them because silence protects the powerful, not the innocent. I write so that the world cannot say: we didn't know.

And so, I begin – at the beginning, where my childhood ended and my fight to survive began.

TABLE
OF CONTENTS

CHAPTER I

GRANDMA'S HOUSE

I t was New Year's Day when I was born into a middle-class family, in the small city of Sarvestan in Southern Iran, the 'Fars' province to be precise. My mother was only 16 years old when I was delivered at my grandma's house. It was a two-floor house and I remember its distinct ten rooms. My grandma was a petite and sweet woman, she had strawberry blonde hair and deep blue eyes. My grandfather I can't seem to remember, I assume he had perished by the time of my arrival. The smell of ripened dates and jasmine leaves will never leave me; the scent engulfed every room and corner in her house. My grandparents were merchants and were relatively wealthy for our small city. As you will come to learn throughout your time reading this, status and wealth was a key driver in my family, as it was for many at that time. I was the first-born son of my father Rostam and mother Touran; he was ten years her senior, which was very much a normality in Iran back in those days.

My father was the youngest of ten children, and in keeping with an old Iranian tradition, I inherited the name of his father – my grandfather – Abdoul Hussein. In theory, it was an honour, but in reality, it felt like a burden I never asked for. The name "Abdoul" always made me feel out of place. It was Arabic in origin – Abd, meaning "slave," and al, meaning "the" – together "slave of the..." followed by one of God's attributes. It carried weight and meaning, but it never felt like it belonged to me. I was a child who wanted to belong, to be accepted, not to be announced with such an archaic label.

My father, however, carried the name with pride, and he made it his mission to make sure everyone else did too – especially me. He would correct anyone who shortened or softened it, almost as if my reluctance to own it was a personal betrayal.

I remember the moment most vividly when I tried to distance myself from it. I must have been around nine. We were enrolling in secondary school. The principal was sat behind a large wooden desk, flipping through papers, and he finally looked up and asked me, "Your full name, son?"

I hesitated. I didn't want to say it. I hated the way it sounded, how kids would tease me, how teachers would pause at "Abdoul" like it was too heavy to pronounce. So I said, softly, "Hussein."

And just then, the door creaked open behind me. My father had arrived, parking his bicycle outside and stepping into the office. I felt his presence before I heard his voice, like a storm creeping over a silent field. Then came the words, stern and loud: "Are you embarrassed of your name?"

Before I could turn around, his hand smacked the back of my head. My ears rang. The principal barely flinched, probably having seen worse. My father stood firm and declared, "His name is Abdoul Hussein!"

I wanted to disappear.

CHAPTER I

Back then, a smack to the head wasn't unusual – it was considered part of raising a child. We were told that it built character. Discipline was measured by bruises, not by understanding.

When I was much younger, around three or four, my father had been a different man, or at least he seemed different to me. He had a bicycle with a small wooden seat fixed to the front, and I used to sit on it as he pedalled through the dust-lined roads of our small town. He was a partner in a sugar and tea shop then, and he'd take me with him on errands, or just for the ride. I think he wanted me to be close, to follow his footsteps – even back then.

But he was always a man of extremes. When I was born, he was working as a site supervisor for a road construction company, building motorways. His job kept him away from home for months at a time. He'd return for a few days, then vanish again into the mountains and deserts with his crew. My early years were spent in my grandmother's house – his mother's house – filled with rooms, relatives, and hard women who did not welcome my young mother kindly.

My mother was just 15 when she married, 16 when she gave birth to me. She was the youngest bride in the family and, by all accounts, not yet ready for the harshness of her new life. She often told me, later, how cruel my grandmother could be, and how the older women of the house bullied her. There was no warmth between them. My mother endured in silence, caring for me the best she could while my father was gone.

I was a sickly child – often ill, with weak teeth and constant infections. Once, I had such a bad toothache that the pain wouldn't let me sleep. My mother didn't have money to take me to the dentist. Instead, in the centre of the room, under the glow of a fuel-fed heater, she held a long needle in the flames until it glowed red. Then, with steady hands and teary eyes, she pressed the scorching metal to my infected tooth. I can still smell the metal, the scorched pain, but the ache faded not long after. That was how poor families managed pain – through fire, courage, and necessity.

There were small comforts, though. In the winter, we'd heat up thin sheets of bread on the same heater, folding them over crumbled Iranian feta cheese, fresh walnuts, and hand-picked mint leaves. The scent was heavenly. An old woman from the neighbourhood famous for her bread – used to come to our house to bake. She'd roll out circles of dough and cook them on a large round dome called a Tanorak. The bread would dry and harden after a day, but if you sprinkled a little water on it and reheated it, it would soften like it had just been made.

On those days, when the kitchen was alive with the smells of ash reshteh (a thick noodle soup) or halva (sweetened saffron pudding), cousins and neighbours would fill the house, laughter echoing off the stone walls. Sometimes, my grandmother would make extra food and send it to poor neighbours, and I was often the one chosen to carry it. In return, they'd give us sweets or small coins, and I'd run home proudly, my hands sticky with sugar and joy.

Despite the name, despite the fear of my father's hands, despite the heavy air of that grandmother's house, there were flickers of childhood. And sometimes, even amidst the struggle, I felt loved.

4

At the time of this writing, a decision has been made to alter the names of those stated hereon, to respect their right of anonymity. My parents went on to have five more children; but unfortunately, my younger brother and sister both passed away. Following on from me, another son was born: Hassan. They say that trauma leads to memory loss, or maybe I was just too young to recall all the memories I had with him. But all I can really remember is playing with him and taking him to our local shop to get him sweets. He was a generous and kind little boy, he would never say no to sharing, no matter the person. I must have been around the tender age of four when Hassan died. I remember him always being ill, my mother would always tell me that he was being seen by a doctor, which considering that there were only one or two doctors in Sarvestan (one being a friend of my father's), it must have been of immense severity. One day he contracted an infection and soon after one morning he just didn't wake up; he was just three years old. I cried for many days and Hassan's death resonated with me for years as being my earliest encounter of pain and sorrow. I would peep through the gaps in doors to find my mum crying and pulling her hair out after his death. My mother was so young and until this day her lack of knowledge or power to save Hassan will always play on her heart strings. My father never showed an ounce of emotion, but I felt captive by the shadow of pain that was cast over our home. I refused to let this become reality, I would still go to the storage room every day and put Hassan's clothes against my body and pretend he was still giggling beside me. He was my only friend, even at such a young and naïve age, I couldn't ever forget him and I blamed my parents for his, what I deemed to be, death at the hands of their neglect. It took me a year to recover from this time, albeit you will never wholly overcome a loved one's death.

To say my father was a complex, serious and strict man would be an understatement. To my delight, after H's passing he surprised me with a bicycle to comfort me, but it wasn't long before he deprived me of its benefit and returned it back to the shop. Unknowingly as an innocent child I let my friends go for a joy ride as they had never seen a bike before, let alone have a friend that could own one. As soon as I handed the bike over, I felt my father's shadow engulf me and before I could spit out a word his coarse and heavy hand knocked me over.

My father had had a difficult time throughout his childhood; being the youngest child of the family he was beaten up and abused by his brother and father. I recall the sole conversation I had with my mother about my father's abusive tendencies; she tried to justify his actions but I never felt that this was good enough or even justified by any means. To this day, I struggle to understand why my childhood took such a sour turn. Hearing stories about my father's childhood now reinforces my realisation that all he knew was a life of abuse and misery. In fact, I wonder whether to my father this was a form of love and affection. I sat with my mother as she began telling stories of my father's experiences. My father had accidentally left his brother's favourite novel outside when it began to rain; when his brother discovered this he tied my father to a tree, punching and lashing him until he fell unconscious. Unsurprisingly, a man who suffered at the hands of people who were meant to be figures of love and protection, would go on to have a very disordered understanding of family ties. I can list the scenarios that would entail and justify a beating in my dad's opinion: not having a nap after lunch, if I was a minute late for dinner, or if I refused to eat a particular food.

My mother left the room each time my father would initiate the act of punishment. As my mother turned to leave the room, I would look at her with tears in my eyes, but nonetheless my father would silence her with his anger if she did try to diffuse the situation, although she only tried once anyway. The hatred that began to build after the first incident towards my mother is something I don't think is forgivable. I would scream and no one even batted an eyelid, he would beat me with the same vigour, and I would scream throughout until he got tired and left me to suffer alone. I can still feel the injuries in my body as if he was still alive – I would usually have bruises on my neck, back and legs followed by debilitating pain in my legs and back for weeks on end. My body eventually began to function with these injuries as it became such a regular occurrence. My father had no limits or guilt; he would even drop me on my head and kick me with his long and skinny foot.

My father had no social boundaries or feeling of embarrassment around other family members; my auntie (Mother's younger sister) would occasionally pay her visits to our home. My father would become fuelled with rage and anger for reasons still unknown. At one point, he lifted me up whilst I cried at the top of my lungs in fear of dying, but ironically fearing that my father may also have a heart attack or sudden death in some kind of form. As he prepared to ungrasp his hands from my body to drop me to the ground, my aunt walked in screaming and pleading for him to let me go. He immediately put me down in a robotic motion and left the room, without even glancing at me. Within minutes he would be around me talking to me again, as if nothing had happened, but more importantly reinforcing to me that this was a normal routine.

I would not be honest if I said it was easy for me to describe these memories. I am left with trauma and conflicting emotions to say the least, but I still cast my mind back to his character and appearance. I remember his slim and tall frame, not forgetting his large slim hands. He was always clean shaven and well groomed. He was also an extremely handsome man – always in a suit and tie, no matter the occasion. My father was a figure of guidance in society, and he would help every person he encountered (except me of course). His popularity was heightened when he was elected to be a member of local council. Young boys would wish they were like him, and young girls would wish to find husbands like him. His appeal had no demographic limit. He was very much an advisor; whether this was for those within his family or those external, such as obtaining a divorce or managing death in one's family. There were always people in our house, whether they were relatives or not. We were never alone as a family – even going on holiday there would always be one or two people accompanying us. We never had quality time as a family, and if we did it was not healthy to experience.

It comes as no surprise that I spent a fair amount of time at my grandparents' houses. As for my maternal grandmother, I would visit regularly until one particular incident. My grandmother would spoil me even though they were on the brink of poverty; she would always make me *ash reshteh*, a soup dish with noodles and whey mashed within it. She would always make sure that my grandpa would bring pomegranates home, as he was a street fruit vendor, she would bring me bread and we would dip our bread into the juice of the pomegranate as if it was a meal of luxury. From the age of six, I terminated my regular trips here for a reason unbeknownst to anyone. My grandma rented out a room to a low ranked police officer. I would regret making this final trip as I learnt that he was the only person in the house at the time. He asked me to come to his room to help him with something, what exactly now I can't be sure. I trusted him to be a man with a strong moral compass. To describe exactly what happened would be too painful for *you* and *myself*, but he proceeded to rape me and deprive me of my innocence. A child experiencing any form of assault but more importantly of a sexual nature, will never come to terms with this reality, but the ability to divulge this information to one's nearest and dearest brings some form of comfort. I couldn't inform anyone of what had happened to me – my own mother and father wouldn't believe me, nor would anyone, especially not when people were so brainwashed to believe that those protecting the nation were figures of authority and of the highest morality. I couldn't bear to face returning, I had to stop my regular trips and somehow be a child again, even though by this age I had experienced things beyond a child's imagination.

I began to find a safe haven in my paternal grandma's house. It was a large house where many of my aunties would also reside. It was a big house with three palm trees that would harvest the sweetest dates imaginable. My cousins and I would climb onto these trees in the hope of picking dates to take back inside and relish in the success of our mission. Our auntie would scream and shout at us with fear saying that we would fall and be killed. Ten metres below sat a '*houz*', here meaning pond, which was layered with blue ceramic tiles. My auntie was correct to fear for our safety, as not long after our palm tree missions we relocated to play in the pond. I have a deep fear of water, regardless of whether this is on a large scale or a small swimming pool. It all derived from my cousins pushing me into the pond and had my grandma not noticed my body submerge into the water, I would have drowned and died within seconds. I can't remember much else after this, probably as I was pulled out of the water unconscious; I do remember my grandma screaming and howling though.

My childhood did have some rare but memorable events; my father bought a black and white television to my delight, which was one of the first in our city. Every evening, we would have friends and people from our little town huddled around the television in astonishment. My mother was the ultimate hostess and would make sure not one mouth went hungry. For a young boy with no friends, happiness or life, the thought of others talking about our accomplishment in affording a television and the envy in their voices made me feel special in some way. I would stay awake throughout the night embracing my newfound hobby of watching films.

We soon had a new addition to our family, a little girl, Juliana, Juli for short. This wasn't a typical Persian name, but my mother and father fell in love with the name when a Belgian princess visited Iran at the time the *Shah*, here meaning king, was in power.

I have little recollection of Juli within her early life, possibly as I was consumed in my own distorted world. Before I knew it, another sister was born, Nikoo, who was beautiful but would cry constantly, at all hours. My mother was busy now with three children and still struggling with Hassan's death and my ever-absent father. It all seemed like the perfect matrimonial home with happy and healthy children to the outside. Unfortunately, the sound of rustling and gathering in the garden led me to take hold of Juli's hand and walk to the balcony which overlooked the garden. I saw countless relatives reciting the *Quran* when my eyes were captured by the washing of Nikoo's body. She was just a year old when she died. I didn't know what to do or what to say; Juli was standing innocently next to me, holding my hand. I didn't know what was wrong with Nikoo, but I knew she had a prolonged illness. This explained her constant crying, she must have been in unbearable pain, though she was always smiling when she had a break from fighting an illness. She had started walking and saying a few words before she died. Her two lower incisors had grown out and I would love giving her carrot batons and watching her use her newfound little sharp teeth to bite into them. Juli wasn't old enough to understand the concept of death or that Nikoo wasn't coming back, but she still understood love and pain. I watched tears roll down her face. She tightened her grip probably as she felt that she may have lost me too. Juli was two and a half years old but still asked me why our mother was crying. I had to explain to an infant that our sister was dead and she would never come back, whilst battling with my grief and the thought that Juli could be next.

I stood on the balcony still and frozen, whilst Nikoo was put into a white blanket; my auntie came up behind me and guided us downstairs. We followed the growing crowd to the cemetery, where a little grave was already made for her. After reciting more from the *Quran,* she was laid to rest. A few days later my father ordered a gravestone and put it on her grave which was situated next to Hassan. The night of her death, friends and family were invited for dinner (which is common courtesy in our culture). I had no time to think about her or what was going to happen thereon. The memories and death of Nikoo made me a very lost child, more lost than I already was. I had to start school and soon realised that life had to continue without her in it.

CHAPTER II

A HOUSE NOT QUITE OURS

I was almost seven when we moved out of my grandmother's home and into what was supposed to be our first proper house. It wasn't finished. The second floor hadn't even been built yet, and the first floor was only partially ours. My father had rented out two rooms to a couple of schoolteachers. We had just one room and a small kitchen to ourselves, and all of us – my parents and I – shared that one space.

The toilet was outside in the garden, among a few plants and scraggly trees. It scared me at night. I hated walking out into the dark to use it. I would lie still, holding it in as long as I could. Sometimes I couldn't. At least once a week, I would wet my pyjamas and sleep in them, not daring to wake my mother to take me outside. By morning, the pee would be dry.

I slept on a doshak on the floor, in the same room with my parents. Even with them near, I cried silently some nights – especially in winter, when the wind howled through the unfinished ceiling above. The upstairs was just a shell of concrete and hollow bricks, not yet covered, so when the wind blew hard, it moaned and whistled like a ghost. I was too afraid to tell anyone I was scared. I didn't have my own space to retreat to, so I retreated into myself.

Later, my father completed the second floor and rented it to two more teachers. The house always felt full of strangers. One of the tenants had a son my age. We fought constantly, but my father always took his side. "He's our guest," he'd say. Even when it was clear the boy had started it, I would be the one smacked – a hit to the head, a slap to the face. I never understood why fairness never applied to me.

Our weekly baths were at the communal hammam, five minutes away on foot. We had no bathroom at home. The bathhouse was old, dim, and always crowded – but also warm and social, a place where people stayed for hours, chatting and escaping the cold.

There were different rooms: some for washing, some for hair, some for removing body hair with a clay-like substance called vajebi. For hair washing, we used konar, a powdered leaf from a tree, mixed with water to make a herbal shampoo. There were no showers – just buckets, large basins, and hot stones. After washing, we'd queue up to get massaged by a bathhouse worker. Every Friday, my father and I would go. It was a ritual.

One Friday stands out in my memory. I had gone with some friends when we saw Habib – a terrifying man in his thirties with a strong build, balding head, and a white glass eye in his left socket. He had a reputation for beating children who played football on the road near his house. He was unpredictable and cruel. That day, we saw him enter the hammam, and since it was dark inside and he couldn't recognise us, we saw an opportunity for revenge.

We swapped the pots – replacing the mud used to remove body hair with the herbal mud meant for hair. He unknowingly smeared it over his head, waited the usual time, and then started screaming. All his remaining hair had fallen out. He stormed out of the bath in fury. Days later, we saw him walking around with a scarf wrapped tightly around his head. He never confronted us, but we knew he suspected the local boys.

Behind the women's bathhouse, my father's brother had a garage with a well. Sometimes, when my uncle wasn't there, we sneaked in and peeked through a hole in the wall – compressed mud, kahgel – to spy on the women. One day, I saw a woman giving birth in the bath. It was terrifying. The image seared into my memory, and I never went back to that garage again. It disturbed me so deeply that even now, decades later, I cannot eat food cooked by a pregnant woman.

From around age five to 11, I also struggled with a painful condition in my heel. I couldn't walk straight – I'd limp painfully for the first ten or twenty steps before the pain faded. My father used to take me to Shiraz for treatment – 80 kilometres away. There weren't many buses, and sometimes we'd travel in the back of a lorry with goats and chickens, dust swirling around us. The animals were loose, no cages – sheep, chickens with bent legs, even sacks of cotton. I still remember the smell of goats and cigarette smoke – thick and choking – as we travelled in buses with no open windows.

The bus rides were overcrowded and chaotic – built for thirty passengers but often holding seventy or more, plus their belongings. It was noisy, uncomfortable, and suffocating. Once, at age seven, I asked a man not to blow smoke in my face. He responded by smacking me on the back of the head. "None of your business," he muttered.

But there were small pleasures. My father loved food. When we went to Shiraz, he always ordered baghali polo ba morgh – rice with dill and broad beans, served with chicken. It was his favourite. He took me with him when he travelled to buy things for his shop: seeds, soap, insect spray. I loved going – not for the shopping, but for a specific store with a cool air-conditioned breeze and the smell of fresh groceries, honey, and chewing gum. The shopkeeper always gave me a small packet of chewing gum balls – strawberry and mixed flavours. I'd chew them for hours, even after the flavour was gone.

I always saved some for my little sister Juliana, five years younger than me. I was eight, and she was three. Every time I gave her the gum, she lit up with joy. It was one of the few things I could give her – and it made me feel like a good big brother.

I loved my sister.

My first day at school, like any child, was filled with an array of emotions. My father had to bring me a chair to school – they had no chairs left as I was a last-minute additional student. I felt isolated and alienated; I was the youngest and all I could engage with was the feelings of missing my mother and N. In those days, a child began school at seven but because, of course, my dad had some form of association with the principal, I started at six. The only way I could manage was by carrying this façade of being a strong boy, but occasionally sliding off my chair under my desk to suck on my saviour: Mr dummy. It was my way of coping day to day, until my teacher found me hidden under a bench with a dummy. I was sent home by the school warden and of course the dreaded walk home meant

I had to have another session with my dummy in order to mentally prepare for confrontation with my father. As soon as he saw me, he smacked me a few times in the face and took away the dummy. It wasn't long before my progression at school became the justification for my father's abuse. I was as usual given homework which I would complete, but for the first time my father seemed to want to have some form of bonding time, by helping me with my homework. I was trying to learn how to write the digit seven. In Farsi, the digit seven is analogous to the English letter 'V'. My fingers were so small that I couldn't grip onto the pen in order for me to draw out this 'V' shaped number. Instead, I kept ending up with a 'U'. Now, when a child is unable to grasp a new task initially, a parent would usually sigh in frustration, but nonetheless plough through until their child masters it. My father, however, adopted a more unorthodox approach, and by unorthodox I mean hitting me on the back of my neck until it made a permanent pattern, both on my skin and in my brain. Unsurprisingly, he never had to beat me again for anything academia-related.

I assume my need to always pioneer in what I do derives from school. I was always the second best student at school, the best being *'Gholam Hossein'*. His father was a poor farmer, and they could barely afford to send him to school. This would explain his tireless efforts to work hard and make his father proud. He would work endlessly to the point that his pen would always shatter and ink would leak all over his hands and onto his trousers. He never had to memorise, revise or even study a subject; he would still achieve 100% in every subject we had. I grew to hate this ability of his, I would try my best to beat him in exams, but he didn't even have to try to override my grades, it became his second nature. Until high school, we would have this bitter, exam-centred feud. But, by high school (aged around 14 to 15), we became very good friends and the competition slowly came to an end. I lost contact with him around the time he was 17, and in a time where mobile phones were not in existence this wasn't too hard to believe. As you will come to learn as we progress through the chapters, I became somewhat politically involved you could say. *Gholam Hossein* and I would attend political meetings together, but at the time of losing contact I have now learnt he had joined *'Mujahedin'*.

By the mid-1970s, Iran felt like it was holding its breath.

Oil money filled the cities with new buildings and promises, but behind the glass walls of banks and ministries, most families still struggled. Wealth belonged to the few; silence belonged to the rest. At home, people whispered. In school, we watched our words. Even a wrong look could bring suspicion.

SAVAK, the Shah's secret service, was everywhere – or maybe just the idea of it was. Students vanished. Clerics were arrested. The newspapers said everything was fine.

But underground, something was stirring. The older boys passed pamphlets in the dark. Names like "Mojahedin" and "Fada'i" began to move through the alleys and late-night kitchens. No one said them out loud.

We all knew something was coming. We just didn't know what it would cost.

The People's Mujahedin of Iran or 'PMOI' for short, was then and still is a revolutionary Iranian organisation, at the forefront of the 1979 Revolution to overthrow the *Shah* of Iran, *'Shah'* here meaning *'King'*. In short, it now advocates for the dissembling of The Islamic regime in Iran. By dissemble, here I mean eradicate. The government had begun to imprison and kill the members of the *PMOI*. Eventually, these members would flee to neighbouring Iraq where they would seek asylum. The Iraqi president at the time, Saddam Hussein, would grant this protection in return for relentless combat and loyalty to the president to fight against the regime in Iran. I discovered a year later, that *Gholam Hossein* had been killed whilst in battle, through the *PMOI* newspaper. A publication which was only readily sought after by anti-governmental advocates, meaning that if this was widely circulated it would result in incarceration, torture and death. As soon as I heard of his death, the combination of sadness and guilt was somewhat overwhelming. I wish I could have repaid the protection he gave me, when he would shield and tower over me to stop the bullies from attacking me at school.

School was quite evidently a rough time for me; but with *Gholam Hossein* it brought sunshine to my life of misery. The other kids would bully and humiliate me constantly, they were jealous of my impeccable 'schoolboy' persona and would do whatever they could to tarnish my only remaining ounce of confidence. If I confided in teachers, the kids would beat me up even more. It was as if everyone was against me and I had nowhere to turn. These boys would touch me and tell others that I was homosexual and that they had had sexual intercourse with me, knowing that this was the ultimate revenge in response to divulging their acts and behaviour to the teachers. There was rarely a day where I would not cry in school – imagine having no safe haven at school, nor at home, what this would do to the psychology of a young child. I tried to confide in my father and tell him what they were doing to me, but he asserted that I was lying and that the reason for their actions was, in fact, perhaps due to me encouraging them in one way or another.

The shades of black and blue soon after starting school, became my permanent skin colour and ironically if the teachers would praise me, I would get beaten up for my efforts. They began to engage in disturbing rituals with me, it's hard for me to fathom now what really had happened throughout this time. They would all corner me into the back of the room – by *they* I refer to around six or seven boys. They would begin to finger me and instead of them being expelled for such acts, they would be expelled for falling below the requisite examination standards. This isn't particularly ironic as this type of sexual abuse was common within primary schools in Iran. I would like to say that my mother was *probably* aware of what was happening, but I am sure she had knowledge but in fact decided not to act upon it. It wasn't even worth speaking to my father as he wouldn't believe me, nor would my pride allow me to overcome revealing this to a male figure, as the male species seemed to only want to bring harm to me and exploit me.

CHAPTER III

THE MAYOR WHO NEVER WAS

I must have been around eight, maybe nine years old, when the school announced a big performance. It was going to be the event of the season. Invitations had gone out across town. Parents, officials, teachers, even a few local celebrities were expected to attend. Tickets were sold in droves. It was all anyone talked about for weeks.

Our part of the show was a play – cleverly written to reflect on power, corruption, and injustice. One character stood at the centre of it all: the mayor of the city, a greedy, ruthless man who accepted bribes and mistreated his people.

That role was mine.

I was proud. Not just because I had a lead part, but because I believed in the lines I spoke. They were bold. They were honest. They mirrored the conversations I had heard whispered by grown-ups behind closed doors – the anger, the disappointment, the weariness of those who had seen too much and hoped for too little. I took that anger onto the stage, word by word.

For weeks we rehearsed. Every afternoon after school, I stood under dim lights with my drama teacher, perfecting my delivery. My monologue, two full pages long, was etched into my mind like scripture. I knew every pause, every inflection. I even practised in front of my little sister, Juliana, who sat cross-legged on the floor, her eyes wide, watching me transform into someone else.

Then, on the final rehearsal day – just hours before the show – the headmaster walked in.

He sat quietly in the front row, arms crossed, expression flat. When my turn came, I walked onto the stage and began my lines:

"People of our city, I come to speak the truth. A mayor who rules through fear, who fattens his pockets while the poor go hungry – this is not leadership…"

I hadn't even made it halfway through when he raised his hand.

"Stop," he said.

The silence that followed felt like someone had turned the oxygen off. He stood, gestured for my drama teacher to follow, and walked out of the room without another word.

Ten minutes later, my teacher returned. His face had gone pale, like all the blood had drained to his shoes.

"I'm so sorry," he said quietly, kneeling beside me. "He says the part must be removed. Especially… your role."

"But why?" I asked, my voice trembling. "What did I do wrong?"

"It's not you," he said. "It's the words. He says it's too political. Too dangerous. He says we have to change it. All of it."

We had three hours. Three hours to re-write an entire performance. Three hours to turn a biting satire into a gentle praise song. The corrupted mayor became a benevolent one – kind, generous, beloved by the people. The speech I had spent weeks memorising was thrown out. A new one, just as long, had to be learned in a single breathless afternoon.

I tried. God, I tried.

At seven o'clock, the house was full. The stage lights burned like fire against my skin. From the edge of the curtain, I peeked out and saw rows upon rows of faces. More than four hundred people, maybe five. Some in suits. Some with notebooks.

I had scribbled down a few cue words on my palm to help me remember the lines. But under the heat of the lights, and the sweat pouring from my hands, the ink melted into my skin and vanished.

The curtains opened.

I stepped forward, legs shaking, heart pounding against my ribs.

"Good evening, ladies and gentlemen, boys and girls…"

And then – nothing.

My throat closed. My mind went blank. I stared at the sea of faces and felt a panic rise in my chest like a flood. My mouth refused to open. I couldn't speak. I couldn't breathe.

Voices rose from the audience.

"Come on!"

"Say something!"

Whistles. Laughter. Murmurs.

I stood there for what felt like a century. My knees locked. My body froze.

And then – I wet myself.

Right there, under the lights, in front of everyone.

I turned and ran backstage, tears streaming down my face. Behind me, I could hear the crowd erupting in laughter.

I hid in the dressing room and sobbed until my whole body ached.

My drama teacher found me and held me close. "It's not your fault," he whispered. "You were brave. Braver than anyone."

But I didn't feel brave. I felt ashamed. I felt broken.

For days after, I stayed home from school, pretending to be sick. I couldn't bear the thought of seeing the other children. Their laughter, their mocking glances. The shame stuck to me like a second skin.

Even now, decades later, I remember the lights. The silence. The cruel laughter.

And I remember what it taught me: that truth, no matter how small or soft, scares those who depend on lies. And sometimes, even a child's voice can shake the walls – if only for a moment.

For weeks after the performance, I couldn't look anyone in the eye. My voice shrank. At school, I walked with my head low, avoiding the boys who had whistled, the girls who had giggled, the teachers who looked at me with pity. The humiliation wasn't just about freezing on stage or wetting myself – it was the theft of something I had believed in.

That play had meant something to me. It was the first time I had seen art speak truth, even if only in a school auditorium. And then it was torn away. Not because it was bad, or wrong, or foolish – but because it was too true.

Something inside me cracked that day. And in the space where embarrassment once sat, a quiet rage began to take its place.

At night, I would replay the original lines in my head – the ones I had practised for weeks, the ones I was never allowed to say. I could still see myself on the stage, standing tall, delivering the words as if they were fire. In my imagination, the crowd didn't laugh. They listened. They clapped. They understood.

It was around then that I started paying more attention. To everything. I listened more carefully to my father's muttering when the news came on. I watched how people lowered their voices when talking politics. I noticed how even my teachers flinched when certain names were mentioned. Fear was everywhere – but no one admitted to feeling it.

That small, ridiculous scandal at my school had shown me something most children my age didn't see yet: that censorship didn't just happen in newspapers or government buildings. It reached into classrooms. Into the hearts of teachers. Onto the palms of little boys who dared to say too much.

In a way, that night became a spark.

Over the next few years, I grew bolder. Quietly, but persistently. I asked uncomfortable questions. I stopped accepting easy answers. I read what I wasn't supposed to read, listened to what I wasn't supposed to hear. And when I eventually joined student groups and underground circles, passing out banned leaflets or sneaking into whispered meetings, I remembered how it felt to be silenced. That bitter taste never left me.

And I remembered the crowd, too. How quickly they laughed. How easily they turned. I learned not to seek validation from them. That night taught me to be strong alone first – before trying to stand strong in front of others.

It took years to heal the embarrassment. But it didn't destroy me. It pointed me toward something much more dangerous, and far more important: the courage to speak truth, even if your voice shakes.

Even if they try to stop you.

Around that time, my father decided we were moving to Shiraz. I was nearly six. We didn't last long there though – only a few weeks. We packed all our belongings into a large lorry and moved into a house he had apparently bought with a friend. It seemed like we were finally settling into something permanent, something better. But then his family – especially his older brother – pressured him into returning. And so we did. Looking back, I think that was one of his biggest mistakes.

He quit his first job as a road manager and bought a chicken farm instead. That farm became the backdrop of my entire childhood. The first one was small, focused on reproducing eggs. We kept a few roosters, but mostly hens. Later, he sold that place and bought a bigger farm – probably about ten acres.

That's when he got serious about hatching and breeding. He bought two old-fashioned incubation machines. They were nothing fancy – just big wooden boxes fitted with light bulbs and thermometers to maintain the heat. After about three weeks, we'd check the eggs one by one. We used a tin can with a hole in it, placing each egg above the opening in the dark. A small bulb inside would shine through the shell so we could see if the embryo had developed. If it hadn't, we tossed it out.

After a few more days, the baby chicks would start hatching. We let them sit in the incubator for a couple of days, then moved them to another room. Most of the chicks were sold – to friends, relatives, or in the local markets. A few we kept, especially the hens and a couple of roosters.

We also sold eggs in our little shop. And often, after school, my father would hand me a basket of eggs and tell me to go door to door and sell them. If I did well, he'd give me half a rial as a reward – a small token to buy something for myself. Eggs were sold for two rials each.

I don't remember spending much time playing with friends. From the age of six or seven, I was always by his side, helping with the farm. That was my life.

CHAPTER IV

THE BARBER'S SNIP

S arvestan, mid-July. The sun blazed overhead, heavy and unmoving, casting a white-hot glare on the baked earth of our courtyard. The sky was a dull, unforgiving blue, and the heat clung to my skin like damp wool. Cicadas screamed from the olive trees, their shrill cries matching the rising tension in my stomach. I was seven years old – old enough to know that men didn't just show up on a quiet afternoon without a reason.

My father was sat under the shade of the mulberry tree, sipping black tea with my uncle, both of them too quiet, too still. They didn't joke as they normally did when visitors came by. They simply stared toward the gate, waiting. I should have seen it then, the omen in their silence. But I was too distracted by a sour unease in my belly that I couldn't name yet.

Then came the knock.

It wasn't the polite, rhythmic tap of a guest. It was a bang – urgent, final. The kind of knock that ends a childhood.

The door creaked open and revealed him: Haj Mahmoud, the local barber. He was a grizzled man, with tobacco-stained teeth, knotted hands, and an apron that had seen far too many kinds of blood. He stepped into the courtyard with his rusty metal kit swinging by his side – a bundle of cloth, half-unwrapped to reveal tools that looked more like farming implements than anything medicinal.

I froze.

It wasn't the haircut I feared. I knew better. In our town, the barber was a man of many trades – some of them sacred, others unspeakable. He delivered babies, stitched wounds, pulled teeth, set bones – and yes, he cut foreskins. Always with the same solemnity, the same grim set of his jaw.

I bolted.

Through the back of the courtyard, over the wall. I heard shouting behind me, the thud of feet, the grating scrape of slippers on stone. But I didn't care. I climbed onto the roof of our neighbour's house, my heart hammering like a trapped bird in my chest. Dust flew under my feet as I jumped from one rooftop to the next. I didn't look down. I knew if I stopped, they'd catch me. I also knew they would catch me anyway.

From the alleys and the rooftops, shouts echoed:

"Gereftimash! Gereftimash!" – "We've got him!"

A rough hand grabbed my arm – then another seized my ankle. I kicked and screamed, flailing like a fish on dry land, but there were too many of them. The elders – neighbours, uncles, even old Mr Asgari from the bakery – joined in the chase. Together, they dragged me back like a captured animal.

At home, the courtyard had transformed into an open-air theatre. Neighbours had gathered, smiling, some even laughing as if they'd come for a comedy. The children climbed onto crates for a better view. Someone brought a tray of sweets. Another waved a fan, shielding herself from

CHAPTER IV

the sun, while I, the trembling main act, was thrown to
the stage.

I tried to beg. "Please, baba, please…"

My father didn't meet my eyes.

Then came the voice, harsh as gravel.

"Ghoftam beshin, pedarsag!" the barber barked.

It doesn't translate neatly, not in spirit anyway. Sit
down, you son of a dog. But in Persian, the insult carries
a violent force – meant not just to command, but to
humiliate, to crush.

I screamed as they held me down.

Hands pressed on my arms, my legs. I recognised some
of the hands – they belonged to cousins, uncles. The very
people who had once lifted me on their shoulders when I
won school races, or tossed me sweets during Nowruz. Now
they pinned me like hunters around a carcass.

The barber squatted beside me, his face stoic, his breath
hot with tobacco. He reached into his bag and began
sharpening the knife. No anaesthetic. No prayers. No
blessing. Just a dull hiss as metal met stone.

I screamed again – this time louder, more animal
than human.

Then, a white-hot fire exploded in my groin.

The world narrowed to that single point of agony. I don't
remember the exact moment the blade touched me – only
the blinding pain, the crushing pressure of limbs restraining
me, the sickening sound of tearing flesh. I remember the
blood. So much blood. I remember the silence that came
afterwards, just before I fainted.

When I awoke, there was cheering.

Cheering.

I opened my eyes slowly. The sun had dipped behind the trees, but the light still burned. My legs were sticky with blood. A thick bandage was wrapped crudely around my penis, tied tightly like a tourniquet. I whimpered. No one noticed.

Someone draped a cotton skirt around my waist – blue with white polka dots. "So it won't rub," someone said, but I knew better. It was humiliation. I was to wear it for weeks, like a badge of shame. The skirt did little to protect me from the ridicule of my classmates. At school, they pointed, laughed, whispered.

"He's the one who screamed like a girl."

"Look at his skirt!"

Each trip to the toilet became its own trial of pain and tears. I had to squat, each drop burning like fire, my body tensing in anticipation. Sometimes I would weep silently afterwards, clutching my knees, waiting for the pain to fade. But it didn't – not for weeks.

Years later, I learned how circumcisions are done in modern hospitals. Sterile rooms. Aesthetics. Soothing words from nurses. Soft music, perhaps. A child goes in and comes out confused, but not broken. They are given ice cream, reassurance, maybe even a toy.

Not me.

There was no ice cream. No comforting hand. No one told me I'd be okay.

There was only pain, and the sound of grown men laughing.

And that memory – unlike so many others from my childhood – has refused to fade. It sits, sharp-edged and glinting, like the barber's knife, in the darkest drawer of my mind.

CHAPTER V

THE ROOM BEHIND THE CURTAIN

I was a child – seven or eight years old – still soft in the face and high-pitched in voice, the kind of age when innocence clings to you like a scent you don't even know you're wearing. My friends and I – Ali, Hossein, Kamran, a couple of others from the neighbourhood – had taken to attending Thursday evening Qur'an sessions at the mosque a few alleyways from our home. We were too young to fully grasp the teachings, too young to question anything. But we wanted to belong. To each other, to our families, to something bigger. We wanted to be seen as good boys.

The mosque was humble – white stone floors worn smooth by generations of feet, cracked walls painted with blue calligraphy, and a scent that was always a mixture of dust, feet, and incense. On those Thursday evenings, we'd gather after ablution, sitting cross-legged in rows on the old carpets, each with our small Qur'an open in front of us. We'd recite the verses in a chorus of high, uneven voices, stumbling over words whose meanings we didn't yet know but were told were holy.

The mullah sat at the front of the room, quietly overseeing us. He was middle-aged, perhaps older, with a neatly kept beard and a soft-spoken manner that, to a child, translated as wisdom. He had a presence that commanded silence without effort. There was something almost gentle about the way he moved, the way he corrected us. We revered him. He was a religious man. In our world, that was sacred.

But there was something else, too – something unspoken.

Every now and then, during or after the session, he would call one of the boys into a small back room, just beyond the curtain behind the minbar. A boy would go in, and the curtain would fall shut. Ten, fifteen minutes later, the boy would return – quiet, subdued, eyes lowered. I didn't think much of it at first. Maybe he was correcting their recitation, maybe helping them memorise. I didn't know. But I noticed that the boys who had been "called" never spoke of what happened. And after a while, they avoided his gaze. But I was still too young to understand the meaning in their silences.

Then one week, it was me.

He placed his hand lightly on my shoulder and told me, almost warmly, to go wait in the room. My feet moved before my mind could catch up. I walked behind the curtain and sat on a worn rug beside a dusty shelf of old Qur'ans. The room was dim, lit only by the faint glow of a single lightbulb overhead. I could hear the faint murmur of boys still reciting in the main hall.

After a few minutes, he entered. Quietly, like he was entering his own home. He didn't say much – just smiled gently and sat down on a cushion beside me. He handed me a Qur'an and asked me to read a page aloud.

I opened the book. My voice was steady at first, rising and falling with the rhythm of the verses, but I was aware – acutely aware – of his body so close to mine. Then, without a word, he placed my hand on his shoulder. It felt… wrong. But I didn't move it. I was confused. I didn't understand the rules of this place. He was the teacher. I was the student. I had been taught to obey, especially in the presence of a man of God.

And then he moved his hand – gently, almost casually – between my legs.

My breath caught in my throat. I froze. My voice faltered mid-verse. Every muscle in my body locked. I looked at him, trying to read his expression – was this normal? Was this a test? Was this what happened to everyone?

He looked calm. As if this moment was as routine as prayer. He must have seen the panic creeping into my face, because then he did something that haunts me to this day: he placed his hand softly over my mouth. Not forcefully – almost tenderly. As if to say, "It's okay. Be quiet. Don't ruin this."

At that moment, I understood everything.

Something inside me cracked open. A memory rose to the surface – sharp, immediate. The police officer at my grandmother's house. The way he had touched me. The same mix of confusion and shame. The same paralysis. And now it was happening again – this time with a man I had trusted, a man everyone trusted, in a house of God.

Then the mullah began to stand. I saw his hand go to his belt. I saw him begin to pull at his trousers. My heart exploded in my chest.

I sprang to my feet.

I screamed – louder than I thought I could. A raw, desperate scream. It wasn't just for that moment – it was for both of them. For every moment I had stayed silent. For the violation that was about to happen, and the one that already had. I didn't care who heard. I didn't care what came next. I just needed it to stop.

I ran out of that room, through the prayer hall, past the curtain, past my friends, past everything. I ran all the way home. I didn't look back.

I never returned to that mosque.

I cut myself off from the boys I had gone with. I couldn't face them. I didn't know what they knew, or what they thought. I didn't want to find out.

But I didn't escape. Not really.

The boys talked. As boys do. The story spread. They said I had consented. That I had "let" him. That I had enjoyed it. Their words turned the shame that belonged to him and nailed it to me. They didn't see me as a victim. In our world, boys didn't get abused – they got corrupted. Tainted. Humiliated. And humiliation had no sympathy in it.

I carried that silence like a secret infection. I never told anyone. Not my mother. Not my father. Not my sister. I didn't have the words. I only had the feeling – the acid of shame, the weight of silence, and the lingering fear that somehow, I had let it happen.

It would take me years to name it for what it was. And even longer to stop blaming myself.

But I remember this clearly: that night, as I sat in my room alone, trying to make sense of what had happened, I felt something break. Not my faith – no, that stayed for a while longer. What broke was my trust. My belief that grown-ups knew best. That religious men were safe. That mosques were sacred. That if you did everything right, nothing bad could happen.

I was a child, and I had done nothing wrong. But the world treated me like I had.

Years later, when I was grown and had stepped far away from that neighbourhood, that mosque, and even that city, I began to understand the invisible scars that the experience left on me. The trauma was not just the violation itself, but the betrayal – by someone who should have been a protector, by a community that turned away, by a culture that insisted on silence.

I wrestled with faith. How could a place that called itself sacred become a hiding place for such darkness? How could a man who wore the cloak of religion use it to mask cruelty? For a long time, I hated the very idea of God, or at least the way people claimed to represent Him. The mosque, which once felt like a place of belonging, became a symbol of fear and loss.

And yet, I also knew that faith was not only found in those walls or men. Faith was something I had to reclaim for myself – outside of dogma, beyond ritual. It became a quiet, fragile hope that goodness could exist even when power was abused.

The shame I had carried alone for so long began to unravel. I realised that shame belongs to the perpetrator, not the victim. The silence that once chained me could be broken – not just by telling my story, but by naming it, by insisting that it be heard.

It took years to find my voice, to confront the past without crumbling beneath it. To see myself not as broken, but as surviving. And to understand that the wounds of childhood can mark us deeply – but they do not have to define us.

As I moved through adulthood, carrying this memory like a hidden burden, I began to see how deeply it shaped not just my sense of self, but my entire relationship with the world around me.

Trust became a fragile, almost foreign thing. I found it difficult to believe in the kindness of others, especially those in positions of authority. The man who had taught me the Qur'an – the one who should have protected me – became a symbol of betrayal. Every time I tried to pray or connect with faith, that shadow was there, whispering doubts and fear.

This fractured my relationship with religion. For years, I wrestled with questions I could not fully voice: How could God allow this? How could sacred institutions harbour such evil? Was my pain some test? Or a punishment? These questions haunted me in silent moments, deepening my isolation.

But over time, I began to understand something crucial. The failure was not of faith itself, but of the human beings who wielded it as a weapon. The mosque was not God's house – it was a place shaped by imperfect people, capable of both kindness and cruelty. That realisation allowed me, slowly, to separate my spirituality from the wounds inflicted by men.

The shame that had felt like a heavy cloak began to loosen. I realised that shame belongs only to the one who commits harm – not the one who suffers it. My silence had not protected me; it had only allowed the damage to fester. Finding the courage to name the truth was not easy. It meant stepping into vulnerability, risking judgment and disbelief. But it was necessary. Each time I spoke my story, I reclaimed a piece of myself.

This journey transformed how I saw power and authority. I learned to question, to doubt, to demand accountability. And I learned, painfully, that silence often serves the abuser, while truth becomes a weapon for survival.

In my relationships, I carried both the weight of my past and the hope of healing. I struggled with intimacy, sometimes recoiling from closeness out of fear. But I also discovered that connection – true connection – was possible. It was built on honesty, respect, and mutual care. Slowly, I allowed myself to trust again.

Healing is not a straight line. Some days, the past feels close, a shadow creeping into the light. Other days, I feel strong, resilient – like a man who has faced darkness and still chooses to walk forward.

Looking back now, I see that this story is not just about pain or betrayal. It is also about survival, about the human spirit's capacity to endure and reclaim itself. It is about breaking the silence, not just for me, but for others who carry hidden wounds.

And it is about hope – that even when the walls we build to protect us crumble, we can build new ones. Ones made not of fear or silence, but of truth, courage, and compassion.

That night in the mosque, and the silence that followed, marked the end of my childhood's innocence. But it was not the end of my story.

Over the years, I learned that surviving such darkness was not about forgetting, but about remembering with courage. About speaking the truths that others wanted buried. About reclaiming the parts of myself that had been stolen – not just my voice, but my trust, my faith, my sense of safety.

I carry the memory with me still – not as a chain, but as a reminder. A reminder that evil can wear the face of holiness. That silence often protects the wrong people. And that healing is a long, difficult path, but one worth walking.

This is why I tell my story – not for pity, but for understanding. For those who have suffered alone, I want to say: you are not alone. Your pain is real. Your voice matters.

And for those who hold power, who claim authority: beware the silence you allow. Because silence does not heal. Silence only hides the wounds until they bleed again.

The mosque was just a place, the mullah just a man. But I am still here. I am still speaking.

And this is only the beginning.

By the time I was 12, my body had grown used to being black and blue. Bruises came and went like shadows across my skin – faded reminders of pain that no one seemed to notice. I had long stopped complaining. Every time I had tried, my father brushed me off with suspicion or indifference. "What did you do?" he'd ask, as if pain only arrived when invited.

Eventually, I stopped trying to explain. I simply endured.

One afternoon, when I was around 12 or 13, I was walking home from school, dragging my satchel behind me, hungry and tired. A boy, maybe a year older than me, stepped into my path. I recognised him from the neighbourhood – not a friend, not quite a stranger. He looked angry, bitter. He asked for money.

I told him no. I barely had enough for myself. Before I could even take another step, he shoved me to the ground. My knees scraped the asphalt. Then came a punch – straight to the face. It was fast, and it hurt. But something in me – some fire that had been building up for years – woke up. I pushed him back, scrambled to my feet, and this time, when he came at me again, I stepped aside and threw my foot in front of his. It was instinct. He tripped, fell hard – his arm landing directly on a sharp rock. I heard the crack. Then the scream.

He lay there writhing, clutching his arm. I didn't wait to see the damage. Panic gripped me. I wasn't afraid of him anymore – I was afraid of my father.

I knew what would come. It didn't matter that I'd been attacked. It didn't matter that I'd defended myself. My father wouldn't care about the truth. He only cared about appearances – about shame, about honour, about being "the man of the house".

I ran.

Out of the neighbourhood, out of the town. I didn't know where I was going. I just knew I couldn't go home. The sun had started to set. The sky turned a bruised orange, and the wind picked up, cold and unfriendly. I was scared – of the dark, of being alone, of what would happen if I went back.

Eventually, I made my way to my aunt's house on the edge of town. She opened the door and saw the fear written all over me. I begged her – please, please go to Baba. Please ask him not to hit me. Just talk to him first.

She nodded, kissed my forehead, and promised she'd speak with him.

Hours passed. Long, slow hours filled with dread. When she returned, she told me what I needed to hear: "He won't punish you. Come home. It's okay."

I believed her.

But my father, like many fathers in our town, believed in a different kind of justice. A justice with hands, with shame, with silence. He had already gone to the boy's family – bringing chickens as an offering of apology, bowing his head on my behalf. But he hadn't come to understand. He hadn't asked me what had happened. He hadn't even waited to hear my side.

When I walked through the door, he punished me anyway. Not as severely as I feared, but enough. Enough to make sure I remembered where I stood in the house, in the family, in his world.

That boy – the one who had attacked me – never came back to school. Word was he broke his arm badly. Years later, I heard that he'd become addicted to drugs. He joined the Pasdaran – the Islamic Revolutionary Guard Corps – like many troubled boys did. Maybe they offered him structure. Maybe they gave him a uniform to hide behind, a reason to feel powerful. But he never came out of that life. He died of an overdose a few years later. Just a passing headline in a local whisper.

And me?

I kept going to school, but joy was rare. I never felt safe – until the day my father sent me to Shiraz for further education. I was around 13 or 14 then. I arrived in that city like a bird suddenly released from a cage. No one knew me. No one had heard rumours about me. I could breathe for the first time in years.

In Shiraz, I loved school. I smiled more. I walked freely. For a short while, I felt like a normal teenager.

But the freedom didn't last forever.

Back home, the weight of gossip never really lifted. Every time I walked down the street in my own neighbourhood, I felt eyes on me. Fingers pointing. People whispering that I was "that kind of boy". That I was soft. That I was gay. That I was "easy". They never said it to my face, but they didn't have to. I felt it like heat on my skin.

We still lived in the same house, up until I was 17 or 18. But I no longer wanted to be seen. I stayed indoors more and more – partly out of fear, partly out of exhaustion. And the more I stayed in, the angrier my father became. "Come help me at the shop," he'd yell. "Don't sit around like a girl." When I didn't move quickly enough, his hands would remind me.

He thought hiding indoors made me weak.

He never understood I was hiding from a world that had already bruised me from the inside out.

Looking back now, I see a boy who was constantly trying to survive. A boy who wasn't allowed to feel pain unless it fitted someone else's version of events. A boy who was punished not just for what he did – but for who he was becoming.

The violence I endured wasn't just physical – it was emotional, psychological. I was being taught to fear my own truth. To hate my reflection. To stay small, stay quiet, stay obedient.

But I remember Shiraz. I remember the feeling of being unknown, and how deeply I longed to stay that way. To be anonymous was to be safe. But eventually, I would learn that survival was not enough. That someday, I would have to stop hiding – not just from the world, but from myself.

My father's shop was a small empire of necessity: sacks of vegetable seeds, chemicals for killing weeds, tiny machines like hand tractors, feed for chickens, and even medicines and vaccines for cattle. He had no formal training, but the villagers trusted him like a veterinarian. He injected lambs, diagnosed infections in goats, and mixed strange powders into muddy buckets with the same confidence a doctor might use holding a scalpel. I spent years watching him perform his village medicine, his hands rough from hard work and stained by the chemical dyes that never seemed to wash off.

From a young age – seven or eight – I was part of this world, working alongside him. School in the mornings, the shop or the chicken farm in the afternoons. Fridays, instead of resting or playing, I'd be there all day: twelve-hour shifts that left my limbs aching. I never received pocket money, not even for sweets or toys. My work was expected, demanded, part of the duty of being his son.

One afternoon, curiosity and hunger got the better of me. I reached into the desk and took two rials – a tiny coin, almost nothing – but for me, it felt like everything. I was trying to hide it inside a massive sack of seeds when my father caught me. The room seemed to freeze. My body went cold. I started shivering, unable to speak, and wet myself in fear.

He didn't say a word at first. He walked over, took the coin out of the sack, placed it back on the table, and then, without a sound, rolled down the shop shutters.

I knew what was coming.

He slapped me across the face, kicked me hard in the backside, and beat me for five, maybe ten minutes. I was crying, screaming, apologizing, begging. He hurled insults at me through clenched teeth.

"Pedarsokhte korreh khar, pol midozdi? Pedareto dar miaram!"

He called me a son of a bitch, a stupid donkey, a thief. He promised to break me. And when he finally tired himself out, he told me to apologize again – this time with my head bowed low. Then he walked away as if nothing had happened and returned to his work.

I kept stealing small coins after that. It wasn't for greed. It was survival. I never truly stopped until I was ten or 11, when he started paying me tiny amounts for helping in the fields. He didn't do this out of kindness. He simply had new land, more work, and maybe realized I was getting older and harder to control.

He would bring home barrels of powerful poisons to kill insects – thick, stinging chemicals that burned your nose and made your eyes water just by opening the lid. He made me pour them into small bottles with no gloves, no mask, no protection. My skin would smell for days, the scent refusing to leave even after ten showers. The toxins would cling to my hair and clothes, like invisible smoke.

One summer, my father had an idea – perhaps his first that felt almost kind. He bought me a lamb to look after. It gave me purpose, something to care for. I fed it grass, corn, and scraps from the farm. By the end of the season, he sold the lamb and shared some of the money with me. I don't remember what I did with it – probably gave it back to him to "keep in my bank account". But it felt like something I'd earned.

The chicken farm was worse. Long hours plucking feathers from freshly slaughtered hens, boiling water under the open sun, the stench of blood and burning feathers mixing with the thick heat of Sarvestan's 40-degree summers. My mother helped, and sometimes cousins joined, but the work felt endless.

Water was another burden. We had no proper pipes in the early years. I was nine or ten when I started hauling water from my uncle's plantation – two 20-litre jugs hanging from each end of a stick across my shoulders. I'd walk 200 metres to the little stream, fill them, and carry the weight back. It left red lines pressed into my skin.

If I complained, my father would call me lazy. He would point to boys like Amrollah, a kid my age who worked in his uncle's shop just down the street.

"Look at him!" my father would say. "Always helping. Not like you."

I hated Amrollah. I hated his smug little face, his uncle's praise, the comparisons. One day, I shot him in the back with my air rifle – the same one I used for pigeons. He screamed, and I ended up locked in the storage room all day without food. No lunch, no dinner. Only kicks and curses.

He wasn't particularly cruel, or smart, or even interesting – but he was everything my father wanted me to be. Obedient. Useful. Presentable. A symbol of what a "good boy" should look like. His uncle's shop sat just across the corner from our house, and every time my father saw him carrying bags of rice, sweeping the floor, or attending to customers, I'd hear the same bitter refrain: "Look at Amrollah. Always helping. Always working. Why can't you be like him?"

I hated him more with every passing day. Not because he had wronged me – but because he was my father's golden standard, and I was always falling short.

There was no way for me to be angry at my father. He was too powerful, too present, too entrenched in every part of my life. But Amrollah – he was within reach. And when I found out he had a girlfriend, a girl named Fatemeh, something inside me twisted. I didn't want her. I didn't even know her. But I wanted to take something from him. I wanted to remind myself – and the universe – that I was not worthless. That I could hurt back.

Fatemeh was pretty in a simple, unassuming way – kind eyes, thick dark hair, and a curious smile that always hovered on the edge of mischief. I had seen her a few times at school, and it didn't take much effort to get close. One day, I followed her after class, caught up with her, and sparked a conversation. A compliment here, a joke there. From the moment we locked eyes, I sensed something – an interest, a warmth. Maybe she was lonely. Maybe she was curious. Or maybe, like me, she needed to feel seen.

Our casual talks turned into deeper exchanges. We started seeing each other more frequently, always in secret. Then, one night, under a moonless sky, I climbed over the back wall of our courtyard, slipping silently through the alleys of Sarvestan, heart pounding, blood hot with risk. It was just after midnight when I reached her home. The main door creaked open, and there she stood in her nightgown, a silhouette in the dim light of the corridor behind her. Without a word, she let me in.

The house was silent. Everyone else was asleep. We walked through the long, narrow corridor that smelled of dust, old rugs, and something faintly floral. That first night, we just talked. Sat on the floor, our knees brushing now and then, our voices barely above whispers. It felt like entering another world – one where time slowed and danger only made desire burn brighter.

Within days, we were kissing. Slowly at first. Then urgently. It wasn't long before we crossed the line – not out of love, but something far more complicated. A need for power. Control. Victory. We made love a few times over the next couple of weeks. And every time, a strange satisfaction washed over me – not just physical, but emotional. I had taken something sacred from Amrollah, even if he didn't know it. He who had everything – the respect, the praise, the girl – had just been humbled, in my mind at least.

I'd lie in bed afterwards, still smelling her perfume on my skin, and think: Now who's better?

But victory comes with a cost.

After a few weeks, I started to feel nothing. The thrill had faded. The war in my chest no longer raged. I wasn't sure if I even liked her anymore – or if I ever had. She would message through friends, send me notes, even wait outside my father's shop pretending to buy something – but I stopped responding. No more midnight visits. No more letters. I shut the door as abruptly as I had opened it.

Looking back, I know I hurt her. Deeply. She didn't deserve that. She was a girl with her own heart, not just a pawn in my battle with another boy. But at the time, I didn't see her. I only saw him.

That chapter of my life left a strange taste in my mouth – not guilt exactly, but something sour. Something that made me realize how easily pain can turn into cruelty. I thought I was proving something to my father, to Amrollah, to the world.

But in truth, I was just trying to prove something to myself – that I was not powerless. That I was not invisible.

And for a little while, it worked.

At first, walking away from Fatemeh felt like walking away from a completed mission. The kind of mission you don't speak of, one you bury under your skin like a wound that's meant to stay closed. No more late-night whispers. No more stolen kisses behind locked doors. No more climbing walls in the dark like a thief.

But what I hadn't anticipated was what came after.

The silence.

The absence.

The subtle but persistent ache that came not from missing her, but from the way I had erased her – as if she had been nothing more than a chess piece I moved and then swept from the board.

She sent word through mutual friends. Quiet pleas disguised as casual messages. "Is he okay?" "Tell him I want to talk." Sometimes, I'd see her standing across the street near the old bakery or wandering past my father's shop pretending to look for something. She never said a word. Just let her eyes speak, and I – too proud, too afraid, too numb – looked away every time.

In the beginning, I told myself I had done what I had to do. That she was part of a game. That she was his, and I had won. But the weeks dragged on, and what had once felt like triumph began to sour into something heavier. Something darker.

Shame.

I didn't feel guilty in a religious sense. Not in the way the local mullahs would preach about sin and hellfire. I didn't believe in that kind of punishment. But I felt something worse: a hollowing out from within, as if I had chipped away at my own soul just to hurt someone else.

She had trusted me. Opened her door. Let me in – into her space, into her body, into parts of her life she hadn't shared with anyone else. And I had taken it all and walked away like it was nothing.

I didn't even say goodbye.

Sometimes at night, I would lie awake and hear echoes of her voice. Not what she said, but how she said it. That soft, nervous laughter when I first kissed her. The way she'd gently fix my shirt collar after we'd hurried to redress in the hallway. The warmth in her eyes when she thought I was someone I wasn't.

What kind of man walks into someone's heart just to prove a point?

What kind of boy does that?

At the time, I didn't know the answers. I only knew that something inside me was broken – and that breaking someone else hadn't healed it. Hurting Amrollah hadn't made my father love me more. It hadn't made me stronger. It hadn't made the loneliness go away.

If anything, I felt more hollow than before.

I never saw Fatemeh again after that summer. Word spread that she and Amrollah had broken up. Some said her parents had found out. Others said she had been heartbroken and had disappeared to stay with relatives in another town.

Whatever the truth was, she vanished from Sarvestan like a whispered secret that no one dared say aloud.

Years later, when I would walk past that same long alley in the middle of the night, I'd sometimes stop at the corner and just…stand there. Imagining her shadow, her scent, her presence. I'd wonder if she ever thought of me. If she hated me. If she ever knew the real reason I had come into her life at all.

And I'd wonder most of all: Was I her mistake?

Or was she mine?

Years later, Amrollah left school, started driving a van, and married his uncle's daughter – a girl who had a reputation, known around the neighbourhood for what the Basiji boys had done to her. What began with assault ended in whispers, and her name was dragged through the streets like trash. She was a victim, but no one treated her like one.

* * *

Chess was my escape. I learned the game at 11 or 12 from my cousin. He taught me the basics, and something inside me clicked. I devoured chess books, played for hours. By the time I moved to Shiraz at 13, away from the constant pointing and rumours in Sarvestan, I found a club. For once, I was somewhere nobody knew me.

One summer, back in Sarvestan, a friend of my father's took me to a local chess competition. Registration was already closed, but he convinced the head organiser to let me play a match against him "just for fun". The man didn't want to – he was well-known, respected, embarrassed at the idea of losing to a boy.

I beat him in ten minutes.

He was shocked. Demanded a rematch. Kids left their own matches to crowd around us. He lost again in 15 minutes. A third time, he challenged me with a bet: if I won, I'd skip the qualifiers and go straight to the final. I beat him once more. And the next day, I won the entire Sarvestan regional tournament – beating a 17-year-old finalist in under five minutes. I was 15.

That same year, I came second in the Fars Province school championship, a region with over five million people. I won cycling competitions. Table tennis tournaments. I was even part of a bizarre footrace where I came in dead last – 45 minutes behind – but somehow, because of the points I earned, my school ended up winning. I found out later a classmate had given me "nabat", sugar crystals before the race to make me thirsty. His mother's idea.

Despite all of this, my father never told me he was proud.

CHAPTER VI

PARASTOU,
THE BANK MANAGER'S DAUGHTER

In a town where every day was measured by labour, sweat, and discipline, Parastoh was a gentle interruption. She arrived into my life like a breeze through the dusty streets of Sarvestan – soft, almost imperceptible at first, then unforgettable.

Her father was the bank manager, and their home sat directly beside the bank like a whitewashed fortress of order and silence. My father's shop was only a few steps away, but it might as well have been another world. I must have been 12 when I first heard about her – whispered rumours from boys in the neighbourhood: "There's a new girl in town. She's very pretty."

That alone was enough to stir something in me. I didn't even know what that "something" was at the time – just that I needed to see her.

So, I began waiting. Each evening after the shop, I'd pretend to play with friends outside the bank, half-hearted games of football or catch, all while stealing glances at the entrance. Then, one day, she came out – just for a moment. She looked around, paused, and went back inside.

That was it. One look. But that single glimpse anchored something in my chest.

Over the next few weeks, I started standing across from her house, pretending to lean against a tree or kick a stone around with my foot, eyes fixed on the door, hoping she'd appear. And when she did – those soft brown eyes, that shy, curious smile – the world seemed to fall away.

The first time we spoke, I just whispered "salaam". She looked at me and replied with a small "hi", then giggled and ran back inside. That moment felt like sunlight on my skin after weeks of rain.

Her presence changed the way I moved through town. Every break I had – after school, between chores, even while delivering something for my father – I drifted toward that white house. She began to notice. Sometimes she would come out on her balcony, wave lightly, then vanish. Sometimes I saw her through the window, pretending not to look, but I knew she was watching.

She always smelled like roses. I don't know how or why – perhaps it was a soap, or her mother's perfume – but every time she passed by, that scent lingered in the air. Even years later, the smell of roses brings her back to me.

I still remember the dress she wore the last time I saw her: light blue, short-sleeved, with a delicate pattern like clouds on the sky. Her long brown hair lay over her shoulders like a soft curtain framing her face. She was taller than most girls her age – graceful, slender, always walking like she carried a secret.

One afternoon, she came outside when no one else was around. We met in the shade of the sarv trees – tall, evergreen, and silent like guards. I was nervous. I didn't know what to say. She smiled and said, "Don't you ever talk?" I stuttered something clumsy, made her laugh, and then she stepped forward and kissed me lightly on the cheek.

My skin burned where her lips had touched.

I didn't move for a long time after she left. Just stood there, hand on my cheek, smiling at the sky like a fool. That kiss felt like permission – permission to feel something pure in a life that was otherwise full of duty and discipline. I floated home that night. My chores, the yelling, even my father's heavy footsteps – none of it touched me.

But nothing stays still in a town like Sarvestan. A few weeks later, she told me that her father had received a promotion – they were moving to a bigger city. She said it quietly, almost like she didn't want the words to be true.

I didn't cry in front of her. I just nodded, swallowed the lump in my throat, and said I understood.

But that night, alone in my bed, I cried into my pillow until I couldn't breathe. I missed her laugh. Her smell. Her eyes that lingered just a second longer than they needed to. For weeks afterwards, I would still go stand under the sarv trees in front of the house that no longer held her. I hoped that maybe she'd come back, even just for a day.

She never did.

It took me years to let her go. Years to stop looking for her in other faces, other voices, other smiles. And even when I finally did, I never forgot her.

CHAPTER VII

SUSAN – THE ONE WHO SLIPPED THROUGH MY FINGERS

If Parastoh was the first drop of rain on dry soil, Susan was the storm that followed.

I was 13 when I met her – not in town, but through family. Her sister had married one of my cousins. She lived in Shiraz, but they visited Sarvestan every few weeks for family gatherings, weddings, mourning ceremonies – the usual rhythms of extended Iranian families.

Susan was older – maybe 14 or 15. She carried herself like someone from another world. There was something modern about her, something bold. Where other girls were quiet and cautious, she looked you in the eyes when she spoke. That first time we met, I think I forgot how to form a full sentence.

We'd sit and talk at family events, surrounded by the chatter of adults and the clinking of tea glasses. Our conversations weren't long or deep – we talked about nothing really. But the way she looked at me, with a hint of curiosity and humour, made my heart beat faster.

I started counting the days until their next visit.

I'd dress a little nicer, comb my hair a bit differently, pretend not to be looking for her while scanning every room. And when our eyes met across a crowded garden or dusty courtyard, I felt like the only boy in the world.

We never held hands. Never kissed. But there was an understanding. A quiet agreement that we liked each other in that way that kids do before they fully understand what love even is.

Then, one day, they stopped coming.

No warning. No goodbye. Just absence. I asked my mother where they'd gone. "Moved away, I think," she said, brushing it off. "Something about new work or problems in Shiraz."

I never saw Susan again.

That kind of disappearance doesn't break you like a heartbreak in adulthood does. It's slower. More confusing. You don't understand why it hurts – just that it does. You replay every word, every smile, every glance, wondering if you missed something.

For years, I wondered what had happened to her. If she remembered me. If she felt even a fraction of what I felt when our knees touched under the sofreh and we both pretended it was an accident.

Parastoh and Susan – the first two to show me what longing felt like. What beauty could exist even in stolen seconds. In a life shaped by duty, silence, and endurance, they reminded me that I had a heart. That I could feel tenderness, even if the world around me did not.

And in some small way, they made survival easier.

Parastoh smiled at me once. Later, she kissed me on the cheek. I was in heaven.

She moved away not long after. Her father got promoted. I cried for nights in bed. I didn't think I'd ever get over her

– until I met Susan at 13, a distant relative visiting from Shiraz. She came every couple of weeks, and our short, shy conversations meant the world to me. Then one day, she too was gone.

Every bit of joy in those years – chess, cycling, a kiss – was mine alone. I carried them like secret treasures in my pocket. Not once did my father tell me he was proud. Not once did he say, "Well done."

But deep inside, I knew I was worth more than his silence.

The first time I saw a banned leaflet, I was barely 13. It was crumpled, half-torn, lying on the ground near the corner bakery in Shiraz. Someone must have dropped it in a hurry. I picked it up, heart racing, and quickly shoved it into my pocket before anyone could see.

That evening, when the house was asleep, I locked myself in the bathroom and read it by the flickering light of the gas lamp.

It was a single page. No pictures. Just words – dense, angry, defiant. It spoke of workers being exploited, young men being imprisoned for their beliefs, and the need for ordinary people to rise up and demand their rights.

I didn't understand everything. But something in the tone felt familiar. Like the speech I never got to give. Like the truth that frightened grown men enough to silence a boy.

From then on, I began to look at the world differently.

In the dusty corners of our school library, I discovered books with bent covers and yellowing pages – translated copies of Gorky, Orwell, Jalal Al-e Ahmad, even bits of Marx hidden behind more innocent titles. I didn't fully grasp all the theories, but I felt the pulse of something powerful: the hunger for dignity. The resistance against lies.

I started asking quiet questions. Why were there always new soldiers in town? Why did some people vanish overnight? Why did my classmate's father stop coming home? Why did no one talk about these things?

At home, my father sometimes scolded me for being too curious. "You'll get yourself in trouble," he warned. "The world doesn't change with questions – it changes with power."

But I couldn't stop.

I began writing small pieces. Anonymous essays. Hand-copied quotes from banned poets. I passed them to trusted classmates, folded them inside textbooks, slid them under classroom doors. It was risky. But it felt like breathing.

Every time I remembered that stage – my knees locked, my voice stolen, the laughter echoing – I reminded myself that I wasn't that boy anymore. I wasn't frozen. I was moving, slowly, deliberately, toward something I didn't yet have a name for.

And though I had once been silenced, I was beginning, finally, to speak.

I was around 13 when my father decided it was time for me to leave Sarvestan and attend a private school in Shiraz. It felt like being exiled. He arranged for me to stay at a friend's house in the city – a modest family with a daughter two years older than me and a younger son. The house was clean, the people were polite, but I felt completely out of place. I missed home with a dull ache that didn't go away. I missed my mother's voice, the smell of her cooking, the warmth of her arms. Most of all, I missed Juliana – my little sister, my shadow, my comfort. I hadn't realised how tightly she was woven into my everyday life until she was gone from it.

The private school itself was another universe. Boys from wealthy families filled the classrooms and corridors. They wore expensive clothes, flaunted new watches, bought snacks at the cafeteria like it was nothing, and talked casually about lunch plans at restaurants after school. Their confidence and ease made me feel like an alien among them. I had no money, no fancy clothes, no one to talk to. I would sit alone during breaks, watching their easy laughter and feeling like I didn't exist. I was surrounded by people but lonelier than ever.

Eventually, I stopped trying to fit in. Some days, I couldn't bear the weight of it all. I'd take my school bag and walk straight past the school gates. Instead of classes, I found solace in the dark halls of Shiraz's old cinemas. I'd sneak in without tickets, slipping between crowds, timing my entrance just right. I'd jump from one screening to another, half-watching films, losing myself in flickering images. Westerns, romantic dramas, old Iranian black-and-whites – anything that would take me out of my own world. The darkness became a second home. The screen was my window into lives where people didn't feel lost or alone.

Of course, the school noticed. My grades fell, and my absence became harder to ignore. The administration contacted my father, and within a few days, I was removed from his friend's house and sent to live with his uncle. That didn't last long. A few months later, I was moved again – this time to an aunt's house. Each move felt like being passed along, like an unwanted parcel with no real destination.

Life at my aunt's was particularly hard. She had two young boys of her own, and her husband worked long shifts at a clothing factory. They barely had enough for themselves, let alone an extra mouth to feed. Meals were sparse. I'd often be given four or five tiny meatballs – each the size of a chickpea – served with a small piece of bread. It wasn't enough. I'd go to bed with my stomach growling, clutching a thin blanket, staring at the ceiling in the cold.

And yet, despite everything, something began to shift inside me during those long, hungry nights. I started reading – books that I found in second-hand stalls, lent by classmates or found left behind in old corners of houses. I devoured them like food. History, politics, literature – especially anything about revolution, justice, and freedom. That's when I began slipping into demonstrations, quietly watching, then eventually marching. I began meeting others – leftist students, young men and women filled with rage and dreams. We'd gather in bookstores, in tea shops, in back alleys. We argued, we listened, we believed. In those secret corners of Shiraz, I began to understand my country, my generation, and perhaps myself.

The hunger I felt wasn't just for food – it was for meaning, for dignity, for a place to stand in a world that never seemed to want me.

CHAPTER VIII

THE IRANIAN REVOLUTION

I was 15 years old when the Iranian Revolution took place in 1977. For completeness, it is worth briefly discussing the purpose and history of the Revolution. The *Pahlavi Dynasty* under the *Shah* (here meaning King) was overthrown and replaced with the order of the Islamic Republic. This was facilitated by the leader of the Revolution, Ayatollah Khomeini. Over the following year, protests and strikes had debilitated the country. The Persian royal reign began to collapse and led to the *Shah*'s exile from Iran in 1979. In the April, Iran by way of national referendum voted to transition into an Islamic Republic, with Khomeini becoming Supreme Leader of the country. By 1977, I had lived in Iran long enough to feel the rhythm of silence – how it curled around conversations, how it waited in rooms. We didn't speak of politics openly. Not at school. Not at work. And certainly not on the telephone. We had learned, quietly and completely, that the walls could hear. Still, something shifted that year. Something subtle, but irreversible. You could sense it in the pauses, in the questions asked with careful curiosity – "Did you hear what happened in Najaf?" or "Did you read what that professor wrote in Kayhan?"

The Shah was still everywhere – in our textbooks, on television, above the chalkboard in every classroom. His regime still projected strength, still wore the mask of progress: oil wealth pouring in, new buildings rising, women walking unveiled in northern Tehran, American companies expanding their footprint. On the surface, it was the image of a modern Middle Eastern kingdom – Western, orderly, and strong. But behind that image was something brittle. Tired. Unsure.

We all felt it, though we rarely said it out loud.

In our family, politics were never discussed directly. My parents had grown up under different kings, seen enough to know when to stay quiet. But even they couldn't help commenting – when prices rose too fast, when another neighbour's son disappeared, or when a cousin from the provinces spoke of land taken or jobs lost. We were not activists. We were not revolutionaries. But we were awake.

That year, Ali Shariati died. I remember how quickly the news spread, how mourners gathered in quiet defiance. Shariati had meant something – especially to the young. His words didn't sound like the sermons of the old clergy. He spoke of Islam in a way that felt urgent, intellectual, and defiant. His death felt unnatural, suspicious. And then, only months later, we heard that Mostafa Khomeini, the Ayatollah's son, had died suddenly in Iraq. Two deaths, close together. Most people didn't believe the official explanations. The whispers began again.

I recall standing in a bookstore that year – the kind where the shelves were too tightly packed, and the shopkeeper always looked twice before handing you what you asked for. A student brushed past me and pressed a folded flyer into my hand. He didn't look back. When I opened it later, it was a copy of a poem – censored verses by someone who had vanished. The ink was faint, like the voice of the country itself: shaken, but still speaking.

In the mosques, in the universities, in the narrow alleys of the bazaar – you could feel a quiet trembling. Khomeini's cassette tapes were circulating again, smuggled across borders and duplicated in back rooms. I heard one for the first time in a friend's home, the volume turned low. The voice was calm but unyielding. It didn't sound like a man in exile. It sounded like a man coming home.

And then there was President Carter, speaking of "human rights" in Washington. It meant little to most Iranians – and yet, somehow, the pressure on the Shah seemed real. Newspapers printed things they hadn't before. A few political prisoners were released. The Writers' Association of Iran began to speak more boldly, holding public readings. Even the language in the press changed – less worshipful, more cautious, but not so fearful. It was as if the country had been holding its breath for too long and had finally begun to exhale.

I don't remember any single moment when I knew that something historic was happening. But I remember a feeling – as if the ground beneath our lives had started to shift. Not violently. Not yet. But undeniably. We didn't call it revolution. We didn't know what name to give it. But we knew we were not going back.

In 1978, Iran stopped whispering.

That year, history came rushing in – not in careful, cautious steps like before, but in fire, in chants, in funerals that became protests, and protests that became riots. It was as if the country had finally found its voice, and it was a voice that would not be silenced again.

At first, it felt like another rumour. Someone said something had happened in Qom – a student killed, a demonstration broken up by police. The newspapers reported a "minor disturbance", nothing more. But we all knew better. It wasn't just one city. It was all of us, finally saying no.

Back then, I was still trying to live an ordinary life. Going to school. Shopping in the bazaar. Drinking tea in the afternoons. But ordinary life no longer held steady. There were strikes. There were roadblocks. One day, you'd hear that banks had been burned. The next, that demonstrators were shot in Tabriz or Mashhad. Black-and-white photos started appearing on walls – of martyrs, of missing sons. Some we knew. Some we didn't. They were all ours, somehow.

It was strange – this mixture of fear and freedom. Fear of the soldiers in the street, of the plainclothes police lurking in crowds. But also freedom in the way people spoke to one another now, without hesitation. Strangers would speak to you on the bus: "Have you heard Khomeini's latest message?" or "They killed three students yesterday – bastards". We had been silent so long that when we finally spoke, it was as if we had forgotten how to stop.

And then came the Rex Cinema fire in Abadan – August 19th. Over 400 people, burned alive. Trapped inside a locked theatre. The government blamed "Islamic extremists". The people blamed SAVAK. I remember the faces of neighbours who had lost relatives, their eyes glassy with grief and rage. It didn't matter anymore who started the fire – what mattered was what it symbolized. That no one was safe. That everything was burning.

By the autumn of 1978, Tehran was a different city. Shops were shuttered. Strikes spread – from the oil workers to the teachers, even the bazaaris joined. We no longer knew when to expect school closures or curfews. We kept candles in the house. We stocked up on rice and bread. We listened to the BBC in secret. The Shah still appeared on television, offering promises of reform, calling for calm. But no one was listening.

Khomeini, now in exile in France, became more present than the Shah himself. His voice, carried on cassette tapes and flyers, echoed in our homes, our mosques, our memories. He spoke not just to the religious, but to the angry, the disillusioned, the poor, the betrayed. For some, he was a saviour. For others, a mystery. But all agreed – he had become the symbol of resistance.

I remember standing in a protest that autumn – not in the front, not shouting slogans, just standing. Watching. Around me, men and women raised their fists and chanted, "Death to the Shah!" I had never heard such a thing in public before. And I felt something then – not hate, not even anger. It was something closer to sorrow. As if we all knew the country we had known was already gone.

Later that year, martial law was declared. More killings followed. More funerals. Each funeral became another protest, each protest another funeral. The cycle was unstoppable. Even the army – long the Shah's final pillar – began to show cracks. Some soldiers refused to fire on demonstrators. Others joined the crowds.

By December, the demonstrations were vast – millions on the streets. I watched them from rooftops, from alleyways, from behind curtained windows. Flags waving.

Black chadors and white turbans. Banners with poetry. Chants that mixed politics with prayer.

"Esteqlal. Azadi. Jomhouri-ye Eslami."

Independence. Freedom. An Islamic Republic.

It was not the same Iran I had grown up in. And I knew then, deep in my bones, that the country would never return to what it had been.

The silence had broken. The future had arrived – loud, uncertain, and unstoppable.

I woke up on February 1st, 1979, to a Shiraz that felt like it was holding its breath.

Outside, the streets were already crowded. Radios buzzed in homes and shopfronts, all tuned to the same voice. People stood on rooftops or pressed together near Mehrabad Airport. Strangers prayed side by side, students clutched cassette recorders, old men wept. After 15 years in exile, Ayatollah Ruhollah Khomeini was coming home.

The Shah had already gone – fled the country in January under the pretence of a "vacation". No one believed he would return. His departure was not met with sympathy. There were no goodbyes. Just the sound of crowds cheering in the streets and the feeling that history had just changed direction. It felt impossible and inevitable at the same time.

When Khomeini's plane finally touched down, it was as if time stopped. Everyone – even those who hadn't fully supported him – knew we were witnessing something immense. I watched it on television, transfixed. There he was: black turban, white beard, eyes as still as stone. As he descended the stairs and walked through the crowd, surrounded by guards and followers, I remember thinking –

this is not just a man. This is something else now. A symbol. A storm wrapped in flesh.

That day, Tehran was transformed. Posters of the Shah were torn down. His statues toppled. Soldiers defected. Women passed out sweets in the streets. Men cried openly. For one strange, impossible moment, it seemed like all of Iran was united – religious and secular, poor and middle class, students and bazaaris – not just against the monarchy, but for something they believed would be better.

But unity, like euphoria, doesn't last.

In the weeks that followed Khomeini's return, the old government collapsed piece by piece. Prime Minister Bakhtiar tried to hold on – a man loyal to the Shah but trying to manage a peaceful transition. It was too late. No one listened. On February 11, the army officially declared neutrality, and the people flooded the streets, storming army bases, police stations, and prisons. That night, the regime fell. We didn't need an official statement. We felt it in the noise – a city erupting with gunfire and celebration.

That week, my neighbourhood became a different world. Revolutionary Committees sprang up overnight. Young men with rifles patrolled the streets. Some were students. Some looked barely old enough to shave. Bazaars hung banners with quotes from Khomeini. Local mosques became command centres. It was thrilling. It was chaotic. It was terrifying.

Everything moved fast.

In March, Khomeini called for a national referendum – a simple yes or no: "Do you want an Islamic Republic?" There was no other option on the ballot. No mention of a constitution. No room for debate. Most people said yes. Many didn't dare say no. Others, still riding the wave of revolution, believed it was a new beginning – that somehow, Iran could be both Islamic and free.

We voted. The result was announced: 98% in favour.

And just like that, the Pahlavi dynasty was over. Iran became something entirely new. Not a monarchy. Not a democracy. But a velayat-e faqih – a government ruled by Islamic jurists, with Khomeini as Supreme Leader.

At first, there was confusion. What did it mean, really? Would life change for everyone? Would women lose their rights? Would music be banned? Would the leftists be allowed to participate? The country was still buzzing with revolutionary energy, and some believed there was room for all – religious and secular, devout and progressive.

But by summer, it became clear: this was no pluralistic revolution. It was becoming a theocracy. Hijab, once a choice, became an expectation. Women were told to "return to modesty". Universities came under scrutiny. Revolutionary courts began trying members of the old regime – many without due process. Executions followed.

Friends began to disappear. Journalists were arrested. Some former revolutionaries – especially those from secular and leftist groups – found themselves now the enemy. The very people who had helped bring down the Shah were being pushed out, silenced, or worse.

At home, we watched it all unfold with a mix of disbelief and resignation. The fear we had once known under the Shah was returning – not in the same uniform, but with the same effect. People became cautious again. Words were measured. Eyes watched you more closely. The chant of "Death to the Shah!" had been replaced with "Death to America!" and "Death to the traitors!".

A new chapter had begun. But it was not the one many had hoped for.

Still, some part of me remembers the hope that pulsed through those early weeks of 1979. The way people hugged in the street. The way strangers handed out roses to soldiers. The sound of collective joy, before it fractured into fear.

The revolution gave us power. But it also took something from us – our innocence, our certainty, and in many ways, our unity. We were no longer whispering. But we were no longer sure what we had said.

The revolution was supposed to free us. That's what we believed in the streets in 1979, when we chanted, when we marched, when we tore down the Shah's portraits with our bare hands. But by 1980, the slogans were no longer ours. They belonged to someone else – someone watching us more closely than the Shah ever had.

The feeling changed quickly. I remember it clearly. One day, people were still celebrating a new republic. The next, it was as if we had walked into a darker version of our old life – same fear, new uniforms.

In early 1980, I began to see the signs. Literally. Posters appeared overnight – Ayatollah Khomeini's image everywhere, along with new rules, new "guidelines for Islamic conduct". Suddenly, you could be stopped for the way you dressed, for playing music too loud, for reading the wrong books. Revolutionary Guards – the Pasdaran – were on every corner, polite sometimes, but always watching.

One afternoon, I passed a wall that had been painted over. Underneath the fresh coat, I could still make out the faded slogan from a leftist group – "Freedom, Justice, Bread". Someone had replaced it with a Qur'anic verse.

That was Iran now: one message silenced, another imposed.

The universities were next.

One afternoon, I was riding my bicycle home from school, pedalling through the familiar streets of Shiraz. It was an ordinary day – dust in the air, the heat rising off the pavement, the usual chaos of traffic and voices – but as I turned the corner near the University of Literature, I saw something that made me stop. The street ahead was packed with people. A demonstration was underway, loud and intense, charged with a kind of electricity that made the hair on my arms stand up.

I stopped my bike and stood there, quietly, as if frozen. The crowd was dense, and the voices loud, but then I heard one voice rise above the rest. It was a woman – her voice calm but fierce, her presence magnetic. She was standing atop something, maybe a box or a low wall, her long dark coat fluttering behind her, her eyes burning with conviction. She spoke with passion and clarity, denouncing the religious authorities and the direction the revolution had taken.

She said we had been fooled.

That replacing one form of tyranny with another – this time cloaked in the name of God – was not liberation. That the Islamic regime was not the answer to our suffering. She spoke of true freedom, of class struggle, of workers and students uniting against oppression. I didn't know her then, not by name. But her words pierced through the confusion and fear I had been carrying inside me since the revolution had turned on its own children.

Her name, I later learned, was Ashraf Dehghani – the legendary woman who had escaped torture and death in the Shah's prison, a living symbol of resistance. She was a leading figure of the Cherikha-ye Fada'i-e Khalq, the People's Fedayeen Guerrillas. And in that moment, watching her speak, I felt something shift inside me – deep, irreversible.

I was mesmerised.

I didn't move. I barely blinked. I stood silently with my bike beside me, the crowd pushing and shouting all around, but I was listening only to her. Every word was like fire and water at the same time – burning away illusions, washing away doubts. She made me realise how blind we had been, how easily we had traded one cage for another. The dreams we had carried before the revolution – the hopes of justice, equality, freedom – had been hijacked by turbans and guns.

That night, when I finally made it home, I couldn't stop thinking about her. The way she stood so fearless. The clarity of her voice. The raw truth in her message.

From that day forward, I made a quiet vow to myself: I will follow this path. I began searching for her writings. I found her memoirs, her political pamphlets, interviews, and underground materials – anything I could read, I devoured. Her words became my teacher. Her struggle became a map for my own convictions.

I was just a boy with a second-hand bike, riding through a city that had become a battlefield of ideologies. But I knew then that I could not remain neutral. I could not pretend. I had seen something real, and it had changed me.

I had found a direction. A purpose. A fight worth joining.

From that moment on, something inside me had changed. I couldn't un-hear her voice, and I didn't want to. The fire Ashraf Dehghani lit in me burned through the confusion and loneliness I had been carrying for years. I was barely old enough to understand the complexity of political theory, but old enough to recognize truth when I saw it – or in her case, heard it.

Back at school, the classrooms and routines felt even more empty and disconnected. I no longer cared about memorising poems for literature class or the dry history books filled with glorified nonsense. What mattered to me now were the ideas that lived underground – the voices silenced by both the Shah and now the mullahs who had taken over his throne.

I began spending my afternoons and evenings searching for anything I could read. At first, it was just books. Smuggled ones. Revolutionary texts passed from hand to hand, hidden inside textbooks or stuffed beneath winter coats. Some were photocopies, the pages warped and smudged, sometimes missing whole sections. But I read every word like it was sacred scripture.

I found a small group of students who shared the same hunger – boys and girls who were angry, disillusioned, and full of questions. We met discreetly in parks, in each other's homes, in teahouses, and sometimes even at the back of mosques that had been reclaimed quietly by the leftist youth. We whispered names of thinkers like Marx, Lenin, and Guevara, but for many of us, it was the Iranian revolutionaries – people like Bijan Jazani and Dehghani herself – who spoke most deeply to our hearts.

I still remember the first time I helped distribute pamphlets. My hands trembled. Not from fear of being caught – although that was very real – but from the thrill of doing something that mattered. I had folded dozens of them in my bedroom the night before, the dim yellow light flickering as I read the words over and over. Words calling for equality, for worker solidarity, for resistance against clerical fascism. I tucked the leaflets under windscreen wipers, slipped them into mailboxes, shoved them through the cracks of shop doors before dawn.

Sometimes I wore my school uniform while doing it, pretending to be on my way to morning classes. It helped avoid suspicion.

There were risks, of course. The pasdars – the revolutionary guards – were everywhere. They roamed the streets in beat-up trucks, armed and eager. They watched the universities. They stopped young men randomly and searched their pockets for "evidence" of un-Islamic behaviour: cassette tapes, political leaflets, even a chess magazine could be enough to raise suspicion. Some of my friends were arrested. One of them, a sweet boy with thick glasses, named Maziar, was beaten so badly in detention that he limped for months after his release. Another girl, Leyla, disappeared altogether. We heard whispers that she had been taken to Evin prison. No one ever saw her again.

But despite all that, I didn't stop. I couldn't.

The more I read, the more I understood that the revolution hadn't failed – we had simply handed it over too soon. The dream of a free Iran was still alive, but it now lived underground, in the whispers and secret meetings of teenagers like me.

By the time I was 15, I was no longer just a boy trying to survive the trauma of a brutal father or the heartbreaks of childhood. I had become someone else. Someone who believed that the future of Iran didn't belong to the clerics, or to the sons of wealthy businessmen, or to foreign powers. It belonged to those who were willing to fight for it, quietly or loudly, in leaflets or protests, with words or with sacrifice.

And I was ready.

CHAPTER IX

WHEN THE STREETS
TURNED AGAINST US

It was a cool, overcast afternoon in Shiraz – the kind of day where the light seemed unsure of itself, flickering between clarity and gloom. I had just left school, my bicycle rattling under me, when I heard the chants. Familiar, rhythmic, filled with a fury that both thrilled and terrified me. Near the Faculty of Literature, a crowd had gathered – students mostly, some workers, a few older men and women, scarves pulled low, collars high. They held handwritten signs and shouted slogans that had become like hymns to me: "Azadi! Azadi!" – Freedom! Freedom!

I stopped.

Something pulled me into the crowd, like gravity. I dismounted and pushed my bike to the side, locking it to a rusted lamp post. As I waded deeper into the group, I saw her. Ashraf Dehghani. Not just a name anymore, but a real woman. The woman. The face of resistance. She stood on a milk crate, her voice slicing through the crowd like a blade.

She wasn't loud – she didn't have to be. Her words were sharp, measured, dangerous. "We cannot rely on mullahs to give us freedom. We cannot trust that oppression wrapped in religion will set us free. The revolution was hijacked – now we must take it back."

I didn't move. I barely breathed. I remember her eyes – not filled with hope, not even fire – but steel. Cold, determined, disciplined. I realized, in that moment, that everything we'd fought for, everything we thought we were building in '79, was gone. Sold out. Repackaged. Drowned in a sea of turbans and blood.

From that day, I stopped being a boy with opinions and became a young man with a purpose.

It started slowly. Books at first – pamphlets, smuggled leaflets hidden inside school folders or under the floorboards of trusted houses. Then came the meetings. Quiet whispers after class. Long, tense walks along alleys where you spoke only when the wind was loud enough to cover your voice. Every face became a question: can I trust you? Every knock at the door a possibility that the Pasdaran had found us.

We weren't warriors. We were kids with ideas, with hearts broken by betrayal and dreams too stubborn to die. But some among us – older students, ex-political prisoners, the ones who'd already seen the inside of Evin – they taught us how to organize. How to move without being seen. How to recognize a plainclothes agent by his shoes or the way he didn't blink when you looked into his eyes.

We had code names. We changed locations for each meeting. We passed notes through third parties who didn't even know what they were carrying.

And then there was the protest that changed everything.

* * *

It was supposed to be small. A gathering in front of the provincial courthouse – no more than 30 of us, holding signs and handing out flyers condemning the latest executions of leftist students in Tehran. We'd timed it just after midday prayer, hoping the streets would be quieter. We were wrong.

They were waiting.

Within five minutes of unfurling our banners, we were surrounded – Basijis, club-wielding and bloodthirsty, some in plainclothes, others in the green of the Revolutionary Guard. The air cracked with whistles and boots. I remember the panic – how quickly courage turns into confusion when you're pressed on all sides.

I ran. I had never run like that before. My feet barely touched the pavement as I darted through back alleys, hearing footsteps close behind. I ducked behind a pile of garbage in an alley behind a closed bakery, barely breathing, heart thudding like a drum in my ears. I didn't know who had been caught. I wouldn't find out for days.

Two of our group were arrested that day. One was beaten so badly he couldn't walk for weeks after he was released. Another – Lalah – was never seen again. Her mother waited at the prison gates every day for a year. Then she stopped coming.

That protest changed me. It taught me the cost. Until then, activism had been words, ideas, a noble defiance. After that day, it became survival. We were no longer a group of dreamers – we were enemies of the state. And they knew who we were.

I had to choose – disappear or double down. I chose the second. But I knew the price might one day come due.

* * *

After the protest that went wrong, nothing felt safe anymore – not the streets, not even the silence of my own bedroom.

I began to walk with my head low, but my eyes always scanning: rooftops, alley corners, the backs of cars. I never took the same route home twice in a week. I didn't linger in shops, didn't answer unknown knocks on the door. Everything about me became calculation. I started memorizing names, addresses, phone numbers – and then destroying the paper trail. I learned how to erase evidence, how to burn pages and flush ashes. I didn't even trust myself to sleep soundly.

I was only a teenager, but I felt like a hunted man.

In one of the underground meetings, I met Faraj.

Faraj was the eldest of four brothers in a family that lived modestly but with deep dignity. His father worked long, punishing hours in a tile factory outside of Shiraz. Every morning, he would rise at four o'clock – while the rest of the city still slept in darkness – catch a crowded minibus, and travel 80 kilometres just to clock in at the factory by seven. He returned home each night close to ten, exhausted, his clothes dusted white with tile powder, his eyes heavy with fatigue. He barely had time to eat, let alone sit with his sons. Yet, even in his silence, there was a kind of pride in his labour. He never complained.

Of the four brothers, Faraj stood as the quiet pillar – the steady heart of the family. The brother after him, through sheer grit and discipline, became a dentist. The third became a lawyer, determined and sharp, always pushing against the system that had robbed his father of time and health. The youngest, full of promise, studied engineering and eventually landed a highly respected position in a foreign oil company – something unheard of in the circles we grew up in.

Their mother was the soul of that household. A housewife by title, but in truth, a miracle worker. I remember her warmth more than anything – how she welcomed us with a kind smile and hands always dusted in flour. Her bread was legendary: thin, soft, perfectly blistered by the heat of the clay oven. You could smell it from down the street, a scent that reminded you of home even if you were far from it. It was no wonder Faraj always had a calm, genuine smile – he inherited it from her.

I only met Faraj's father once. He was a quiet man, reserved, with the air of someone who had witnessed more struggle than he let on. Years later, we received the devastating news. A tyre on the minibus he rode daily had exploded on the highway. The vehicle rolled, and all the passengers were killed. Just like that, he was gone – his hard life ending not in peace, but in a tragic, violent moment.

His mother never broke. She grieved, but she carried on. She raised all four boys alone, supported only by a meagre pension. And still, she worked – baking bread in other people's homes, kneading dough with aching arms, standing for hours at stoves just to put food on the table. I don't think she ever took a day off. But her sons flourished. And I believe it was because of her. Quietly, with no recognition, she had built a legacy of resilience.

Faraj and I became inseparable. He wasn't just a friend – he was a brother in every sense of the word. In those years when everything was uncertain – when protests turned into raids, and meetings were laced with fear – he was the one constant. We studied revolution together, whispered names like Ali Shariati and Ashraf Dehghani under our breath, passed folded notes in cafés and back alleys, convinced we were on the edge of history.

But our bond would be tested in ways we could never have imagined. We would soon find ourselves caught in a storm far greater than anything we were prepared for – through war, betrayal, impossible choices. And Faraj... he would leave a mark on my life that I carry to this day.

Faraj and I grew closer with each passing month. We were both young, burning with ideals, but it was more than just ideology that bonded us. There was an unspoken understanding between us – two boys from different kinds of hardship, drawn together by a sense of injustice and a dream for a freer Iran. He had a way of calming the fire in me. I, often impulsive and angry at the world, admired the way he could laugh, even when we were sitting in dark rooms whispering about revolution while the city outside brimmed with fear.

We began taking more risks together. Faraj was the one who taught me how to avoid surveillance, how to memorize sensitive addresses without writing anything down, how to use innocent-sounding code words in casual conversations. He was always prepared, always thinking two steps ahead. If someone handed out a leaflet in public, it was likely Faraj who had printed it, folded it, and slipped it into someone else's hand with a smile that disarmed suspicion.

I remember one night vividly. We were both out distributing leaflets calling for a protest – small, yellow slips of paper printed with a quote from Ashraf, smuggled through photocopiers in the backs of shops and basements. We knew there was increased patrol activity after the crackdown two weeks earlier, and we had a curfew of sorts – if we weren't home before 10:30 pm, we risked being picked up. Faraj was supposed to head back early that night. But he stayed with me, said, "I don't like you walking alone. One day your anger will outrun your caution." I laughed it off, but he was right.

That same week, we had a meeting in the house of a retired schoolteacher in the outskirts of Shiraz. It was supposed to be safe. It wasn't.

They came in just before the meeting ended. A group of Pasdaran, shouting, guns raised, smashing through the front door. The moment I heard the crash of the door, my heart froze – but Faraj grabbed my hand, pulled me through the back corridor, and we ran across the neighbour's garden. I never saw him run so fast. We didn't stop until we were almost a kilometre away. Our clothes were soaked in sweat, our breath burning in our lungs.

But not everyone was as lucky. Five of our friends were taken that night. One of them, Hassan, never came back. The others emerged weeks later, thin and broken, refusing to speak of what had happened. That raid marked a turning point. Everything became more secretive after that – smaller meetings, less contact, more distrust. The group began to fracture, and fear began to settle like dust in every corner of our lives.

I began to see the toll it was taking on my family. My mother grew quieter with each passing day, worried sick but never asking questions. My father remained distant – he had always been strict, but now I sensed something deeper, perhaps fear, perhaps shame. But Juliana... she noticed everything. Her eyes followed me every time I left the house, and though she never said a word, I could feel her questions weighing in the silence between us.

Faraj remained steady. If I was the flame, he was the stone that held me from burning out. But soon, even he would be tested in ways neither of us could have predicted. We didn't know it yet, but our friendship – and our convictions – were headed towards the fire.

My mother had begun to notice after Auntie sent her messages about me and talked to me. She decided to come over with my sister and stayed for a few weeks in order to convince me about going back to Sarvestan. At first, it was subtle – she'd watch me as I came home late, tired and nervous, my eyes red from late-night meetings or reading banned books under dim lights. One night, I came home soaked in sweat, shirt torn at the collar after almost getting cornered by two Basiji on motorbikes. She didn't ask questions. She just looked at me for a long time, then quietly went to boil tea – her way of saying, "I'm here, even if I don't know what this is."

But one evening she broke.

She sat me down at the kitchen table, placed her hand on mine – her fingers rough from years of cooking, scrubbing, working – and asked in a trembling voice:

"Do you want to die, azizam?"

I didn't know how to answer. I couldn't tell her that I already felt half-dead inside from watching what had become of our revolution. I couldn't tell her that the only thing keeping me alive was the belief that I could somehow, someday, help build something better.

She cried softly. Not loudly. Just a few tears running down her face. Then she whispered, "Your father doesn't see it. But I do. They will come for you. They always come for boys like you."

Juliana, my sister, was still young, but not too young to notice the change in me. I had always been protective of her – teased her, played with her, told her silly stories when she had nightmares. But I had grown distant. The warmth between us had cooled, replaced by a kind of forced maturity on my part – and confusion on hers.

One afternoon she slipped a small note into my pocket. I found it later that night. It read:

"Why don't you smile anymore? I miss you."

I sat in the dark with that note in my hand and cried like a child. The burden of what I was doing, who I was becoming, suddenly felt unbearable.

The risk was everywhere now. Our network had been infiltrated in another city. Names were being passed. A few comrades had been dragged out of their homes at night – some resurfaced, broken and unrecognizable. Others didn't resurface at all.

And yet I couldn't stop. Every time I heard about another execution, every time I walked past the Evin prison wall on a trip to Tehran and saw the silent crowd of mothers clutching photographs, I knew why I had to continue. Their children were gone. But I was still breathing. That meant I had a responsibility.

I became more careful. I began using different names. Started hiding microfilms in pen barrels, in shoe soles. I was taught how to spot surveillance – even how to memorize the licence plates of suspicious cars following us. Once, I was told not to go home for three nights after someone reported they'd seen me at a meeting. I slept on a rooftop one night, on a cold mosque floor the next, and once in the back of a bakery where the old owner – a sympathiser – let me curl up beside sacks of flour.

But what haunted me most wasn't fear of arrest. It was the quiet pain I saw in my mother's eyes every time I walked through the door and she knew I was still intact. Still breathing. Still not one of the "disappeared".

It was the way Juliana looked at me when I left the house without saying where I was going – the mixture of curiosity, admiration, and growing fear.

We all lived in silence, pretending nothing was happening. But every glance, every quiet dinner, every night that passed without me getting home on time – it all added up to a weight my family carried without ever being told why.

I wasn't just risking my life anymore.

I was dragging them into it too. After I spoke to some of my friends, they gave me the mission of going to Sarvestan to spread the news and distribute leaflets, and I took this opportunity to visit my family.

* * *

If my mother's reaction was grief stitched with love, my father's was suspicion carved from iron.

He had always been a hard man. Discipline to him wasn't a tool – it was a language. He spoke it fluently, through silence, orders, slaps, and expectations. When I was young, he had tried to mould me into his image: strong, emotionless, industrious. But I had become something else. I was no longer the obedient boy in dusty sandals hauling water or plucking feathers beside the fire. I was now coming home with ink-stained fingers, smelling of fear and smoke and secrets.

He noticed. Fathers like mine always noticed – not in words, but in the way their eyes narrow, the way they linger a little too long on your posture, your silence, the subtle shift in your routine.

One night, when I came home later than usual – shirt buttoned wrong, collar damp with sweat – he was waiting.

He stood by the doorway, arms crossed, his face a tight mask of judgment.

"Where were you?" he asked, not kindly. Not with curiosity. But like a man already convinced he wouldn't like the answer.

I shrugged. "At the library."

He didn't believe me. He didn't say so, but I saw it in the way his lip curled and his jaw clenched.

"You think you're smarter than everyone," he muttered. "Walking like a man with no father. Like someone who doesn't owe anyone anything."

That stung. Not because it was true – but because it was the opposite. I owed everything to too many people: the ones who had died already, the ones still risking their lives with me, and especially the ones who waited at home for me to come back every night. Including him.

But my father couldn't see that. He didn't understand why I was doing what I was doing. He saw politics as poison – not a cause, but a curse. He had survived the Shah. He had found his place in the new order, awkward and resentful as it was. And to him, all this defiance meant one thing: danger.

He began to follow me sometimes – or have others do it. I'd hear from neighbours that he'd been asking where I went after school, who I sat with, what books I was carrying. He questioned my cousins, interrogated shopkeepers. I once found my notebooks in the bin – torn apart, some pages burned. He never admitted it, but I knew it was him.

My mother, on the other hand, had no such weapons. She didn't try to control or threaten. Her resistance was quiet, but no less powerful.

She would leave warm food on the table even if I came home at midnight. She stopped asking where I went. Not because she didn't want to know – but because she did. And the truth would break her.

Sometimes, when I'd sneak out at night, I'd turn to look from the street and see the curtain in her room swaying – just slightly. She'd wait for the sound of my steps, watch the dark swallow me, and whisper prayers under her breath.

One day, I overheard them arguing in the back room. My father's voice thundered like a storm:

"He's going to get himself killed! And you just feed him and cover for him like he's a little prince!"

And my mother – quiet, steady, exhausted – replied something that stopped me in my tracks:

"At least he believes in something. Let him be a man you'll be proud of one day."

There was silence after that. Heavy, thick silence.

I don't know if my father ever became proud. I don't think pride was a language he spoke, either. But after that night, something shifted. He still didn't approve, didn't understand, but he stopped trying to break me.

Or maybe he just gave up.

We were a house of unspoken things. My mother loved with warm food and silent prayers. My father punished with cold eyes and withheld affection. And I, caught between them, carried both of their fears inside me – but neither of their tools.

I was making my own way now, even if it led into the fire.

CHAPTER X

A CHOICE IN THE DARK

It was the winter of 1980, and fear had crept into every corner of our lives. In Shiraz, the streets were quieter now – not because things had calmed down, but because people had learned to disappear. Some vanished by night. Others in broad daylight, right outside their homes, or schools, or corner stores. There were whispers that the prisons were full, that they were building new ones, that confessions no longer needed evidence – only suspicion.

And I was no longer just another angry teenager with leaflets stuffed into my coat. I was now involved – properly, dangerously, deeply. Meetings in cellars. Couriers who didn't share their real names. Coded messages. Burned papers. Trust that stretched thin across too many secrets.

And then there was her.

Laila.

She wasn't a comrade. She wasn't political. She wasn't "useful" to the cause. She was just... someone I loved.

I met her at a friend's house, where I had gone to borrow a banned copy of Che Guevara's diaries. She was his cousin – visiting from Tehran for a few weeks. A girl with olive skin, quiet eyes, and a mind that saw through me before I even opened my mouth.

We started talking in the kitchen, far from the boys in the other room whispering about checkpoints and paper trails. She asked me what I was reading. I lied at first – said it was just some old poetry.

But she smiled, gently. "You don't lie well."

And somehow, I didn't want to. Not with her. She didn't need to know everything. Just enough to see who I was beyond the anger. Beyond the danger.

Over the next few weeks, we'd steal hours together – walks under quiet skies, shared bread in alleyways, her fingers brushing mine like it meant something. I found myself wanting something I hadn't dared to want in years: a future. One with her in it.

She was my breath of warmth in a world gone cold. But I knew it couldn't last.

And then the warning came. One of our members – older, careful, respected – pulled me aside one day after a meeting.

"They're asking about you," he said, not unkindly. "You're too visible. Too active. There's talk that someone close may have already been taken. You need to disappear for a while. Maybe Tehran. Maybe further."

Disappear.

And that meant leaving her.

I remember sitting with her by the river the night I told her. It was cold. She brought a scarf I had once said I liked. She had knitted it for me.

When I told her I had to leave, I expected tears. But she just stared at me with that same deep quiet I had first fallen into.

"Is it worth it?" she asked. Not like someone begging. But like someone demanding the truth.

I didn't know how to answer. I wanted to say yes. I wanted to say no. I wanted to say, You're worth more than all of it. But instead, I said what I thought was the truth:

"I don't know how not to do this."

Her face softened, but her voice didn't. "Then go. But don't come back unless it's for something more than anger."

That was the last time I saw her.

For weeks after I left, I carried that scarf with me. I slept with it like a child clinging to some memory of safety. I read her letters – brief, rare, cautious. She wrote about Tehran, about books she was reading, about nothing and everything. Then the letters stopped.

I never knew what happened to her. Maybe she moved on. Maybe someone found out who I was to her. Maybe silence was her only way to protect herself.

But I chose.

And that's what haunts you. Not just the danger. Not just the risk. But the choosing. The understanding that love – real, soft, living love – will sometimes stand at the threshold of your revolution and ask, Is this more important than me?

And if you say yes – even just once – you never really get to take it back.

THE PAIN OF BETRAYAL AND MY BOND WITH JULIANA

The revolution and its aftermath brought with it an emotional brutality that no prison or interrogation could rival. It wasn't just the violence or fear that scarred me the most – it was the betrayal. The quiet, soul-tearing realization that people you once trusted had turned their faces, that friends whispered your name to the wrong ears, and that love, once solid and safe, could dissolve into suspicion and silence.

Some of them I had marched beside, eaten with, studied with, and even hidden secrets with. But fear changes people. It makes them dangerous. One friend I had once helped escape a raid later gave my name to the authorities. I never found out exactly what he said, but I knew it was him. After that, I never saw him again. Maybe he thought he was saving himself. Maybe he was. But something in me broke that day. It wasn't just betrayal; it was the slow death of trust.

In the midst of this darkness, the one thread of light was Juliana.

Juliana was always five years younger, but in those years, the gap felt like a lifetime. Still, she was the one person who seemed untouched by the poison spreading in every corner of our lives. Her innocence wasn't naivety – it was grace. Somehow, she saw me – not the activist, not the hunted boy, not the failure of a son in my father's eyes – but her brother. Just her brother.

She used to sneak into my room late at night when she could sense something was wrong. She never asked questions I couldn't answer. She just sat with me, sometimes bringing me a small plate of food, sometimes telling me a story about her day at school, sometimes just being silent beside me as I stared at the ceiling, wondering who else might betray me next.

When I was at my lowest – when I had to go into hiding for weeks after a failed protest – she was the only one who dared bring me food, slipping it quietly into the space behind the shed. I never asked her to. She just knew.

In many ways, Juliana became the anchor I clung to when everything else felt like it was drifting away. My love for her was one of the few things I could still believe in. I never told her everything I was involved in, not out of secrecy, but out of protection. I didn't want her drawn into the shadows I had chosen. I wanted her to have something I had lost: the right to be a child, the freedom to believe in the good of people.

But I think she always knew more than I admitted. One night, after I returned from a meeting shaken and bruised, she looked at me and said quietly, "Promise me you'll survive. Not for the cause – for me." And I nodded, but deep inside I didn't know if I could keep that promise.

The betrayal from others taught me how easily people bend under fear. But Juliana taught me something more enduring: that love, when it's pure and selfless, doesn't bend. It holds.

And perhaps that's why, even now, when I remember the revolution – not just the fire and slogans, not just the risks and the dreams – I think first of her. Of her small hand slipping into mine when the world felt cold. Of her belief in me when I no longer believed in myself.

Juliana was the revolution I didn't deserve – but the one that saved me.

As the years passed and my involvement with the underground networks deepened, so did the danger. I began moving more carefully, speaking less, trusting no one. I changed my routines, stopped going to familiar places. I burned letters before they could be used against me. I memorized faces and exits wherever I went. I learned to live like a shadow.

But even shadows leave traces.

One evening, I returned home to find Juliana waiting at the gate, arms crossed, her eyes heavy – not with anger, but with worry. She had grown taller, her voice calmer, more steady. She was no longer a child. She had become a woman in a world that demanded women grow too fast.

"They were asking questions at school today," she said, without greeting me. "About you."

I stood still. "Who was?"

"I don't know. A man. He wasn't a teacher. He asked the principal if I was related to you."

Her voice broke on the word "you". That word now carried weight. It didn't mean brother anymore. It meant "the one in hiding", "the one in danger", "the one who brings risk to everyone near him".

I felt sick. I wanted to grab her and take her far away from all of it. But I couldn't. I had nowhere safe to take her. I had long since crossed a line. And the people I loved were beginning to pay for it.

"I'll leave," I said. "I'll go tonight."

"No," she said quickly, stepping closer. "That's not what I want."

"What do you want, Juliana?"

"I want you to promise me," she said, her eyes locked on mine. "Promise me this will end before it destroys you. Before it destroys us."

But I couldn't promise her that. The truth was – I didn't know how to stop. I didn't know how to be anything but the person I had become. The movement gave my pain a purpose. It gave my betrayal a direction. And even though it was devouring me piece by piece, it made the chaos make sense.

Still, I nodded. I lied to her. Because the truth would've broken her heart.

A few weeks later, I heard whispers that my name had been added to a list. A list of those being watched. A list that too often became a death sentence.

Juliana found out before I did.

She burst into the house one afternoon, shaking, her hands full of crumpled paper and a half-torn notebook she had pulled from one of her classmates. "They have your name," she whispered. "It's real. They're going to come for you."

That night, we argued. I told her I had to finish what I started. She told me she didn't want to lose me.

And then she said something that cracked me wide open:

"I've already lost one brother to this country. I won't lose another."

I didn't know who she meant. I didn't ask. Maybe it was someone from her dreams, someone she had imagined I could have been if we had lived in a normal world. Or maybe it was the version of me she still held onto – the boy who used to play chess in the backroom, who used to make her laugh when the power went out, who used to sneak her extra bread when she was hungry and ashamed to ask.

I had become a stranger to her.

But she had never become a stranger to me.

Juliana remained the one face I couldn't bear to lose. The one person whose opinion still had the power to cut through the noise of ideology, fear, and the fog of war. She was my compass. And in the end, it was her voice that pulled me back from the edge when I had gone too far.

* * *

In the spring of 1980, they shut them down — all of them. Khomeini called it the "Cultural Revolution". We were told the universities needed to be "purified" — to remove Western influence, to make education Islamic. But we knew what it really meant. Professors were fired. Students were arrested. Libraries were purged. My cousin, who had studied political science, was expelled. Too many questions, too many opinions.

We were watching a purge — not just of people, but of thought.

At home, the air changed. We didn't talk the way we used to. Even inside our own walls, we became cautious again. We had learned this kind of fear before, under the Shah. But this one cut deeper — because it wore the face of religion, and it called itself righteous. Dissent wasn't just criminal now. It was sinful.

Still, we tried to live our lives. We had work. We had families. We still gathered in kitchens and whispered our doubts. But the joy had faded. There were no more roses in the streets.

And then — as if all of this weren't enough — the war came. September 1980. Saddam Hussein invaded.

At first, it was distant. A border dispute, we were told. Nothing serious. But within days, the truth exploded: Iraq had launched a full-scale invasion, trying to take advantage of the chaos in post-revolutionary Iran. Cities in the south — Khorramshahr, Abadan, Ahvaz — were under attack. Missiles fell. Soldiers bled. Civilians fled. And we... we stood in line for rice and watched it all on grainy television.

Young men volunteered to fight. Some were barely 18. Others didn't wait for conscription. They tied green bands around their foreheads and went to the front, chanting Khomeini's name. The government called them martyrs. The streets were plastered with their faces, their smiles frozen in photographs printed on cheap paper.

One boy on our street – Reza – left for the war. His mother clutched his hand all the way to the bus. A month later, they brought back his name, written in black calligraphy, and a small framed photo. The neighbourhood set up a black tent. We all went. We all cried.

And yet, despite the tragedy, there was something else – a tightening. A hardening of resolve. The war gave the new regime exactly what it needed: a reason to silence opposition, a reason to call for unity, a reason to postpone freedom. "We are at war," they said. "Now is not the time for questions."

But for many of us, the questions only grew louder inside.

Where had the revolution gone? What had we done with our voices, our dreams? Why had we replaced one cage with another?

In those years, I learned to carry two selves: the one I showed, and the one I kept hidden. The outer one prayed, smiled, obeyed. The inner one remembered – the marches, the hope, the brief taste of freedom before it vanished like smoke.

By the end of 1981, everything had hardened. The opposition had been crushed. President Banisadr was dismissed. The Mujahedin-e Khalq turned against the regime. Bombings shook Tehran. Executions followed. Fear returned – not whispered, but declared.

And still, the war raged on.

In the winter of 1980, I made a decision that would change everything.

The war with Iraq was intensifying by the day. Cities were being shelled. Young boys, barely out of childhood, were being drafted and sent to the frontlines. Yet, despite the chaos, I had made up my mind – I wanted to leave the country. I didn't yet know how or where to, but I felt a growing sense that if I stayed, I might not survive. The regime was tightening its grip, and the underground circles I was part of were becoming more and more dangerous. I needed a passport. But in Iran, no young man could get one unless he completed his military service.

It felt like a cruel paradox: to escape the war, I had to step directly into it.

I gathered four of my closest friends from high school – Amir, Asghar, Ahmad, and Mansoor – and told them of my plan. We had all just graduated, full of uncertain hope and vague dreams. We were young, reckless, and desperate for freedom. To my surprise, they agreed. Together, we would join the military, complete the compulsory service, and try – somehow – to find our way out of Iran.

My father was furious when he heard my decision. He had always been a stern man, but this time, there was fear in his voice when he told me not to go. He had seen enough of the world to know what lay ahead. My mother, though heartbroken, said little. She always knew that once I had made up my mind, I wouldn't turn back. I left for Tehran in silence.

A few days after we arrived, I called home. My mother picked up the phone, and the moment I heard her voice, I felt like a boy again – ashamed, vulnerable. I asked to speak to my father, but he refused to come to the phone. That cut deeper than I expected. He wasn't just angry; he was afraid for me. And he was right to be.

CHAPTER XI

THE CALL TO KILL OR DIE

Tehran in winter was unforgiving – cold, grey, and filled with restless tension. Our military training began immediately. We were part of a special intake: 220 young men, all of us with high academic scores. We were the generation who could have become doctors, engineers, teachers – the minds meant to rebuild Iran. But none of that mattered now. The war didn't care about our dreams.

Most of us had never held a weapon, let alone imagined ourselves marching into battle. We weren't soldiers. We were students. Yet the regime had plans for us.

Our group was part of a larger cohort – over a thousand recruits crammed into training barracks under the open sky and brutal cold. The first three months were relentless. From dawn until nightfall, we ran drills, carried heavy loads, endured shouting commanders, and tried to pretend we weren't afraid. They pushed us hard, as if war was just a matter of stamina.

But behind all the discipline and marching was something far more chilling – a quiet, methodical process of selecting who would be sent to the frontlines. As the weeks passed, one by one, the names were called. They were given rifles, uniforms too large for their thin shoulders, and sent away on buses. Most of them never returned.

Of the 220 boys in our group – brilliant, full of promise – 212 would die in the war.

I still remember some of their faces. Ali, who wanted to become a civil engineer. Reza, who had read every Russian novel he could get his hands on. Mehran, who never stopped joking, even during training. None of them were meant for the battlefield. They didn't choose this war. It was chosen for them. They went not with courage in their hearts, but with fear, obligation, and hope that maybe – just maybe – they'd survive.

When I think of them now, I feel rage. Not just at the war, but at the system that devoured them. The dreams they carried died with them. The homes they could have built, the families they might have had, the ideas that could have changed Iran – all gone, buried in trenches and mass graves along the border.

Two weeks after our first brutal training in Tehran, they gathered us in the cold dawn for what they called "second-phase training". They said we'd be relocated to a new camp outside the city. There was a strange sense of anticipation in the air – a flicker of hope, maybe – because they promised us that this time, we would begin the practical work of becoming drivers. "You will be the army's lifeline," they told us. "Your hands will steer the machines that support the front. You are not fighters, you are supporters."

It sounded, for a brief moment, like salvation. We clung to that lie like a rope thrown into a sea of dread.

But when we arrived, after a long silent journey and a freezing night in an open tent, they woke us early and marched us through fields and broken terrain. "We'll show you your cars," the officer barked, "you'll get familiar today." We walked for miles. Then, finally, beyond the next ridge, we saw them.

Not cars. Not trucks. Tanks.

Massive, rust-streaked Soviet-era tanks. Monsters of war. Some of them barely operational. Some leaking fuel. All of them cold and dead-eyed, waiting for frightened hands to bring them back to life.

The shock that hit us wasn't sudden — it was like drowning in slow motion. I remember the murmurs among the boys, the disbelief. Then the rising voices, the shaking heads. They lied to us. There would be no safe job behind the lines. No driving. We were being turned into soldiers, whether we liked it or not.

The next month was a haze of drills, weapon instruction, endless shouting, and exhaustion. Every day, they stripped away another layer of our identity – student, dreamer, son, brother – and tried to replace it with "warrior". But none of us wanted to fight. Not one of us had chosen this path. They had chosen it for us.

And then, one morning, they gathered us again. We stood in formation. Dirty, sleepless, hungry. The commander stepped forward with a smile that didn't reach his eyes and said, "You are now heroes. The homeland needs you. You will be sent to the front."

That word – "heroes" – felt like poison. We didn't want to be heroes. We just wanted to survive. We were 17, 18, barely men. We wanted books, cafés, music, a future.

My father's words echoed in my mind that day: "Don't go. They'll send you into a war you don't understand."

He was right. This wasn't our war. It wasn't our fight. It was decided by men in palaces and war rooms. The Islamic regime had used the war as a cloak to tighten its grip, to silence protests, to flood the streets with fear instead of freedom. And the foreign powers? They had played their part too – fuelling Saddam with weapons and encouragement, turning the Persian Gulf into a chessboard of blood.

That war, the one we were being fed to, would eventually kill nearly two million Iranians. Boys just like us. Millions more would flee the country, forced into exile. And those who remained would live in the shadow of a regime that grew bolder with every martyr's blood.

They sent twelve-year-old boys to the frontlines, wrapped plastic keys around their necks – keys to paradise, they told them. They marched them across minefields with no weapons, just Qurans in hand. And when they realized they were losing too many, the government began using animals – donkeys, goats – to trigger the hidden mines left behind by the retreating Iraqi forces. That was how cheap life had become. That was what war had reduced us to.

Then they gave us a "choice" – if you could call it that. We were told we would be sent either to Kurdistan, to fight against our own people – the Kurdish Iranians – or to Khuzestan, where the Iraqi forces were pushing deep into Iran's oil-rich south.

It wasn't a real choice. We were already puppets in a larger plan.

No one wanted to fight their own countrymen. None of us wanted to be traitors to our own soil. So we chose Khuzestan. Fighting a foreign army felt less filthy than killing fellow Iranians who only wanted autonomy and dignity.

Three days later, they loaded us onto old, rusting military buses. No words were spoken as we sat shoulder to shoulder. I remember the silence on that bus more vividly than the noise of war later. We weren't joking anymore. No one was smiling.

It took 20 hours to reach Ahvaz, the capital of Khuzestan. The roads were broken, and the air grew hotter with every kilometre. You could smell oil and dust long before you arrived – an eerie foreshadowing of what lay ahead.

When we stepped off the bus, a soldier pointed at the horizon and said:

"The front is that way. Walk carefully. There may be mines."

That was our welcome to the war.

We were so worried when we arrived at the front. Fear clung to our skin more stubbornly than the sweat under the blistering southern sun. It was 44 degrees Celsius when the buses dropped us off in Ahvaz – thick, suffocating heat that pressed into your lungs like a wet rag. There was no shade. No relief. No air conditioning, of course. We were at war, and comfort was a luxury reserved for the generals, not for the sons of farmers, workers, and teachers.

They split us up into smaller groups, dividing the new recruits like cattle. I was lucky to stay with two of my friends, but the other two – Amir and Mansoor – were assigned elsewhere. The very next day, a dusty, battered army lorry came and took us deeper into the war zone. We were no longer "tank drivers", as they had promised. That fantasy had evaporated in Tehran. Here, in Khuzestan, we were just more bodies for the front line. More fuel for the fire.

They dropped us off and assigned us to sections along the trench line. I ended up in a small, dusty bunker – really nothing more than a hole dug into the scorched earth – with three other soldiers. It was about 200 or 300 metres from the Iraqi positions. At night, you could hear their voices drifting over the no man's land. You could hear the metallic clank of weapons being cleaned, the low murmur of their radios. Sometimes, you could even smell their cooking. That was how close we were – so close you could almost convince yourself that you weren't enemies, just tired boys on the opposite side of some terrible misunderstanding.

There was no cold water. They brought it in battered tankers, and it was scalding hot from sitting under the sun. We were allowed to wash ourselves maybe once or twice a week, but always quickly, always watching the horizon in case of shelling. Our clothes stuck to our skin. The dust coated our lungs and the back of our throats. You couldn't tell sweat from fear anymore. Everything blended.

Then, just two days after our arrival, the unthinkable happened – Mansoor shot himself.

The news spread through whispers. He'd used his own weapon and fired into his arm. I couldn't believe it. We went to see him, but he was gone – already transferred to the medical post. A few days later, after treatment, he came back to say goodbye. He looked like someone who had survived a plane crash. His face was pale, sunken. There was no light in his eyes.

He told us what had happened. On the first night after arriving, he had been assigned to help an ambulance as an assistant – just moving stretchers, helping load the wounded. But that night he had to help retrieve nine bodies, some alive, many not. Mangled, bloodied, silent. He said he vomited repeatedly. He said he could still hear their moaning when he tried to sleep. And he knew he couldn't do this night after night. He couldn't watch boys his age bleed out in the back of a rusty truck. So, he did what he thought he had to do. He shot himself. His father had connections – an influential friend with ties to the army – and they pulled him out.

I didn't blame him. In fact, I envied him. He had escaped. The rest of us were still stuck in this nightmare.

One day, I heard from another soldier that Faraj was also somewhere in Khuzestan, assigned to a different unit just a few kilometres away. The moment I heard his name, I felt this deep, almost irrational urge to see him. I needed to talk to someone who knew me from before all this. Someone who had laughed with me, marched with me, read books with me under candlelight back when we thought change was possible.

I knew it was risky to try to reach him. The roads were exposed and watched, so I decided to go through the hills, on foot, moving quietly and carefully. Every step could be my last – there were mines everywhere, especially in the areas the Iraqi forces had pulled back from. It was like walking across a forgotten chessboard, with death hiding in every square.

As I climbed over one ridge, the smell hit me first – a sickening, sweet-sour stench that turned my stomach. Then I saw them.

Dozens of rotting Iraqi corpses, abandoned where they fell. Some were missing limbs. Others had clearly been lying there for weeks, their bodies bloated and blackened by sun and time. Crows perched on ribs. Dogs gnawed on exposed muscle. No one had come to bury them.

I froze. My knees weakened. My body went cold despite the heat. The silence was unbearable. These weren't enemies. These were boys. Just like me. Just like Faraj. Just like Mansoor. Boys with mothers waiting. Sisters crying. Fathers crushed by guilt.

I stood there, staring at them, my stomach churning with a storm of anger and grief. What were we doing here? What madness had brought us all to this? Politics? Oil? Flags? A dictator's ego? A theocracy's thirst for martyrs?

Tears welled up in my eyes. My whole body trembled. I began to cry – not softly, but like a dam had broken. For the dead around me. For the friends I had lost. For my mother who probably lit a candle for me every night. For Juliana, my little sister, whom I promised I would protect. And for myself – because I knew, in that moment, that even if I survived this war, I would never return as the same boy.

I turned around. I never reached Faraj that day. The risk was too great, the road too full of ghosts.

The war did not end when I left the battlefield. It followed me like a shadow, clinging to every part of my being. Long after the explosions faded, I still felt their echoes in my chest. I would wake in the middle of the night drenched in sweat, gasping for breath, the images of mutilated bodies and the sound of mothers wailing seared into my mind like burns that never healed.

The day I saw those corpses on the hills, picked apart by animals, changed something inside me. I had seen death before, but not like that – not so meaningless, not so forgotten. These weren't just enemy soldiers. They were sons. Maybe they were brothers, students, lovers – boys like me. We were all boys. It didn't matter what side of the line we stood on. We were all being sacrificed.

After that, I withdrew into myself. The laughter came less often. I stopped writing in my notebook. I stopped speaking unless I had to. There was a numbness that settled over me, thick and unshakable. I hated the war, but more than anything, I hated how powerless I felt. I hated that I couldn't cry openly. I hated that I couldn't scream without risking punishment. I hated that I had to keep surviving, pretending, pushing forward like it didn't break something deep inside me.

I carried guilt too – guilt for surviving when others didn't, guilt for not being brave enough to resist, and even guilt for thinking of escape while others were still fighting. I thought often of my mother and Juliana, of the worry in their eyes when I had left. I thought of my father, who had tried to stop me, and how maybe, for once, he had been right.

The war didn't just take lives – it carved invisible wounds in the minds of the living. I returned home a different person. I no longer fitted into the world I had once imagined for myself. The dreams I had before the war seemed naive, almost embarrassing. I questioned everything – my purpose, my country, even my faith in people.

And yet, I couldn't share any of it. In those days, there was no space to speak of trauma, no understanding of what war did to a soul. We were expected to be proud, to hold our heads high, to carry on as if we hadn't seen the worst of humanity with our own eyes.

But I couldn't carry on – not in the way they expected. Something in me had shifted. I wasn't just angry anymore. I was awake.

After the war, nothing felt the same.

The fire of activism that once burned so brightly in me – driven by hope, defiance, and a fierce hunger for justice – had turned into a quiet, smouldering grief. Before the war, I believed that we could fight the system, organize, resist, overthrow. We had ideas. We had faith in the people. But after seeing so many of my generation – those bright boys full of promise – slaughtered like pawns in a political game, something cracked in my belief that we could change it all.

I no longer saw revolution as something noble. I saw it as a graveyard filled with the idealistic, the young, and the expendable. I didn't lose my values, but I lost my innocence. I became more cautious. My activism grew quieter, more secretive, more paranoid. I trusted fewer people. I second-guessed every meeting, every whisper, every knock on the door. I had seen what betrayal looked like. I had felt the cost of being caught. I knew now that sometimes the people who stood beside you in a protest could be the same ones who handed your name to the authorities.

And then there were the relationships I tried to keep – family, friends, even love. I came back different. Juliana said she could see it in my eyes. The softness in me had hardened. I no longer knew how to laugh the same way, or how to sit with someone without scanning the room for danger. I became quieter, sometimes cold. I wanted to protect the people I loved, but the way I withdrew hurt them too. Juliana didn't understand why I wouldn't tell her anything about what I'd seen. My mother said I barely spoke to her anymore. And when I tried to be close to someone – to love, to let them see me – I found I couldn't. There was always something held back, buried, locked away.

The long-term cost of war wasn't just physical danger. It was psychological erosion. Every day was a balancing act: between who I used to be and what I had become. Between holding on and letting go. I began having nightmares – flashes of gunfire, cries in the dark, the sharp metallic smell of blood. I would wake up with my jaw clenched, sheets soaked in sweat, heart racing as if I was still in uniform.

Even years later, I would find myself flinching at loud sounds, avoiding crowds, sitting near exits. I became deeply distrustful of authority, of organized ideology, even of myself at times. Was I a coward for surviving? Was I a traitor for not doing more? The questions never stopped. They gnawed at me like old wounds that never fully healed.

But in all that pain, I still held onto one thing: memory. I knew I had to remember everything – the friends I lost, the mistakes we made, the crimes committed in the name of religion or nationalism or control. Because forgetting would be a second death. And if I couldn't fight anymore in the same way, I could at least bear witness. I could tell the story. I could be the keeper of truth in a country that had tried so hard to bury it.

And maybe, someday, that would be my real form of resistance.

But in my heart, I carried that moment like a scar. The day I stood among the forgotten dead, and truly understood the cost of war.

I tried. I really did.

After the war, I told myself I had to move on. I had survived. Others hadn't. That had to mean something. I owed it to the boys who never came back, to the mothers who never saw their sons again, to the people who still believed in change – even if I no longer did. I told myself to focus on the future. To study, to work, to create some kind of life that looked like healing.

But I never really succeeded. Not fully.

There was always a part of me still stuck in those trenches, still hearing the distant thud of mortars, still seeing the bloated corpses rotting under the desert sun. My body walked forward, but my mind – my soul – lagged behind. I would smile at gatherings, pretend to listen to small talk, laugh when expected, but the laughter never reached my chest. People said I was quiet, mature, withdrawn. They didn't know it was grief disguised as control.

I tried different jobs. I tried to study. I tried to love again. I even tried to reconnect with old friends who had survived, like Faraj. But we were no longer those boys who used to sit under mulberry trees and talk about a different Iran. The war had taken that from us. Even our silences had changed. We talked less about the future and more about the past – or not at all.

My relationship with my father remained strained. He never forgave me for going to the front. I never forgave him for staying silent all those years when I needed his voice the most. My mother tried to bridge the gap, but some distances are too wide. Only Juliana, my sister, seemed to see the wounded boy still living inside the man. She would touch my arm gently, say my name with a softness that almost made me cry. But even with her, there were things I could never speak of.

I didn't return to politics with the same fire. I followed from the sidelines, signed things anonymously, passed along the occasional message. But I no longer believed that change would come quickly — or at all. I didn't trust leaders. I didn't trust mass movements. I had seen how easily the noble can become cruel, how revolutions devour their own children. I had seen boys used as martyrs by men who had never once touched the front lines.

So, I lived quietly, mostly. I built something that looked like a life, brick by cautious brick. But it never felt stable. I never felt fully at peace. Joy would visit, yes — but always as a guest, never a resident.

Sometimes I wonder who I might have been if the war hadn't happened. If the revolution had taken another course. If the betrayal hadn't cut so deep. Maybe I would have been a teacher. Or a writer. Maybe I would have learned how to sleep through the night.

But those versions of me didn't survive.

What did survive was a quieter man. Still principled. Still haunted. Still stubbornly carrying the stories of those we lost, in the hope that someone, somewhere, would listen and remember.

Because if the world won't give us justice, at least we can keep the truth.

* * *

After one month at the front, one endless month of fire and sand and death, we were finally given a brief permission — 48 hours of reprieve. We were allowed to travel 25 kilometres back to Ahvaz, the battered capital of Khuzestan, for what they called "buffing" – a time to shower, wash clothes, make a few phone calls, and remember we were still human.

Ahvaz. Even the name carried a scent from my childhood. I remembered it differently – warm evenings beside the Karun River, where the breeze smelled like date trees and jasmine, and the music of old radios drifted like perfume into the night air. I remembered families strolling through lush gardens, the sound of children playing, the rhythmic clang of boats tying into the banks. The river, wide and proud, moved like a poem through the heart of the city.

But what I saw now was a city that had lost its soul. The gardens were gone, turned into smoking craters or piles of rubble. The trees were blackened skeletons, the flowers long dead. The Karun River looked like sewage now, cloudy and stinking. There was no music, no laughter. No women on the streets. Only silence, broken by the occasional thud of a distant shell or the groan of a collapsing wall. Most people who could flee had already left. Those who remained wore eyes that had forgotten how to hope.

I took a lorry from the outskirts into town, packed in with other soldiers and civilians. We barely spoke. War had made us mute. After three hours, I climbed out and flagged one of the few taxis left in the city. The driver looked like a ghost – skin clinging to his bones, his hands trembling slightly on the wheel. I gave him the address of the safe house – our organization's centre for Cherikah-e Fada'i in Ahvaz, the heart of war itself.

The city passed by in fragments – burned-out apartments, shattered shop windows, graffiti half-erased by smoke and dust. And as I looked out, memories collided with the present. In every ruin, I saw a place where something beautiful once stood. And I thought, What if we hadn't helped tear it all down? What if we hadn't been so young, so sure, so angry? Had we traded one form of oppression for another, only to end up here – suffocating under the weight of both?

I was lost in thought when the driver snapped, "Are you getting out or not?" I realised we'd reached the neighbourhood. I handed him the money, but he didn't thank me. He stared at me with sharp resentment in his eyes – as if I, in my military uniform, was one of the men who had done this to his city. Maybe he was right. Maybe we all were.

I stood in front of the house. The front was riddled with bullet holes, jagged and ugly. A chunk of the porch had been blown off. The doorbell wire had been yanked out – stolen maybe, or destroyed by a blast. I knocked softly. For a moment, nothing. Then I caught a twitch in the curtain. Someone was watching.

A few tense seconds passed. Then the door creaked open. A man stood there, mid-thirties, dark-skinned, with tightly curled hair and tired eyes that had seen too much. He looked like he was born of this soil, one of Khuzestan's sons. His eyes flicked over me quickly, assessing, calculating.

"You came alone?" he asked.

I nodded.

He stepped aside, motioning me in.

Inside, the house was dim, its windows covered with thick cloth to keep out light and prying eyes. There were mattresses on the floor, maps pinned to walls, books – our books – piled in quiet reverence in a corner. A transistor radio hummed low in the background, someone speaking in code.

"I'm Reza," the man said, offering a calloused hand. "You're from the front?"

"Yes," I replied. "I'm with the comrades in the south. I heard this place was still... active."

He nodded solemnly. "Not for much longer."

His words hit like a gust of cold wind.

We sat. He poured me lukewarm tea. As I sipped, I looked around and realized how fragile everything had become – how quickly our dreams had turned into ruins, just like the city around us. But still, we held on. Still, we tried.

And in that moment, I knew this fight wasn't just in the trenches. It was in rooms like this. In whispered plans. In ideas that couldn't be bombed into silence.

There were seven of us in the room. The air smelled of sweat, tea, and something else – hope, maybe, or fear. Six boys in worn uniforms stood up when I entered, each one no older than 20, eyes bright with the kind of conviction that only the young still have. Only one of them wore civilian clothes. He was calm, poised, and older than the rest. I could tell by his tone and posture that he was the leader, the courier, maybe, sent from Shiraz to carry messages and instructions between cells. He didn't talk much. When he did, everyone listened.

We spoke in low voices for hours. Mostly about what remained of our network, the safe points, the scattered comrades, and what we might still do from within the military. I told them I had to return before midnight – if I missed the food lorry, I'd be stranded, and worse, I'd raise suspicion. Before we parted, they handed me a small, worn satchel filled with folded leaflets, banned pamphlets, and a list of names. I was now responsible for the others stationed at our front line, to keep them connected, informed, and – somehow – hopeful.

We set another meeting for two months later. It never happened.

A few weeks later, I received word: of the seven of us in that room, only one survived. Some had been bombed by Iraqi artillery, but others – most – were captured and executed by our own government's security forces. Silenced for believing in something better. I could still see their faces. I remembered one boy who smiled as he offered me a cup of tea, another who hummed quietly to himself as he folded the pamphlets. That room had been filled with life. And now it was only ghosts.

What a waste.

These weren't traitors. They were poets, teachers, future engineers and writers. They could've rebuilt this country. But they were gone, like so many others, buried beneath rubble and ideology.

CHAPTER XII

THE LINE THAT TOOK ME DOWN

I rode back to the front in the back of the food lorry, numb. We arrived at noon, dust kicking up from the road. The lorry couldn't go farther – it was too dangerous – so we had to walk the rest. I saw the sand stir under our boots, and I knew even this dust was watching. The sound of the truck's approach had drawn Iraqi gunfire, and we sprinted to cover as bullets traced lines through the heat-hazed sky.

That night, I began my task. Quietly, one leaflet at a time. I'd stick posters to the backs of tanks, to water tanks, inside bunkers, beneath blankets. I passed messages in code and asked the right questions in hushed tones. I trusted too easily.

Three days later, I was caught.

They found me mid-act, just as I pressed a damp poster to the side of a supply barrel. I don't remember the blow that knocked me down. Only the way the guards looked at me, like they already knew I wasn't coming back.

They questioned me for hours. Not with fists, but with silence and stares – until they decided what to do. That night, they handed me back my weapon – but I noticed it immediately: no ammunition.

They said I was being reassigned to a special unit, a reconnaissance mission near the front line. It was a lie. They didn't expect me to come back. One of them walked behind me the whole time as we moved through the dark.

We walked for over an hour. The night was so still it felt like the whole world had stopped breathing. Finally, we reached a group of bunkers. It was too hot inside, so the others decided to sit outside, resting, smoking, murmuring plans.

I sat quietly, waiting – my body on alert, my mind racing.

I didn't know what would happen next, only that it would.

Then it came.

The familiar whistle of a rocket sliced through the air. We had seconds. The others scrambled for the bunkers and one reached out to block me. They didn't want me to live.

I dived to the ground, a few metres away. The explosion shook the sand from under me. Heat, dust, screaming – and then nothing. Silence. I lifted my head. The bunkers were gone. Just a mess of charred metal and limbs.

They were dead.

I wasn't.

I wanted to feel relief. Instead, I felt sick.

Before I could move, I heard it again – a second rocket, closer this time. I ran, crawling toward a shallow ditch. The sound hit before the blast. Something struck me in the stomach.

Hot. Blinding. Wet.

I fell.

At first, I thought it had hit my groin. The pain was sharp, unbearable. I reached down. My hand came back soaked in blood. But it wasn't my groin. It was my belly, the side of my stomach torn open by shrapnel.

I lay there, alone, shaking. The night sky above me blurred. I thought of my mother's hands. Of Juliana's laughter. Of the way Faraj smiled with one side of his mouth.

I thought: This is how it ends. This is where it all stops.

And then I thought: I don't want to die. Not like this. Not forgotten.

And the moment they lifted me out of the jeep, I felt the pain all over again. It came like a flood – sharp, burning, twisting inside me, as if the metal was still lodged in my side, reminding me with every bump and jolt that I was still alive, but only just.

The hospital wasn't really a hospital either – just a concrete building in Ahvaz, barely holding together under the weight of war. Lights flickered, some rooms had no electricity, and the halls were filled with moaning, blood, and the smell of disinfectant and death. They didn't ask for my name. They didn't need it. I was just one more broken soldier.

They rushed me into surgery. I remember the glare of the light above the table and the surgeon's eyes behind his mask. I could tell he was tired. He looked like he hadn't slept in days. I tried to speak, to ask something, anything – but my mouth was dry and heavy, and my words fell apart in my throat. The last thing I remember was the cold steel of the scissors cutting through my shirt, and the sting of something sharp in my arm. Then everything went black.

When I woke up, it was daytime. I was bandaged from my chest to my waist. A nurse was wiping sweat from my face. She didn't say much. No one did. There were too many of us and not enough of them.

My body was weak, but my mind was screaming. I thought about what had happened. I was left for dead. I was sent to be killed by my own. They gave me an unloaded weapon, a mission that was just a cover for an execution, and then tried to keep me from shelter during the rocket strike. And still – I lived.

But what kind of life was it now?

I felt alone in a way I had never felt before. Not just physically, but stripped of something deeper. Trust, perhaps. Or belief. Or the illusion that I mattered to someone in this machine of war and betrayal.

For days I lay in that bed, barely able to move, listening to the cries of other wounded boys around me. Some screamed for their mothers. Some spoke to God. Some just wept quietly, the sound of their tears louder than any bomb I'd ever heard.

I couldn't sleep. When I closed my eyes, I saw the dead boys in the bunkers. I saw the faces of the six young men in the house in Ahvaz, laughing and full of purpose, now all gone. I saw the posters I never got to put up. I saw my father's angry face the last time I called. I saw Faraj. I didn't know if he was dead or alive.

The pain in my body slowly dulled, but the one in my chest remained sharp. It would never really leave.

That was the moment something inside me changed forever.

I no longer believed I could save my country. I no longer believed the cause would win. I no longer believed I could come out of this whole, or sane, or even free.

But I did believe one thing now: I had to get out.

I didn't know how. I didn't know when. But I could no longer survive in a place that had tried to kill me not once, but twice – first by war, and then by betrayal. I had escaped death by accident. I wouldn't wait for them to try again.

That moment in the hospital, when my father walked in, weeping at the sight of me alive, shattered something deep inside me – and perhaps healed something else, too. I had seen so much death, and had stood on the very edge of it. The reunion was not just emotional – it was surreal. To be counted among the living, after I had already been grieved for, felt like stepping into another reality. And in a way, it was another reality.

My father's hands trembling as he lifted the blanket to check if I still had my legs – that image would stay with me for years. It wasn't just about the fear of physical loss; it was about how close the war had come to taking everything. And in that instant, I saw not just his pain, but also the quiet, private guilt he must have carried for being right all along. He had tried to stop me from joining the military. He had warned me and now he was holding my hand as if to say: My son, you're still here. Somehow, you're still here.

And then there was Mansoor. His presence was another jolt of memory and meaning. I looked at him – not with judgment or resentment, but with deep, aching understanding. He had done what I wished I had done. He had taken a bullet to the arm to escape, and yes, some had gossiped, some had laughed, some had scorned him. But I had seen the real cost of staying. I had walked among the dead and carried leaflets in the night. I had laid in a bunker expecting to die. And so I knew: Mansoor was not a coward. He had simply survived in the only way he could. And now, both of us sat in that hospital – changed, broken, but alive.

What followed was not easy. Recovery was long, and the physical pain – though intense – was nothing compared to the emotional wreckage inside you. I had survived something most could never fully understand. I had seen too much. I had come too close.

I was haunted by faces – those of my comrades in the leaflet house, of boys who laughed in the training grounds, of the man in the bunker who wouldn't let me jump in. The war had taken them all. And worse – it had almost taken me quietly, without justice, without recognition, as if I was nothing more than a minor inconvenience in someone else's war plan.

From that hospital bed in Tehran, something hardened in me. Not out of bitterness, but out of clarity. I knew now that the war was not about defending Iran. It was about controlling it. About silencing those who resisted. About using the lives of the young to bury the hopes of the people.

And while I was still healing, I had already begun to plot the next phase of my life. The war had nearly ended me. It would not end my story.

* * *

From that hospital bed, with my body torn and my mind fractured, I began planning my escape – not just from the war, but from everything that made life in Iran unbearable. The regime, the fear, the silence, the endless loss.

I remained in the hospital in Tehran for 14 days, a stretch of time that felt endless and fragile all at once. Every moment was marked by pain and uncertainty, surrounded by the sterile walls and the distant hum of machines. My father was there when I finally received permission to go home, his tired eyes filled with both relief and worry. The journey back to Shiraz was a daunting ordeal – 14 hours squeezed into a cramped bus and then a car, each jolt sending sharp reminders of my injury through my body. Sitting still was torture; the rough seats, the jolting road, every bump a fresh wave of pain. Strong painkillers dulled the worst of it, but never enough to make the trip comfortable.

As the dusty roads stretched out before me, I found myself wrestling with a swirl of thoughts. The front lines, the endless sound of gunfire, the faces of fallen comrades – was this really the end for me? The doctors had said my injury excused me from returning to war, and yet the war had marked me in ways that no official papers could erase. I wanted to believe this was a second chance, a moment to rebuild. But deep down, I knew that the scars, both seen and unseen, would remain with me forever.

Once home in Shiraz, I tried to breathe again, to taste life outside the shadow of death. A few weeks passed in a blur of exhaustion and quiet moments. One afternoon, seeking a fleeting respite, I joined friends on a walk in the mountains – the cool air and greenery a sharp contrast to the battlefield dust. But the relief was cruelly short-lived. After barely an hour, a searing pain exploded in my belly, forcing me to my knees. The world spun; I was helpless, trembling, unable to stand. My friends carried me back to the city, rushing to the hospital where they administered intravenous painkillers. The doctors ran an X-ray, but it revealed nothing – no clear reason for the pain that wracked me.

Sent home, I hoped the worst was over. But at midnight, the agony returned, more intense and unrelenting. We raced back to the hospital in a panic. This time, after countless tests and frantic searching, the grim truth emerged: during my initial surgery in Ahvaz, surgical gauze had been left inside me, now festering and causing infection. The doctors looked grave as they explained the urgency. Without immediate surgery, the infection could spread and kill me.

So once again, they cut me open, crawling through layers of pain and fear. The gauze was removed, but the damage lingered. I stayed hospitalised for several more days, each one a battle against pain and weakness. Though I survived the operation, I never truly healed. Every few days, sharp pangs would flare inside me – reminders that the war's wounds were far from healed.

Yet, even as my body betrayed me, my spirit remained restless. When I finally recovered enough and learned I was excused from further military service, I refused to let my injury silence me. I threw myself back into the struggle with fierce determination. The meetings, the plans, the small but daring acts of rebellion – each was a lifeline, a defiant stand against the forces that had shattered so much.

I worked tirelessly to weaken the regime's hold – targeting government offices, local enforcers, and militia stations. Protecting our caches of weapons and ammunition was crucial, as was collecting funds from charities and families who had lost loved ones to the conflict. These acts were more than resistance; they were a form of survival. They gave me a reason to endure the endless pain, the sleepless nights, and the haunting memories.

In those moments, I realised that though the war had taken so much from me, it had not taken my resolve. Every scar, every ache, was a testament to survival. And in the quiet, burning fight of everyday resistance, I found a fragile hope – a hope that one day, maybe, we could build something better from the ruins.

For days after my injury and return from the hospital, I couldn't stop thinking about Faraj. We had been so close, yet I didn't know if he had survived the frontlines. The war had scattered us all like dust in the wind. Finally, during one of our secret gatherings, I saw him again – alive. He was thinner, paler, with eyes that had seen too much. But he was smiling, and just seeing him again made my heart lighter. Others were there too – old friends, familiar faces from Sarvestan – some of them barely recognizable, aged far beyond their years.

CHAPTER XIII

EVEN MY DREAMS HAD EARS

There came a time when even silence became dangerous. After the war, the streets of Iran no longer felt like home. The same slogans still screamed from the walls, the same faces still peered from giant posters – martyrs, ayatollahs, the dead and the powerful locked in a dance of control and obedience. But I had changed. The war had stripped away my illusions. I no longer saw ideology – I saw blood. I no longer heard speeches – I heard the sobs of mothers.

The whispers had started again. Friends disappearing. Someone from our old meetings arrested, tortured, or simply vanished. A name we once shared leaflets with, now whispered with fear. I tried to stay low, tried to live a quiet, ordinary life – but there was no such thing anymore. Even breathing freely felt like defiance.

It was during those nights – long, haunted nights – that the thought took hold: Maybe I have to leave. Maybe Iran is no longer mine.

At first, it felt like betrayal. I had fought. I had lost friends. I had risked everything. How could I abandon the soil where they bled and died? How could I leave my mother, my sister, the streets where I had marched and shouted and dreamt?

But then I looked around. What was left for me? The regime had become more brutal, not less. The war had made them stronger, not weaker. People were tired. Hope was a whisper. I couldn't teach. I couldn't speak. I couldn't even trust.

I thought of Juliana. Her voice on the phone, quiet and trembling, telling me that our name had come up in a meeting. That someone had asked about me. That she was afraid. I had put her at risk too. My baby sister, who had always protected me, now living in fear because of me.

That was when I knew – I had to go.

Planning an escape was like planning a second war. Quiet, paranoid, exhausting. I spoke to no one except one trusted contact, a man who had helped others leave through the mountains to Turkey. He didn't ask questions. He only gave instructions. "You must be ready to walk. Days, maybe a week. There are smugglers. There are police. There are bullets."

I wasn't ready yet. Or so I told myself.

But I still had something left: the will to be free.

There were millions of us – young and old – who, one by one, quietly slipped through the cracks of our beloved country, like water escaping through broken walls. We left Iran not out of desire, but out of despair. We weren't chasing a dream. We were running from a nightmare.

I wasn't alone in my thoughts. Everywhere I looked – on the road, in whispered rumours, in smugglers' safehouses – I saw pieces of a broken nation. The same stories played on repeat: "We had to leave", "We couldn't breathe anymore", "There was nothing left for us". But the price of leaving was steep.

So many of them never made it beyond the waiting rooms of exile. Stuck in Turkey. Stuck in Pakistan. Living on the edges of cities that never wanted us. They sold whatever jewellery they had brought. They worked in kitchens, on construction sites, sewing clothes for pennies, cleaning toilets. And when the money ran out, and when hope ran dry, some did what they had to just to survive.

I heard about girls – some younger than my sister Juliana – forced to sell themselves in dirty alleys or behind locked doors. Not because they were weak. Not because they wanted to. But because no other door opened for them. And once that door closed behind them, they couldn't open it again. They couldn't go home. How could they face their fathers? Their brothers? A society that would blame them for what desperation had forced on them?

Many had no passports anymore. The smugglers had taken everything – their documents, their dignity, their dreams. They were invisible people in countries that didn't want them, and unwelcome in the country they'd left behind. They were owned, in a way – trapped between nations, between identities, between lives.

And I kept asking myself: What am I doing? Will I become one of them? Will I be another lost name in a foreign place, forgotten by those I love and haunted by the past I tried to escape? The weight of these questions stayed with me like stones in my stomach. I wasn't ready yet.

Sometimes I would lie awake, curled in a blanket that smelled of damp and fear, asking myself: Was it right to leave? What if I vanish in a place like this – will anyone know? Will anyone care?

I wasn't sure if I was saving myself – or slowly losing what was left of me.

But I knew one thing with certainty: Iran had pushed us to this. A country that raised us with poetry, with history, with beauty – had turned its sons and daughters into exiles, fugitives, bodies sold for bread, and souls slowly starving for dignity.

* * *

CHAPTER XIV

NO FORGIVENESS GIVEN

It was during this time that things in our town grew darker. More and more, Basiji informants – zealots loyal to the regime – were appearing in our neighbourhoods. Some were our former classmates, even our neighbours, and they had turned into eyes and ears for the government. They would follow us, report us, betray us. Families were ripped apart because of their whispers. Young boys and girls we knew – who once dreamed of freedom and change – were being arrested, tortured, executed. And some of those responsible for giving names lived among us, walking the same streets, sitting in the same teahouses, selling bread and milk like nothing had happened.

One evening, Faraj and I, along with a few others from our circle, sat together in silence. No one needed to say what we were all thinking. The pain, the fear, the anger – it had been building for too long. One of us finally said what we all felt: "They've taken enough. It's time we hit back."

Revenge. It wasn't justice, but it was the only thing we could grasp.

I still had a motorbike – fast and quiet. We bought a five-litre container of petrol and hid it in a canvas bag, along with a plastic siphon pipe and a few bundles of our resistance leaflets, thick with glue. That night, under the cloak of darkness, we rode through Sarvestan's narrow lanes. Our first target was a shop owned by a man and his sons who had been openly cooperating with the Basij. Their names were tied to arrests. Some of our friends had never returned after they were taken because of them.

We parked quietly a few metres from the shop. It was shuttered for the night, silent. I crouched beside the door, heart pounding in my ears, and slipped the siphon into the petrol container. As I sucked to start the flow, the bitter taste of gasoline filled my mouth, and I choked – but I didn't stop. I guided the petrol beneath the metal shutter, soaking the base of the door and the wood behind it. Faraj handed me the matchbox. My fingers trembled. I struck it once – nothing. Again. A small flame. I lit the edge of the soaked fabric and stepped back. Within seconds, the fire erupted with a roar. The flames leapt up, licking the shutters, then bursting higher, swallowing the entrance. Orange and red lit the narrow street like day.

We ran.

My lungs were burning. My heart felt like it would explode – not from fear, but from something else. A terrible mix of satisfaction and guilt. We had done it. We had struck back. We had sent a message.

Later that night, as we sat in the orchard behind Faraj's house, breathing heavily and watching the flicker of light in the far distance, no one said much. We had done something irreversible. I couldn't stop thinking about the faces of the people who lived in that house above the shop – traitors, yes, but also people. I told myself they were responsible for deaths. I told myself this was justice. But a part of me, deep inside, wasn't sure. The fire we started that night burned more than a building – it began to burn something inside me too.

And in the days that followed, when whispers began circulating in Sarvestan about who might have done it, the paranoia returned. We knew we had crossed a line. We were now more than activists. We were now hunted.

Two weeks after our first action, the memory of the fire still lingered in Sarvestan like the lingering smoke that had drifted through our alleyways. But it hadn't silenced the informers – if anything, the Basiji network grew more emboldened, more vicious. More arrests. More disappearances.

We had to act again.

Our next target was another well-known collaborator – a grocery shop owner whose family had been whispering names into the regime's ears for months. His two daughters and one son were said to be among the most active informants in our town. Some of our closest friends were behind bars – or worse – because of them.

The plan was similar. We'd distribute leaflets that night across the neighbourhood – sticking them to doors, walls, shutters – urging people to resist, to question, to open their eyes. Then we would return to the shop under the cover of darkness and burn it down.

His shop was near a construction site, which gave us some cover. Faraj and the others were stationed at different ends of the street to keep watch. I had the petrol again, hidden in a canvas bag slung over my shoulder. My hands trembled slightly as I pulled the plastic siphon from the bag. I crouched low beside the shop's gutter and poured the petrol out, just like before. The darkness made it hard to see clearly, and I didn't realize that some of the liquid had splashed onto my shoes and the bottom of my trousers.

I struck the match. The flame hissed to life, and in one quick movement I dropped it near the gutter.

In an instant, the fire burst upward with a roar – but something was wrong.

I felt the heat first, then a flash of pain as flames climbed up my leg. My trousers had caught fire. My shoes too. I panicked. The fire was alive, wrapping around my calves like a furious animal. I screamed – not loudly, but enough to break the silence – and I ran.

Instinct kicked in.

I remembered the construction site just metres away and sprinted towards it. I threw myself onto a mound of loose soil and gravel, rolling furiously. The dry dirt stuck to my wet clothes and singed skin. I clawed at my trousers with both hands, trying to smother the fire. Every movement was agony, but the fire slowly died down.

When I stood up, I was breathing hard, heart pounding. The pain was intense – sharp and pulsing – but I was alive. My leg was burned, patches of my trousers charred and sticking to the skin. I couldn't afford to stay a second longer. Sirens might come, or worse, someone might recognize me.

I limped away, keeping to the shadows, eventually circling back around to where my motorbike was parked. My hands were shaking as I started it, and the vibration of the engine sent jolts of pain through my burned leg. I rode through the silent streets, trying not to think about the pain, the failure, the risk. I couldn't be caught – not now.

Faraj was already waiting at his house when I arrived, his face pale when he saw me. He didn't ask questions. He just helped me inside, sat me down, and quietly fetched some ointment and bandages his mother kept in the kitchen. I winced as he dabbed at the burn, biting my lip to keep from crying out.

We didn't speak much that night. The adrenaline was wearing off, and a heavy silence settled between us. For all the anger we had, all the reasons we told ourselves that what we were doing was right, it was moments like this that stripped everything bare. We were still just boys, playing with fire in a world far too cruel for our age.

That night, as I lay on Faraj's floor with my leg bandaged and throbbing, I stared at the ceiling and thought about what we were becoming. I didn't feel like a hero. I didn't feel victorious. I just felt pain – and a growing sense of isolation. We were losing pieces of ourselves, one burn, one secret, one lie at a time.

The next morning, the town was buzzing. People stood in small clusters outside shops and tea houses, whispering and chuckling, casting suspicious glances at the charred remains of the grocery store. The smell of smoke still lingered in the air, clinging to the early morning breeze like a stubborn ghost. And though no one dared speak openly, you could feel the energy shifting – like a breath being held and suddenly exhaled. Everyone knew what had happened, and while no names were spoken, the silence carried a strange kind of approval.

For the first time in a long while, the fear wasn't only on our side.

But by the following evening, I was sitting in front of a few senior members of our organisation, being sharply criticised. Not for the act itself – they knew as well as I did what the informants were doing – but for the motive behind it. They said I had allowed personal feelings to infiltrate the movement. That our resistance had to be disciplined, strategic, not ruled by emotion.

I sat quietly, listening, though my heart was burning more fiercely than my wounded leg. It wasn't personal, I wanted to scream. It was justice. The owners of those shops and their children had pointed fingers that led to the imprisonment and execution of dozens of our comrades – some of whom I had grown up with, studied with, played chess with under the mulberry trees of Sarvestan.

They were dead. Or still rotting in Evin prison. Their parents lived with unanswered questions. Their younger siblings still searched for them in dreams.

So no, it wasn't personal. It was necessary.

Still, after that meeting, something inside me shifted. I began to distance myself from our official handlers, the older "responsible" members who preached caution while others bled and died. Faraj understood. He had also lost people – his cousin had vanished the previous month – and he, too, had grown tired of waiting.

We planned one more action. But this time, before striking, we decided to send a message to the community. We distributed leaflets in neighbourhoods known for informants, warning that if anyone else gave names to the police or collaborated with the regime, they would lose their businesses. Their standing. Their safety.

We wanted to shake the foundation they stood on, to remind them they were not untouchable.

The next night, just before midnight, we gathered again – six of us, adrenaline humming through our bodies like static electricity. Faraj and I rode my new motorbike together, parking at the edge of town where the dusty road met the orchard. From there, we continued on foot, keeping to the shadows.

We had studied the patrol schedule carefully. At midnight, the Basij guards were supposed to switch shifts, leaving a brief gap in surveillance – a few crucial minutes of vulnerability. It had worked before. We hoped it would again.

The plan was to plaster our posters right in the centre of town, on the wall of the community board – the most visible spot in Sarvestan. We moved quickly, silently. The moon was high and the streets were eerily quiet. Just two minutes after midnight, I had climbed halfway up the low wall, my fingers gripping the edge, glue brush in one hand and leaflet in the other.

That's when we heard the voice.

"Don't move!"

It cut through the silence like a blade.

I froze.

In the distance, under the flickering streetlight, I saw the shadow of a man holding a rifle. Then a second. And a third.

They weren't changing shifts – they were waiting. Maybe they'd changed the schedule, or maybe they'd suspected we'd return. Either way, it was a trap.

My heart exploded into motion before my body did. I leapt from the wall and hit the ground running. Behind me, I heard Faraj shout, then the heavy thud of boots on pavement. They were chasing us.

We sprinted down the narrow alleys, our feet pounding the earth like war drums. The sound of barking dogs echoed through the streets. My lungs screamed for air, but I didn't stop. I didn't look back. I knew if I did, it would be over and Faraj was just behind me.

We ran with everything we had left in us – hearts pounding, breath heaving, chased by the echo of shouted orders and the distant clatter of boots. Our minds were blank with panic, guided only by survival. We turned a corner and spotted a derelict, crumbling old house – the kind long abandoned, forgotten by time and untouched by the war's propaganda. I remembered it vaguely from my childhood. If we could just get inside, I thought, we might have a chance.

I grabbed Faraj's arm and we vaulted the broken perimeter wall, landing hard in the courtyard. The place was pitch dark inside, shadows heavy and suffocating. But I knew – somewhere in the back of my mind – I remembered that there was roof access, and from there, we could reach neighbouring homes and disappear.

We crouched in silence behind a section of collapsed plaster wall, holding our breath. Outside, we heard the shouts – "Come out! We know you're in there!" – followed by the sudden crack of gunfire into the darkness. The bullets tore through the air, wild and blind, but close enough to feel death breathing on the back of your neck.

I whispered to Faraj, "You go. Take the roof. Run. Don't wait for me."

He hesitated, his face pale even in the shadows. I pushed him. "Go! I'll distract them."

Before he could say anything else, I stood and yelled into the night: "Stop! I'm coming out! Don't shoot!"

The firing stopped. For a moment, there was only silence – tense, waiting silence. I moved slowly, raising my hands, stepping into the pale light spilling through the broken entrance.

That's when I saw him.

One of the Basij standing at the edge of the rubble was my cousin. His eyes locked onto mine, his face contorted with disbelief and rage. Before I could say a word, he stormed toward me, raised his rifle, and slammed the butt into my shoulder. I stumbled back, gasping.

"Who was with you?!" he shouted.

"No one!" I lied.

He struck me again, this time across the head. Pain bloomed like fire. I felt something warm trickle down my face – blood. My knees buckled, but I didn't fall. I didn't give him the satisfaction.

Desperate to buy more time, I said, "It was just one friend… his name's Abbas."

"Which Abbas?!" he demanded.

I gave him the name of a Basiji – someone I knew was on their side. Confusion flickered in his eyes.

"Come out, Abbas!" he shouted towards the building.

And that's when I saw movement in the doorway.

My stomach dropped.

It wasn't Abbas.

It was Faraj.

He stepped out slowly, hands raised. His face was pale, his eyes filled with a mixture of fear and guilt.

I stared at him in disbelief, fury rising in my chest. "Why didn't you run?!" I hissed under my breath.

He looked at me, ashamed. "I tried. I got to the roof... but they were up there too. I couldn't go anywhere."

I turned my head away, biting back my frustration. I had risked everything – everything – so he could escape. And now we were both caught.

The night swallowed us whole.

They didn't waste a second.

The moment we were in their hands, the blows began again – sharp, furious strikes from fists and rifle butts landing across our backs, shoulders, legs. "Tell us who else was with you!" they kept shouting. We both stuck to the same answer, our voices strained but firm: "No one."

We were sure the others had scattered safely into the night. It was only me and Faraj who'd been caught – wrong place, wrong moment, wrong move. But we weren't going to betray anyone else. That was clear to both of us.

They handcuffed us – tight, digging into the skin – and shoved us forward, forcing us to walk as they kicked and hit us along the way. My head was pounding, my shoulder felt like it was broken, and I could feel blood drying in thick lines down the side of my face. Every step was agony.

After a few minutes of being marched through empty streets, we reached their van. They threw us into the back like sacks of meat. It was pitch dark inside, and the metal floor was cold and sticky with some kind of dried liquid – sweat? blood? engine oil? I didn't want to know.

The ride didn't take long, but every second stretched out. We could hear their laughter in the front, jokes made at our expense, and even now, I remember thinking: They don't even see us as human anymore.

When we reached the station, it was just past 1 am. They dragged us out again and gave us one more round of beatings – this time quieter, more methodical. Like they were taking their time. We didn't cry out. We didn't give them that.

Finally, they led us down a long corridor, past locked doors, and opened a tiny, suffocating space that reeked of mould, piss, and old sweat. It wasn't a holding cell – it was a tiled utility closet, probably once used as a bathroom. There was nothing in it. No bench, no light. Just a cold floor and dirty walls.

They pushed us in and locked the door behind us.

I collapsed in a corner, my back against the tiles. Faraj sat nearby, breathing heavily. In the dim light leaking in through the broken vent, I could see how pale he looked. He was in pain. We both were.

My shoulder throbbed. My head pulsed with a dull ache, dried blood crusted in my hair. I turned to Faraj and whispered, "We need to agree now. If they question us separately tomorrow, we say it was just the two of us. Nobody else."

He nodded silently, then said, "And if they push harder?"

"Still just us," I replied. "If they believe we were acting alone, they won't search for the others."

We spent the rest of that night huddled together, aching, bruised, too sore and scared to sleep. Every sound in the hallway made our hearts jump. I thought about what might happen to us next. Would we be handed over to the intelligence service? Would we disappear, like so many others had?

But even in that awful, stinking cell, even with blood on our faces and pain burning through our bodies, there was something else, too – a kind of fierce, silent loyalty between us. We weren't going to break. Not yet.

The day after our arrest, they came for me first.

I was dragged down a narrow hallway, the echo of their boots on the concrete like a drumbeat announcing pain. I didn't ask where they were taking me – I knew. I'd seen others before. Heard the screams.

They accused me of arson – setting fire to the shops. I denied it, as planned. I told them we were only putting up posters, exercising our voice, our protest. But they didn't care for truth or explanation. To them, silence was guilt, and defiance deserved punishment.

CHAPTER XV

DAYS WITHOUT A NAME

They took me into a room with no windows, just a rusted metal post bolted into the centre of the floor. One of them grabbed my arms and pulled them around the post. I heard the clank of handcuffs snapping shut. Then they tore off my shirt.

A rubber belt. Thick. Heavy. The kind used in machinery – oiled and cruel.

The first lash took the breath out of me. I clenched my teeth, digging them into my lip. I wouldn't scream. I couldn't. That would be giving them what they wanted. The second and third lashes came quickly, each one cutting deeper. I could feel the skin on my back swelling, rising in ridges like ropes under the flesh.

They said lying cost 72 lashes. I tried to count. I lost track somewhere around 20. After that, it was just pain. Raw, unending, blinding. I bit down so hard I tasted blood.

I must have blacked out, because the next thing I remember was silence.

And the pain.

I opened my eyes slowly. The ceiling spun above me. My face was sticky with sweat and blood. My shirt was gone, my trousers too. I was left in just my underwear, half-conscious, shivering on the cold floor.

Then I saw him.

Faraj.

He was lying not far from me. Unmoving. Pale. His body bare, his back covered in dark welts and open wounds, a grim mural of brutality. Blood had dried and cracked on his skin. His head was tilted to one side, his lips parted. His chest rose and fell slowly, weakly.

My heart broke.

He was never supposed to be here. I was the one who had pulled him in, who should have protected him. He had a life – a family, younger brothers, a mother who baked bread every morning to feed them. He wasn't a fighter. He was a friend. My brother.

I tried to move, crawling over broken floor tiles, every movement burning across my back and abdomen. I reached his leg and touched it gently, trying not to hurt him. I whispered his name, choked with guilt. "Faraj... My dear friend..."

He stirred. Slowly. His eyes fluttered open – red, swollen, and distant. He looked at me, a flash of recognition in the pain. I could see he was holding it in, trying not to cry, not to scream. That quiet courage only made it worse.

"I'm sorry," I said, my voice barely more than a whisper. "I shouldn't have let this happen."

He blinked slowly, then turned his face away. "They asked names," he murmured, barely audible. "I said nothing. They beat me."

We were kept in that dark, putrid room for days. They didn't ask us anything else. Just left us in silence to stew in pain and fear. There was no medical attention. Just a trickle of dirty water from the sink and a plate of rice or bread once a day, if they remembered.

After about a week, they moved us again. This time, to one of the Pasdaran's main stations – a more formal prison, but no less cruel. They put us in a cramped holding room with a filthy toilet in the corner, no privacy, no comfort. We barely spoke anymore. We were afraid the walls had ears. And they probably did.

Our backs were inflamed, crusted with blood and infection. Even putting on clothes was torture. But they forced us to wear prison uniforms when they took us into the yard.

It was the first time we had seen the sky in over a week.

The light hurt our eyes. I remember blinking hard, trying to adjust, seeing shapes of other prisoners – boys, some even younger than us, hunched over or limping. We had one hour. Just one hour to stretch our legs under a watchful guard's gaze.

Then they took us back.

Still no answers. No charges. No trial. Just silence and fear.

But in the darkness, despite everything, I still had Faraj beside me. And that mattered. We weren't broken yet. We hadn't given up the names. We hadn't betrayed anyone. Somehow, that tiny sliver of pride – of resistance – was still ours.

We had been locked up in Sarvestan's pastoral station for what felt like forever. The days blurred together – there was no calendar, no sense of time. Maybe it had been two weeks, maybe three. All I knew was the ache in my back, the hunger in my stomach, and the steady throb of shame and fury in my chest. The pain came in waves, but worse than the pain was the silence. The not knowing. What would happen next? Would we be sentenced? Released? Disappear, like so many others?

Then one morning they told us to get ready.

It was Friday. I remember because the streets were quieter than usual, and the air carried that strange mix of fear and ritual that always hung around Friday prayers. They marched us out of the prison and into a van. I knew something was off – they weren't cuffing us this time. No blindfolds. No beatings. Instead, they dressed us in clean prison clothes, handed out from a plastic bag, and told us we were being taken somewhere "important".

The van stopped by the main park – the largest one in Sarvestan. The centre of the town's Friday prayers. There were already hundreds gathered, sitting on their prayer mats, heads bowed toward the temporary pulpit they'd set up, where the local mullah would soon speak. I could hear the rhythmic call to prayer echoing off the trees and the nearby shops. It was strange hearing it again, after so many weeks in darkness. It felt surreal – too quiet, too clean, too disconnected from the suffering we'd just come from.

They led us out into the open, under the sharp gaze of the crowd. Two Pasdars stood on either side of us, and another followed behind. They didn't say much. Their posture was strict but rehearsed. They weren't trying to hide us – they were displaying us. Parade us like two sheep caught straying too far from the flock. Like examples. Warnings.

I could feel the stares immediately. Some people were whispering. I looked up, slowly, and saw them – faces I recognized. Neighbours. Shopkeepers. Classmates' fathers. A few kids from school. And then I saw him.

My breath caught in my chest.

My father.

He was standing further back, half-shaded under a tree. He was wearing clean clothes, a white shirt tucked into old trousers, and he had a thin prayer mat folded under his arm. He never used to come to prayers. I knew that. Growing up, he never prayed – not publicly, not privately, not even when our mother begged him. But now, here he was, among the faithful, trying to look the part.

And then I saw it.

Tears. In his eyes. He was trying to hold them back, but I knew him well enough to recognize it. His face was tight, his lips pressed thin, but the tears betrayed him.

And in that moment, something in me broke.

* * *

The mullah climbed up onto a plastic stool and began his sermon. He spoke about mercy. About justice. About the purity of Islam and the wickedness of the West. He quoted verses from the Qur'an about forgiveness, about patience. And the whole time, my blood was boiling. The hypocrisy. The lies. They had tortured us, beaten us till our backs were split open, and now they brought us here to perform kindness in front of the community?

I couldn't take it.

I didn't plan it. I didn't even think. Something snapped.

I stood up, my legs trembling, and I screamed.

I shouted curses at the mullah, at the Pasdars, at the entire performance. I told them what they really were. I told the crowd what they did to us behind closed doors. I screamed that they were liars, cowards, torturers hiding behind God's name.

Gasps. Someone shouted. A few people stepped back.

I barely got five seconds out before I felt the heavy crack of a rifle butt against my shoulder, then another to the side of my neck. Everything spun. The heat disappeared and all that was left was darkness.

I hit the ground hard.

The next thing I remember, I was being dragged – my feet scraping over gravel and dirt. My head was spinning. I could taste blood in my mouth. They were yelling at me, but I couldn't make out the words. I was in too much pain. The van doors slammed shut behind us, and they threw us back into the station like garbage.

I never got to see my father's reaction.

Did he try to help? Did he look away in shame? Did he pray harder, in the hope it would wash away his son's rebellion? I didn't know. I would never know for sure.

But in that moment, I wasn't afraid anymore. I was hurt – physically, yes – but what they didn't realize was that they'd made something even stronger in me.

They thought they were humiliating us.

But what they did was turn my anger into purpose. They made me more dangerous, because they revealed who they really were – openly, shamelessly, in front of my father, in front of the town.

They stripped me of my dignity.

But they also stripped themselves of any illusion.

After a few more days locked in that same cell, they told us we'd be transferred again – this time to a central prison in the county, where a proper court would decide our sentence. I don't know if I was more afraid of being sentenced or simply being forgotten.

They loaded us into the back of another prison van. It had no windows. The inside was made of dark metal, and the floor was cold and slick. The kind of space that swallowed hope. We could hear only the rattle of the engine and the chains of others shackled nearby. You lose track of time in those steel boxes. Minutes stretch into hours. Fear mixes with exhaustion, and even silence sounds like a threat.

We arrived at a larger city – Estahban. I had never been there before, and I wouldn't see much of it anyway. They dragged us out one by one and pushed us through a heavy metal door. And there it was – the prison room they would keep us in.

A single, filthy room, no more than 30 square metres. It held 50, maybe 60 men. Most of them were just boys. And there was nowhere – nowhere – to move.

The air hit me like a punch. The stench was unbearable – like sweat, urine, old wounds, and something rotting in the corner. I saw a large rubbish bin overflowing with food scraps, flies circling it like vultures. There were two small windows on the far wall, sealed with rusted metal shutters. Not a single ray of sunlight reached inside.

When they shoved us in, the room seemed to shift – bodies adjusting, pressed tighter. An elderly man – maybe in his late 60s – looked up at us and raised a hand. He murmured to the others, telling them to make space. Slowly, a few of the inmates shuffled, repositioned themselves, and carved out a little patch of floor just big enough for me and Faraj.

We thanked him softly, sitting with our backs to the wall. I felt like I had sat in the centre of hell.

Someone whispered, "Don't worry about the smell. They usually empty the bin once a week. Just... try to survive."

Try to survive.

That night, the cell fell into a ghostly silence. The air thickened, the breath of 60 men merging into one long wheeze of despair. And then, I heard it – a sound I'll never forget. A woman crying. Softly, desperately. Her sobs filtered through the concrete, from a cell next to ours.

The next day, I asked one of the prisoners quietly, "Who is she?"

He leaned toward me and whispered, "They say she's been here nine months. She was caught with some of her friends... political. But they never charged her. She's been in that room alone all this time."

Later – months, maybe years later – I learned the full story. After finally arresting her friends and gathering enough information, the authorities discovered she was innocent. Just in the wrong place, at the wrong time. No apology. No compensation. They released her quietly, without ever saying a word of regret.

But what they did say – without speaking – was far louder. The damage was done. The isolation, the shame, the dehumanisation. She took her own life not long after. That memory haunted me for years. Still does.

We stayed in that cell for nearly three months.

Each day bled into the next. There was no sense of time – no morning, no night. Just hunger, heat, sickness, and waiting. We were given food only when leftovers were available. Often, the only thing they fed us were stale crusts of bread or cold rice from the Pasdaran's meetings or religious gatherings.

Most of the prisoners had lice crawling through their clothes and hair. There was no medicine. No doctor. I was still struggling with stomach pain from the surgical complications I had after the war. Some nights I couldn't sleep from the pain, and still, nobody cared.

We were allowed outside for air just two hours a week – on Fridays, between two and four. But that wasn't relief – it was another reminder of how long we'd been caged. The sun hurt our eyes. The guards shouted at us like animals. We were never truly free, not even in the yard.

And then there was the horror.

CHAPTER XVI

WHERE TIME HAD NO MERCY

During our time there, three inmates were taken – young men I'd spoken to, some not older than 18. They were dragged out of the cell on Friday mornings and hanged in the town square, in full view of the crowds after Friday prayers. The guards came back afterwards, laughing and joking. They even brought photos of the executions – holding them up for us to see, passing them around like gruesome souvenirs.

The message was clear: Stay quiet, or you're next.

It was state-sponsored terror. A psychological war inside the prison walls.

And yet, somehow, we kept going.

We waited. We prayed, if we still believed in anything. We hoped, if we still had hope left. Until one day they said the court was finally ready to see us. The county court would decide our sentence. And just like that, the months of waiting came to an end.

But what waited for us next... we still didn't know.

It was one of those rare moments – Friday afternoon, our two hours of "fresh air". They called it a break, but it wasn't anything like that. The garden was just a courtyard – concrete, surrounded by high, stained walls with rusted barbed wire above. A square of dust and silence.

But that day, something inside me snapped.

I had had enough.

We had been locked in that foul, overcrowded room for weeks – over 50 men packed into a space no bigger than a classroom, choking on the stench of the overflowing rubbish bin, breathing the rot and filth day and night. Flies and mosquitoes bred in the damp corners. Everyone was coughing, many were running fevers, and no one cared.

I walked straight toward one of the Pasdars standing guard. He was young – maybe just a few years older than me – but he stood with his rifle slung over his shoulder like he was a god. I didn't shout at first. I asked.

"Why haven't you taken the bin out? People are sick. Can't you smell it yourself?"

He sneered at me, unimpressed. "This is none of your business. Go back."

I shook my head. "No. We live in that room like animals. If you don't take it out, more people will die."

He took a step towards me, his hand twitching near the weapon. "I said, move. Now."

By that time, I wasn't alone. Faraj had walked up behind me, his face as hollow and pale as I'd ever seen it. A couple of other inmates followed. You could feel something stir – a quiet rage spreading. They didn't shout, just stood behind me in silent protest.

That's when the Pasdar reached for his walkie-talkie. He mumbled something quickly, and within less than a minute, three more guards stormed in.

They didn't ask questions.

They started beating us.

The punches were wild and fast. One grabbed me by the back of the neck and slammed me to the ground. The others pulled Faraj and the others away, kicking them in the ribs, shouting insults, calling us traitors, cowards, scum.

They dragged me off on my own. Blood dripping from my lip. A bruise already swelling on my cheekbone. My back still raw from older wounds.

They threw me into a solitary cell, no larger than two metres. The metal door slammed behind me like a final judgment. No light. No voice. No sound but the distant echoes of shouting guards and the faint sob of someone crying in a nearby cell.

Time stopped.

There was no bed, no blanket. The floor was concrete, cold and damp. I tried to sit, but my body hurt too much. I leaned against the wall and closed my eyes. At some point, I must've slept, though sleep in a place like that isn't really sleep. It's just blacking out.

After a while – hours, maybe days – I began to recognise patterns in the distant noise. A change in guard voices, a door slamming in rhythm. I started to guess when it was day and when it was night.

In one corner, I found a metal bucket and some torn paper. That was the toilet.

I lost all sense of time. My thoughts ran wild. Was Faraj okay? Had they beaten him too? Was this just punishment – or were they planning to transfer me somewhere worse?

I didn't know anything. I just waited.

Finally, after what felt like two or three days, they opened the door.

The light from the hallway burned my eyes.

Two guards stood there, one of them with a smug look on his face.

"You're going to Adelabad," one said. "You should consider yourself lucky."

I had heard of Adelabad Prison. Everyone had. It was one of the most notorious high-security prisons in Shiraz – a place built for the "most dangerous enemies of the state". Torture, disappearances, forced confessions. It was the end of the road for many.

I nodded, numb. I didn't speak. Inside me, the fear coiled tighter than ever.

But there was also something else – something defiant.

If they thought they could break me, they were wrong. I had survived worse. And somehow, I would survive Adelabad too.

They couldn't send us to Adelabad until we had a formal court ruling. But "court" in those days meant something far more terrifying than justice. A few days later, they gathered ten or 11 of us young boys, barely older than children, handcuffed us together, and loaded us into a van. We were surrounded by six or seven Pasdars, each with a weapon slung over their chest and a hardened look on their face, as if we were already guilty of the worst crimes imaginable.

When we arrived at the main county court, it didn't look like a place of law – it felt like a trap. They led us inside a large, dimly lit hall, and told us to form a circle in the middle of the room. No lawyers. No family. No right to speak freely. Just fear, and the weight of the unknown.

Then the door opened.

A man in clerical robes entered, flanked by two Pasdars. He was short, fat, with a sharp nose and dark, piercing eyes. At first, we didn't know who he was, but whispers filled the room almost immediately.

Sadegh Khalqali.

The infamous judge. The man Khomeini himself had sent to clean out the prisons, to deliver "swift justice". But what he brought wasn't justice. It was death, terror, and arbitrary judgment.

He didn't sit. He didn't look at us as humans. He just walked slowly around the circle, stopping in front of each prisoner.

He pointed at the first boy on his right.

"What have you done?"

The boy's voice shook. "I belonged to the Mujahideen… I was distributing leaflets."

Without blinking, Khalqali said, "Enough. Ten years."

No questions. No trial. Just a number.

He moved to the next boy. He looked even younger – maybe 13. He and his older brother had been arrested with us.

"What have you done?" Khalqali asked again.

The boy lifted his head, anger flashing in his eyes.

"It's none of your business," he snapped.

A silence fell over the room. One of the Pasdars shifted his weight, gripping his weapon.

Khalqali's voice lowered, as if amused. "I'm asking you one more time."

"I told you," the boy repeated, louder this time, "it's not your business." And then, without warning, he cursed the judge.

Khalqali didn't flinch.

"Take him away," he ordered.

No sentence. No explanation. We all knew what that meant.

He was dead.

We stood frozen. His older brother, clearly a respected figure in our organisation, was next. Khalqali approached.

"What have you done?"

The boy swallowed hard. His voice was calm, almost rehearsed.

"I didn't do anything. They made a mistake. I may have helped with some leaflets."

Khalqali gave a slight nod.

"Ten years."

And just like that, his fate was sealed.

He came to Faraj and me.

I couldn't feel my legs. My heart was beating so fast I thought I'd faint. My mouth went dry, but I had to speak.

"Brother," I began, choosing my words carefully, "we don't know... they arrested us and said we put fire to a shop, but we didn't do anything like that."

He glanced at me – just a flash of his eyes.

"One year," he said.

He turned to Faraj.

"Same for him."

And that was it. Our trial lasted less than 30 seconds. No witnesses. No evidence. No defence. Just a sentence thrown at us like scraps to a dog.

They led us back out. The van was waiting. This time, we knew where we were going:

Adelabad Prison.

The name itself sent a shiver through my spine. We had heard stories – torture, disease, executions. It wasn't a place for rehabilitation. It was a place where the regime sent people to be broken – or forgotten.

But I remember thinking in that moment: at least it wasn't a death sentence.

At least we had one more day to breathe.

Still, the cost was high. And for some of the boys we left behind, it was their last day.

That evening, they came for Javad!

He was just a boy – small, wiry, with eyes too big for his face – and when they called his name, something inside all of us stopped. We said goodbye to him, quietly, without ceremony. None of us wanted to believe it was real, but somehow, we knew: we would never see him again.

The next day was Friday.

After the prayers, they hanged him.

By a crane.

In the middle of the square.

They said people came to watch, as if it were a spectacle. Like a show. Like something righteous. The crowd stood there – eyes vacant, mouths shut – and we realized then how blind people had become. Or maybe how afraid.

Back in our cell, we kept silent. Five minutes. Not because someone told us to, but because that was the time we knew they would be tying the rope, lifting him up. No one could speak. Not even whisper. Javad's brother – only a year or two older – wept into his hands, trembling. We tried to comfort him, but what could you say to someone who had just lost his brother to the jaws of cruelty?

It wasn't long after that they came for us.

There were seven of us that day, packed into the back of a van – me, Faraj, and five others. They didn't say where we were going, but we heard the name murmured between guards: Adelabad.

The van rumbled through the narrow streets of Shiraz, and as we passed through Sarvestan, memories surged up like a flood.

My mother's gentle hands brushing my hair.

My father's tired eyes, looking over his fields.

Juliana, my sister, laughing and chasing after the chickens when we were children.

Everything from before.

Tears slid down my face before I even realized I was crying. I turned to Faraj – he was the same. Silent, eyes brimming. But we didn't speak. What could we say that hadn't already been ripped from us?

Eventually, the van slowed. Ahead stood a massive gate – tall, maybe six or seven metres high, just as wide. The driver leaned out, handed a paper to the guard. They nodded. The gate groaned open.

Inside was another wall, another iron gate. Heavier. Meaner. As if Adelabad needed to remind us again of where we were.

The paper was shown again. The second gate opened. The van rolled forward into the belly of the prison.

They took us into a small room. It smelled of sweat and old metal. No one said a word. The door closed behind us with a heavy click.

The silence in that small room was almost holy – the kind that wraps itself around your body like a shroud. None of us dared to speak. We were surrounded by thick cement walls, but it was the silence that made it feel like a tomb.

I sat against the cold floor, knees pulled to my chest. My head leaned back against the wall, and I let my eyes close – not to sleep, just to escape. Just for a moment.

And then the past came rushing in.

CHAPTER XVII

GREEN FIELDS, GREY WALLS

It was summer, in Sarvestan. I must have been nine or ten. The air was thick with the scent of dust and wheat. I was running barefoot through the fields behind our house, chasing after Juliana. She was five years younger than me, a wild little thing with hair that tangled in the wind and laughter that carried across the rows of barley.

"Mano begeer!" she screamed – "Catch me!" – her voice a mix of challenge and glee. And I ran. Not because I wanted to catch her, but because I wanted to keep hearing that laugh.

Mum was calling from the veranda in the chicken farm, warning us not to go too far. Baba was in the distance, bent over his work in the chicken coops, his hands crusted with feed and soil. He never looked up, but I knew he heard us. I always knew he heard everything.

That day, Juliana tripped – knees scraped, palms bruised. She started to cry, but before the first sob could escape, I picked her up and held her, pressing her dusty face into my shirt. I told her she'd be fine. That I'd never let anyone hurt her.

I believed that back then. That I could protect her. That I could protect anything.

The memory sliced through me, sharp as broken glass. What would she think of me now? Sitting in a prison. Waiting for... what? Judgment? Punishment? Another rope, another crane?

A cough snapped me back. One of the boys shifted, cracking his knuckles nervously. But the silence still held.

I glanced at Faraj. His eyes were closed too, his lips moving – a prayer maybe, or a conversation with someone who wasn't here.

I knew what he was seeing. He'd told me once, during a long walk back from a secret meeting, about his mother – how she used to sing lullabies when the lights went out in their small flat in Namazi Street. Her voice, soft and steady, like a river smoothing over stones.

"I'd fall asleep before the song was over," he said. "Always."

Now we were here. Seven boys in a concrete room, trying to stay human. Trying to hold on to fragments of life before the darkness came.

Still, we waited. The fluorescent light above us flickered, humming faintly like a dying wasp. Nobody moved. Nobody asked questions. It was as if we had all agreed – without a word – to retreat into ourselves. To go back to the only place that still belonged to us: memory.

Another wave came.

I was 15. Autumn in Shiraz. The skies had turned grey, and the wind carried with it the scent of rain and wet stone. That was the year I first beat Mr Nakhjavani in chess – my old teacher, the one who once said I thought too fast and felt too much.

We were in the back of the classroom, hunched over a worn wooden board. A dozen boys circled around us, whispering, half-mocking, half-rooting for me. I don't know what it was – maybe just instinct, or maybe rage from something I couldn't name – but that day, I played like a machine. Every move was exact. Every piece, a weapon. When I finally cornered his king, the room went still.

Mr Nakhjavani smiled – not the condescending kind he usually gave, but something deeper, almost proud. "You've grown teeth," he said.

That win tasted better than any meal I had ever eaten.

The wind outside the prison moaned low, like a ghost dragging its feet along the wall. I looked down at my hands – cracked, dirt beneath the nails. Those same fingers had once moved bishops and knights like they were born to it. Now they trembled.

I closed my eyes again.

Another memory. This one warmer.

Faraj and I on the rooftop of his house, a month before the crackdown. The sky above Sarvestan was brilliant with stars. His younger brother had brought up hot tea in chipped enamel cups, and we were talking about leaving – maybe getting to Ahvaz, or even across the border, if we could make it. We knew it was risky. But Faraj had laughed.

"If they catch us," he said, grinning, "we'll just say we got lost looking for the moon."

He always had that in him – a kind of defiance that didn't need shouting.

I told him that night that if anything ever happened to me, he should go on. Run. Start again somewhere. I didn't say it, but I was thinking of Juliana. Of how much she'd already lost. Of how she might never survive losing me too.

Back in the prison room, I dared a glance at Faraj. He was still sitting cross-legged, hands resting on his knees, eyes distant.

Was he remembering that night, too?

Or was he thinking of the minibus – the one that took his father away forever?

He once told me the whole story, late one night. The roads were slick with rain, and the brakes failed. His father had gone through the windscreen. He was ten years old when it happened. And from that day on, his mother carried everything – work, grief, and the hearts of four boys.

He never cried when he told me. But I did.

A sudden bang – metal on metal – jolted us all.

The door was opening.

But for those few quiet minutes, we weren't in Adelabad. We were home.

We were free.

* * *

ANSWERS WERE NEVER ENOUGH

The metal groaned as the door swung open, harsh and sudden – the kind of sound that tears through your thoughts like a blade. The cold light from the hallway spilled into the room, bleaching the edges of our faces. We blinked, our eyes unprepared for it. The moment of memory vanished, like smoke sucked out through a vent.

Two guards stepped in. One was older, his beard dusted with grey, eyes sunken but alert. The other was younger, barely older than us – nervous in his uniform, clutching a baton like it might slip from his fingers.

"Stand," the older one barked.

We scrambled to our feet. My legs ached from the cold floor, but I stood straight, refusing to show it. Faraj was already up, his face blank, unreadable.

The older guard looked us over like we were sacks of rice. "Follow."

We were herded down a narrow corridor, walls painted a sickly yellow that seemed to drain the colour from everything. A bulb flickered above us every few steps. The smell was overwhelming – bleach, mould, and something sour, human.

We passed other doors. Heavy, iron, sealed. From behind one of them came the muffled sound of weeping. From another, a cough so violent it echoed like a gunshot.

They led us into a larger room. No windows. Just a concrete box with a desk in the centre and three chairs lined up against the wall. On the desk sat a single black folder. Nothing else.

Behind it, a man in plain clothes – civilian, but unmistakably an interrogator. His hands were folded, his knuckles large and white. He didn't look at us at first. Just opened the folder, slowly, like it was part of a ritual.

"Sit," he said without lifting his head.

They brought us in two at a time. Faraj and I were last.

We waited outside that room in silence, backs against the wall, while the others were taken and returned – some pale, some sweating, one boy trembling so hard he couldn't sit afterward.

When it was finally our turn, the guard shoved the door open again.

Inside, the interrogator was still seated, unmoved, as if he hadn't blinked the entire time.

He looked at me first.

"Name?"

I answered.

"Father's name?"

I answered again. My voice came out lower than I expected. I could feel Faraj beside me, solid, steady.

He closed the folder.

"You've been seen at meetings. You've been distributing material. You've been talking to people. Teaching."

He leaned forward.

"Why?"

I hesitated.

Not because I didn't know the answer – but because I did.

Because we were tired of being lied to. Because the dreams they fed us had turned to ash. Because I wanted a future for my sister that didn't smell of blood and fear.

But I said none of that.

Instead, I said, "I was helping."

He stared at me, unsmiling.

"Helping who?"

Faraj spoke before I could.

"Each other."

The man leaned back in his chair. His jaw twitched.

"You think that makes you a hero?"

"No," Faraj said. "It makes us human."

That was the moment I knew: he would remember Faraj's face. Whether we left this place or not – whether they broke us or didn't – that answer would stay with him.

And perhaps, it would frighten him more than any weapon ever could.

The man stared at Faraj for a long time. The silence stretched, and in that gap, something shifted – not in the air, but in him. Maybe it was the way Faraj looked back at him, unblinking. Or maybe it was the weight of the truth in those four words:

"It makes us human."

The interrogator didn't reply. Instead, he opened the folder again, took out a sheet, and scribbled something quickly, almost angrily. He tore it off, folded it twice, and handed it to the guard.

"Take them."

We were led out without explanation.

Back into the corridor. Back past the locked doors. But this time, they didn't return us to the same small room. We were brought deeper into the prison, through a second set of gates – these rusted and loud, screaming as they opened.

The air grew heavier.

We passed a row of solitary cells – tiny spaces like vertical coffins, just enough room to sit or squat. In one of them, a boy not much older than me stared out through the slot in the door. His face was bruised purple, his lip split and raw. He didn't blink when we passed. Just stared. Like he wasn't inside anymore. Like something had already left him.

They took us into a dim hall. There was no light except for a small barred window near the ceiling. It was enough to see what they wanted us to see.

A boy – maybe 18, maybe 20 – hung from the ceiling by his wrists. His feet dangled, barely touching the floor. His shirt was soaked through with sweat and blood. Strips of his back were raw, lashes carved deep into the skin. You could see the bone through parts of it.

A guard nearby saw us look. He smiled, just slightly.

"This is what happens when you don't cooperate," he said, almost casually.

The boy lifted his head slowly. His face was swollen, one eye shut. But the other eye – the one still open – met mine.

He wasn't crying.

He wasn't broken.

He looked at us like we were already free.

The guard didn't like that. He spat on the floor and turned away.

We were shoved into another cell after that – larger than the last, but darker. Cement floor, no blankets. A single bucket in the corner. No windows this time. Just one slit high in the wall, where you could hear the distant sound of men yelling, doors slamming, sometimes crying.

That night, no one spoke.

Not even Faraj.

We lay side by side, our backs against the cold floor, eyes open. And though the room was silent, I could still hear the guards. The boots. The screams. The boy with the eye that wouldn't stop looking.

And I thought: this is how they do it. Not all at once.

Not with bullets.

But with silence.

With time.

With the sound of your own heart beating in the dark, wondering if tomorrow it will still be yours.

CHAPTER XVIII

WHEN THE DAYS WERE QUIET, THE MEMORIES WEREN'T

The dark pressed in so thick it felt alive, like something breathing over our skin. No one had spoken for hours, maybe longer. Time didn't move inside that cell – it folded in on itself, wrapped in shadows and fear.

I couldn't sleep. My body ached in places I hadn't known existed – shoulders stiff from the cold, stomach twisted from hunger, but it was the silence that gnawed at me the most. The kind that eats through thought until only dread is left.

Somewhere outside, metal scraped against metal – a gate opening, then closing again. A faraway shout. Then silence once more.

I rolled to my side.

Faraj lay beside me, his face turned towards the wall. For a moment I thought he was asleep. But then I heard it – so soft I almost missed it.

He was humming.

A tune with no words. Just a few low notes. Barely audible.

I recognised it instantly.

It was the lullaby his mother used to sing. He had hummed it once before, back on the rooftop in Shiraz, when we were hiding leaflets in our shoes. Back then, it made me smile.

Now, it brought something else – something deeper. It was like a hand reaching through the dark, reminding me: we are still here.

He stopped after a few bars. Silence returned. But something had changed.

I leaned closer. Whispered, "Do you think she sings it to the little ones still?"

He didn't turn. Just whispered back, "Every night."

We didn't say more. We didn't need to.

But the song opened something in me. And with it, a memory – sharp, sudden.

I was 12. It was a hot afternoon, and I was sitting on the cracked tile floor of our house in Sarvestan, flipping through an old English reader Mama had found at a second-hand stall. The ceiling fan clicked overhead. My father was asleep on the divan, his chest rising and falling like a tired engine.

Juliana came and sat beside me, swinging her legs, watching the book upside down.

"Read to me," she said.

So I did. Slowly, haltingly. She didn't care that I stumbled. She clapped when I finished.

Then she said, "One day, you'll read stories to big rooms. And I'll sit in the front."

I laughed, told her that no one would come to hear me. And she said something I never forgot.

"Then they'll be stupid."

The memory hit me so hard I had to cover my face to keep from making a sound. My chest tightened, and the tears came without asking. I let them come, quietly, so the others wouldn't hear.

In that moment, in that cell, surrounded by darkness, I felt something I hadn't in days.

Not fear. Not pain.

Love.

And maybe that was the worst thing to feel in a place like Adelabad. Or maybe it was the only thing worth holding onto.

I reached out in the dark, found Faraj's arm. Gave it a slight tap – just once.

Still here.

He tapped back.

Still here.

It had been four days.

Or maybe five. Time inside Adelabad didn't pass – it dissolved. Meals, if you could call them that, were bowls of lukewarm rice or thin soup with floating slivers of nothing. The guards barely spoke. The hallway screams had lessened – not because the cruelty stopped, but because those who screamed no longer had the strength.

That morning – or night, we couldn't tell – the slot in our door scraped open. A tray slid through.

Bread. Cold. Water in a tin cup.

And something else.

Tucked beneath the bread, almost invisible: a tiny slip of paper, no bigger than my thumb.

I looked at Faraj. His eyes widened, then narrowed in warning. Slowly, I slid the tray towards me, careful not to draw the guard's attention. With trembling fingers, I peeled back the crust of bread and palmed the note.

We waited until the echo of boots faded completely. Then I unrolled it.

The handwriting was rushed, angled, almost childlike. "Room 31. Tell him the river still runs."

That was all.

We stared at the message. My heart pounded like a drum in my throat.

Room 31.

That meant someone was trying to reach us – someone who still remembered the underground network. The river still runs was a phrase we used during leaflet drops – code for "the network is alive". We'd whisper it when we passed messages, when we found safe houses, when we thought the regime had burned every bridge.

Faraj's jaw clenched. "Could be a trap."

"Or a lifeline," I whispered.

He nodded, eyes darting to the door. "We can't ask for Room 31."

"I know."

We didn't have a plan. Not yet. But that scrap of paper became a heartbeat in the room. A pulse of maybe. Something outside these walls still existed. Someone was still fighting. Someone knew we were here.

That night, we were taken one by one for more questioning. Nothing brutal this time – just long silences, repeated questions, writing down names we refused to give. The guards were tired too, or bored, or both.

When they brought me back, we passed the hallway lined with numbered doors.

I saw it.

Room 31.

The guard was distracted, chatting with another.

And in that moment, from the tiny square window of Room 31's door, a hand appeared.

Not waving. Just flat against the glass.

Slow. Deliberate.

I don't know why I did it – it was stupid, reckless – but I let my hand drift to my side and graze the wall as we passed. A small touch. A mirror.

A breath later, the hand inside Room 31 curled into a fist, then opened again.

Twice.

Twice. That was the signal. Message received.

Back in our cell, I whispered it to Faraj.

"Room 31 answered."

He closed his eyes. "Then we're not alone."

And for the first time in days, I believed it.

CHAPTER XIX

A NEW ARRIVAL

A few days had passed – time moved strangely in there, either too slow to bear or gone in a blink without anything having changed. Then one morning, the heavy metal door creaked open. We all turned to look. A tall, blond man entered, flanked by a prison guard. He didn't speak right away. His presence filled the cramped room, not just because of his height but because he didn't look like he belonged there. He seemed like someone who'd come from a different world.

He looked around, unsure, but quiet. The Pasdar said, "He'll be staying here now." And that was it.

We had only three bunk beds, each stacked three-high – nine beds in total, but there were already 14 of us crammed into that tiny, airless room. Some slept on the cold concrete floor in the corner, others on thin blankets spread in the narrow space between the beds. At night, if someone on the top bunk needed to go relieve themselves, they'd have no choice but to step on someone else's body to climb down. Personal space didn't exist.

Now we were 15.

His name was Farrukh. He moved slowly, as if measuring every step, and then sat down silently. He was striking –

tall, with sharp, thoughtful eyes and a quiet strength that seemed to come from somewhere deep inside him. We all glanced at him, suspicious. In a place like that, trust wasn't given. It had to be earned, or forced. And so, no one asked him anything. He didn't offer anything either. We all kept our walls up, including him.

Days passed like that – monotony wrapped in tension. Once a day, we were allowed outside for exactly one hour. They'd herd us into the prison yard – if you could call it that – just a walled rectangle of dust and concrete, open to the sky. Sometimes the sun broke through. Sometimes it was just wind and grit. But we all lived for that hour. It was the only time we could breathe.

They blasted Quranic verses over the loudspeakers during those breaks, their voices echoing through the concrete walls, chanting again and again. We were expected to repeat after them, to mouth the verses back with conviction. Guards watched us from the roof, rifles slung over their shoulders, eyes sharp and dead. Speaking among ourselves was nearly impossible. The noise, the fear – it made it all but pointless to try.

But somehow, over those days, I began to speak with Farrukh. First just nods. Then a few words. Then whole whispers. He had a calm way about him, one that made you forget for a moment where you were. He told me he had been a soldier, stationed in Shiraz during his military service. He'd taken leave to visit his family – just a normal visit, just a few days off.

But it was during that same period when there was an armed clash between the government and the Chirikha in Amol. And when he returned to duty, they pulled him aside for questioning. They claimed the timing was too perfect – that he must have been involved in the uprising. He said nothing could convince them otherwise.

They told him to prove his loyalty – go stand in line for the Friday prayer. Just blend in, pray like the rest. But the guards were watching. He didn't know how to pray properly, hadn't been religious. They saw through the act, exposed him. That's when the beatings began.

Seventy-four slaps. He counted them. One by one. Then the sentencing: five years in prison. No trial, no defence.

He had been brought from another wing of the prison – transferred to ours for reasons he didn't fully understand. Maybe it was to break him down further. Maybe it was just bureaucracy. But now he was here, and little by little, he and I found some kind of friendship in that place where friendship was rare.

In the quiet moments – when the guards weren't watching too closely – we'd talk. Not just about our cases or who we were, but about what we missed. The sky. The smell of bread. The sound of a bicycle rolling down a street. In a room full of ghosts, Farrukh became someone real.

And maybe I became someone real to him, too.

In that overfilled, foul-smelling cell, surrounded by men too broken to speak or too scared to breathe deeply, Farrukh became my anchor. We never called it friendship – not out loud. That word didn't belong in prison. It was too fragile. But in the silences, in the way we sat side by side during the breaks, in the way we'd lean just a little closer when speaking so others wouldn't hear – that was something. Something more human than anything the guards could understand.

Farrukh had a soft way of speaking, almost careful, like every word had weight. When he told me stories of growing up in the north of Iran, of how he used to swim in rivers and run barefoot down gravel roads, I could almost feel it – the texture of the stones underfoot, the heat of the sun on my neck. He'd laugh sometimes, just a little, when he remembered his sisters yelling at him for being late for dinner. That laugh was rare. It cut through the thick air like a knife.

In return, I told him about my childhood in Sarvestan, about my father's chicken farm, about Juliana. I don't know why, but I told him things I hadn't told anyone else in there. About the beatings. About the protest that went wrong. About the times I had felt brave – and the many more times I had felt terrified. Farrukh listened without judgment. He never tried to fix anything, never offered false hope. He just listened. And in prison, that was worth more than food or rest or even freedom.

One night, the guards came in shouting names. Random, as always. The sound of boots echoed down the corridor like thunder. We all sat up. No one spoke. Farrukh's name was called.

He stood up slowly. I remember he looked at me – just a glance, but it said everything. No panic. No fear. Just that calm resolve he always carried, like a man who had already died once and knew there was nothing left to lose.

They took him away.

I didn't sleep that night.

Three days passed. No sign of him. I feared the worst – solitary, beatings, or worse. Then, just before lights out on the fourth day, the door opened again. He stepped back in.

His lip was split. One eye was swollen. He limped slightly. But he was alive.

He lay down beside me on the floor that night – there was no room in the beds. I asked him nothing. He said nothing. But as we lay there, back to back in that narrow space between the beds, I felt a kind of safety I hadn't felt in months.

Later, he would tell me they had interrogated him again about the Chirikha. Same questions. Same accusations. They were trying to break him. And maybe, just maybe, they were starting to.

Still, he didn't give in.

As weeks passed, we carved out small rituals. He would whisper verses he remembered – not from the Quran, but from Hafez or Khayyam. I would hum melodies from the old days, songs my mother used to play on the radio. Tiny things. Useless things. But they kept us alive.

In a world that was designed to erase us, Farrukh reminded me I was still someone. And I think – I hope – I did the same for him.

A GLIMMER OF MERCY

Months had passed since Farrukh first joined us in that overcrowded cell. By then, the stench of sweat, fear, and rusted iron had become a permanent part of our lungs. Time had lost its shape. Days blurred into nights, and names were called at random for beatings or worse. But somehow, we endured. Farrukh and I had grown close. Not in the way people imagine friendship – but in the way soldiers cling to each other in a trench, bound by silence and the unspoken knowledge that only the other understands.

One afternoon, we were sitting against the far wall of the yard, pretending to soak up sun under the eye of the guards. Our voices barely above a whisper, we talked about the future – not in grand ways, but in simple things: hot tea in the morning, a walk without chains, the sound of a door opening without dread. Then he told me something I hadn't expected.

"They haven't called me in weeks," he said.

It was true. The interrogations had stopped. No more threats. No more questions about Amol or the Chirikha or the prayer line. It was as if, suddenly, he no longer mattered to them.

Word came that they had quietly downgraded his case. Not innocent, of course – they never said that – but no longer a priority. The reason? A quiet favour behind closed doors. His older brother, it turned out, had connections in high places. Not a regime loyalist, but someone clever. Someone with reach. With bribes passed and hands shaken, the system that crushed so many had chosen – for once – not to grind him into dust.

Then came an even greater surprise: they allowed a family visit. Not in Shiraz, where his family lived, but here, near the prison far to the south. His mother and sister were given permission to see him, but for just a couple of hours.

Farrukh was excited, but his face clouded with worry. "They don't know anyone here," he said. "They've never been this far south."

Without even thinking, I said, "They can stay at our house in Sarvestan."

He looked at me, eyes wide with disbelief. No one made such offers in those days. Not with the fear, the watching eyes, the way one wrong move could mean another arrest. But I meant it. My parents would understand. My mother had always had a soft spot for kindness, and my father – though hardened by life – respected loyalty and quiet resistance. I trusted they would open their door.

Farrukh hesitated. "Are you sure?"

I nodded. "They're welcome."

He wrote to his mother, and to his brother and sister. Weeks passed. Then, one bright morning, I learned that they had arrived.

My parents welcomed them like their own. His mother was quiet, dignified. Wore her pain like a heavy shawl across her shoulders. His sister – barely in her twenties – looked older than her age, eyes tired from worry. They stayed a few days in our home, slept in the guest room, helped my mother with tea and meals. They shared stories over rice and yogurt soup, sat with my father on the veranda, talking quietly about the state of things, the dreams of sons, the cost of silence.

And then they visited him. For two precious hours. I wasn't there to see it, but later Farrukh told me what it meant to him – to hold his mother's hand, to see her eyes in person and not just in memory. It gave him strength, he said. And for once, his voice trembled.

After that, something changed.

Every few months, they returned. Not just for him – but for us. They stayed with my family, shared meals, brought dried fruit and little gifts. They brought pieces of the outside world with them: stories, music, fabrics that smelled like northern rain. They made our home a bridge between prison and freedom, between despair and hope.

And in the shadows of those visits, I understood something: the smallest kindness, offered in the darkest places, can become a kind of light.

* * *

Farrukh and I had started as cellmates. We became friends. And through that friendship, our families – so different, from distant corners of Iran – became bound together by shared suffering and quiet courage.

I saw it every day. How they cornered the prisoners – especially the young ones. They brainwashed them, threatened them, dangled their families in front of them like bait. They broke them down piece by piece. And then, once they were shattered, they demanded they inform on their friends – on her, on him, on anyone.

Some of them – unfortunately, and who could blame them? – they gave in. They leaked everything they knew. Names. Locations. Secrets.

Every day, we saw new people being dragged in. Every night, we heard the screams through the walls. Not a soul spoke, but the night was never silent. Gunshots cracked through the darkness. The sound of death became familiar. Sleep became impossible.

We didn't know who to trust. We didn't know how many weeks – or months – had passed. Talking was dangerous. So was thinking.

They chose the books for us – only what they deemed safe. We had to pretend to be devout, to attend evening prayers, Friday prayers, to keep up the performance 24/7. Loudspeakers blared Qur'anic verses day and night, drilling it into us, always watching, always listening.

When they allowed us outside for that single hour of "break", we were forced to sing, to chant along with the speakers, to repeat their slogans, their verses, their words.

And then, something terrifying began to happen: after enough months of repetition, you start believing. The chants lodge into your mind. The Qur'an replaces your thoughts. Their voice becomes your inner voice.

My mind wasn't my own anymore. Everything I thought, everything I saw, was filtered through them. I couldn't think clearly. I was in a different place – a place inside myself that wasn't mine anymore.

I remember one boy – his name was Farid. He couldn't have been more than 17. Quiet. Smart eyes. He lasted two weeks. After that, he was different – eyes dull, face blank, like someone had turned off the light inside him. He wouldn't meet anyone's gaze. A few days later, they raided the women's wing. They dragged out Laleh and two others. We knew then. Farid had talked.

There was a woman – Zahra. Maybe in her thirties. I don't even know what she had done to end up there. But she refused to bend. She never gave them anything. They beat her, isolated her and there was a story whispered among us – one of many, yet this one etched itself into my bones. She was just a girl, a prisoner like so many others, accused of opposing the regime. She was a virgin. And in their twisted logic, rooted in a corrupted interpretation of faith, they believed that if a virgin died, she would go to paradise. So they made sure she wouldn't. They sanctioned rape – systematic, deliberate – carried out by prison guards or, horrifyingly, by men posing as religious authorities. They lined them up. Pasdars, soldiers, cowards with beards quoting verses they no longer understood. She was raped the night before her execution, stripped not only of her life but of her dignity, her right to hope for the afterlife they stole from her. This wasn't justice. It was cruelty wrapped in piety, sanctioned by silence, and fed by fear.

But even in that fog, somewhere deep down, I was still there. A small voice. A flicker. A tiny, stubborn ember that refused to go out.

I remember once – maybe in the fourth or fifth month – they handed out small Qur'ans with the prison logo stamped in the corner. We were told to memorise passages, repeat them aloud, and reflect in writing. I went through the motions. I even convinced myself, for a while, that I believed.

But one night, as I sat on the cold floor, repeating verses under my breath, I realised I was saying the words without meaning them. My lips were moving, but my heart wasn't in it. That tiny part of me – what was left of me – was still resisting.

It became a secret ritual. While others bowed or chanted, I would repeat verses in my head but replace certain words – just slightly, barely noticeable. "Obedience" became "dignity". "Submission" became "remembrance". I don't know if it made a difference to anyone else, but it helped me survive.

Even walking across the yard became a silent form of resistance. I counted my steps in French – one of the languages I used to teach. I recited poetry under my breath, the kind I had loved in school before the arrests. Sometimes

I even imagined a chessboard in my mind, placing my opponents and strategizing silently while pretending to listen to the loudspeakers.

They could take everything from us – sleep, privacy, freedom, even our names. But they couldn't touch the last quiet corner of the mind. Not unless we let them.

And that became my focus: don't let them in. Don't give them that last room.

I didn't speak of this to anyone. You couldn't. One wrong glance, one misplaced word, and it was over. But in the silence, in the watching, I realized I wasn't alone. There were others holding on in their own way. A blink. A footstep out of rhythm. A moment of eye contact. That was how we recognized each other.

We were still alive – not just breathing, but alive.

CHAPTER XX

AND STILL, I LIVED

I began to survive in ways I hadn't imagined possible. Not by strength or clarity – but by fragments. By holding on to pieces of memory, of meaning. A line of poetry. My sister's face. The smell of orange blossoms in spring. The way sunlight used to fall across the kitchen table in Sarvestan when I was a boy. These were my talismans. I would gather them quietly, one by one, and carry them in the back of my mind like contraband.

Sometimes at night, while the others whispered prayers or lay silent in the dark, I would press my fingers into my palm – not hard enough to bruise, just enough to remind myself: This is my body. This is mine. It became a strange comfort, grounding me, telling me that not all of me belonged to them.

The walls pressed in. Time stretched and collapsed. I began to lose track of how long I had been there. Weeks? Months? I measured time by executions. By the sound of screaming. By who disappeared and didn't come back.

There was a day – one of many – when I came close to breaking. It was after they dragged out a boy named Mehdi. He had been kind to me. We never spoke much, but once he had slipped me a folded scrap of paper torn from a children's book. A drawing of a red kite flying over a hill. He'd said nothing, just passed it to me with a look. I had kept it hidden under my mat for weeks.

Then one morning, he was gone. They came for him before the call to prayer. No explanation. No noise. Just absence.

That night, I sat in the yard during our one hour of "freedom" and looked at the sky. It was almost clear – just a single faded star visible through the clouds. And I thought: If I scream now, if I throw myself at the wall or curse the guards, it won't matter. They've already won.

And then I thought of Juliana – my sister. Five years younger. The way she used to tug at my sleeve when she was scared. Her laugh, sharp and mischievous. I imagined her voice saying, Don't let them take you, agha joon. Not all the way.

So I didn't scream. I didn't throw myself at the wall. I stayed very still. And I survived that night.

Over time, I learned how to float above things. How to nod without agreeing. How to speak without saying anything real. How to look down when my eyes wanted to burn holes in the floor.

But I also learned something else: there is power in endurance. In choosing, even silently, not to disappear.

We became ghosts in that place. Shadows. But some of us – some – were still ourselves. Just enough to matter.

There was one day – one moment – that never left me.

It was in the third or fourth month, though time had already lost its edges. I had been called in for questioning. Nothing official. No paperwork. Just a voice barking my name from the hallway.

The room was small, stifling. No windows. One bare bulb swung overhead. A single chair. A metal desk. And behind it, a guard I had seen before – young, maybe early twenties, but hardened already. His eyes were dead. Like he had long ago made peace with whatever darkness he served.

He didn't ask questions right away. He stared at me. Long and hard. Then he said, flatly, "You still think you're better than us. I can see it in your eyes."

I didn't speak. I was too tired for games.

He stood and came around the desk. Walked slowly, deliberately, until he was inches from my face. "You think you know what truth is? What faith is? You're nothing. You're dust under my boot. If I spit in your face right now, you'd still have to thank me for not putting a bullet in your head."

I should've looked down. I knew the rules. Keep your head down. Keep your mouth shut.

But something in me snapped.

Maybe it was the hunger. The sleeplessness. The weight of too many nights listening to people scream, vanish, go mad. Maybe it was Mehdi's kite. Maybe it was Zahra's silence, her unblinking defiance. Or maybe I had just reached the point where fear no longer mattered.

I looked him in the eye.

Not with anger. Not with hatred. Just… stillness.

And I said, quietly, "You can kill me, but you can't make me believe you."

For a second – just a second – his expression faltered. Not much. Just the slightest shift in his eyes, like he wasn't expecting that. Then he backhanded me so hard I hit the wall. I tasted blood.

But in that moment, I knew something important: I had touched a nerve. Not his – but mine. I had found a boundary they couldn't cross. My body belonged to them. But not my mind. Not my truth.

They didn't call me in for questioning again for weeks after that.

The bruise faded. The blood dried. But what stayed with me – what still stays with me – is the look on his face before he struck me. That flicker of doubt. That recognition, however brief, that I was still free in a way he would never be.

After that moment – after the slap, the blood, the ringing in my ear – I didn't feel weaker. I felt clearer.

Something inside me had shifted. It wasn't that I stopped feeling fear. The fear was always there – it curled in my gut, it tightened my throat, it stood behind my every breath. But now I understood something: fear doesn't have to own you. You can walk beside it. You can carry it. And still, you can choose.

That guard, for all his threats, was more trapped than I was. He had power, yes – the kind backed by uniforms, guns, orders shouted down hallways. But what he didn't have was freedom. Not real freedom. His soul had long been mortgaged to the system. I saw it in his eyes – the flicker of uncertainty when I met his gaze without flinching. The fear he felt when he realized he couldn't reach the part of me he most wanted to break.

That moment hardened something in me – not into stone, but into steel. Not brittle, but flexible, forged by pressure.

I began to move through the prison differently – not recklessly, not loudly, but with a deeper sense of who I was. I no longer chased hope like a desperate man. I held it quietly, like a secret language only I understood.

The rituals they forced on us no longer disturbed me as they once had. I played the part, but I knew I was performing. The Qur'anic verses, the chants, the staged prayers – they became like background noise. They no longer entered my mind the way they used to. I had found a wall they could not breach.

And I watched the guards differently, too. I started to notice their patterns – the ones who lingered too long during inspections, the ones who looked away quickly when someone cried. I saw cracks in their armour. I saw humanity trying to crawl out from under their roles. Most buried it. Some drank after hours. Some kicked harder, shouted louder, trying to bury what was left of themselves beneath violence. But I could see it now: power built on fear is always trembling, always afraid of its own collapse.

That gave me something to hold on to. Not pride – not exactly. But dignity. A sense of quiet resistance. The knowledge that even if they took everything else from me, they could not make me become like them.

And that was enough. Enough to endure. Enough to survive. Enough, even, to imagine a life beyond those walls.

We had been there for a year.

Twelve months. Three hundred and sixty-five days. We counted every one. Each day carved itself into us – etched into the bones, the nerves, the breath. So much had happened in that time. So many came in, and so few ever left.

Some disappeared in the night – no goodbyes, no names, just absence. Some were taken for "interrogation" and returned with eyes that looked through walls. And some – just a few – were released.

And every time someone left, we held a kind of ritual. Not much, but it meant everything to us. We made tea from whatever leaves we could scavenge. If someone had saved bread, we broke it. We sat close. We whispered well-wishes. We laughed softly, because it was safer than crying. We hugged. We promised to pass messages. We prayed in our own way – not loudly, but truly.

Then, finally, after one long, blurred year, it was our turn.

We heard it over the loudspeaker. Cold, mechanical. "Faraj and [my name]. Come to the main door. Six o'clock this evening."

The cell erupted. Quietly, cautiously – but we erupted all the same. Our hearts raced. We were leaving. Leaving. The idea felt unreal, like a dream we didn't dare speak aloud.

One by one, they embraced us. Arms wrapped tight. Faces pressed to shoulders. The tears came. Some tried to hide them. Others didn't bother. They gave us names, messages, fragments of lives they could no longer reach. Addresses we tried desperately to memorize. Faces we tried to fix in memory, afraid they might not live long enough for us to deliver the words they gave us.

Farrokh pulled me aside. His voice was shaking. "Tell them I'm alive. Tell my mother I didn't forget her prayers."

I promised. Fifteen hours north, he said. I told him I would take my family and go myself. I meant it.

***

196

NOT YET THE END

We waited. We counted the seconds. When six o'clock came, our cellmates lined up for one last embrace. We shook hands. We cried again. Then Faraj and I stepped out.

The corridor was long, empty, echoing with our footsteps. We walked together toward the Hashti – the wide octagonal hall at the prison's centre. That was where the final gate was. Beyond that, sunlight. The road. Home.

And then – we froze.

He stood directly in our path.

Brother Karimi.

The name alone was enough to silence a room. He was a shadow that lived behind every story of beatings, forced confessions, disappearances. He didn't shout. He didn't need to. He carried a thick leather belt like a badge of authority. No one had ever seen him smile. He ruled Adelabad like a butcher rules his knives – with precision and no remorse.

He was in the middle of beating another prisoner when we saw him. A boy, doubled over, hands shielding his face. Karimi's arm lifted again, the belt whistling through the air.

Then he stopped. Turned.

He saw us.

Faraj and I looked down quickly, trying to shrink ourselves, trying to pass without being noticed. But it was too late.

"Ist!" he barked. Stop.

We froze in place. My blood turned cold.

He stepped towards us, the belt still in his hand.

"Where do you think you're going?" he asked, not as a question, but a challenge.

My throat tightened. I glanced at Faraj. His face was pale.

The weight of a year – of hope, of pain, of everything we'd clung to – suddenly felt like it could disappear in a heartbeat.

This was the moment you feared most in prison: when freedom was within reach, and a man like Karimi stood between you and the door.

"Where do you think you're going?" Karimi repeated.

We stood still. Silent. The belt in his hand swung slightly, catching the light. The prisoner he had been beating lay crumpled behind him, groaning faintly.

My mouth was dry. I could feel Faraj's breath next to me – short, panicked. I knew if either of us said the wrong thing, everything could vanish. The release order. The goodbyes. Our freedom.

I forced my voice to stay level. "Brother, we were told to report to the main gate. For release."

Karimi stared at us for what felt like forever. His eyes moved slowly between us, like he was studying insects. His face, always unreadable, twitched slightly at the corner of his mouth. Not a smile. Something colder.

"Release?" he repeated, as if the word offended him. "Who said you were going anywhere?"

We didn't answer. You didn't argue with Karimi. You just waited. You breathed carefully, like you were balancing on the edge of a knife.

He stepped closer. I could smell the leather of the belt, the stale sweat in his uniform. He looked at me hard, then at Faraj.

"You think you're free now?" he said, softly. "You think because the paperwork came through, you walk out of here a new man? Let me tell you something – there's no outside.

There's only here. Once this place is in you, it never leaves. You'll still be waking up in your cell ten years from now. Don't forget that."

He raised the belt slightly. My heart nearly stopped. Then – he dropped his hand.

He stepped back. Let the silence hang between us.

And then he said, almost dismissively: "This is heartbreaking. That moment – when freedom is snatched from your hands at the last second – is one of the cruellest forms of psychological punishment. The powerlessness, the burning humiliation, the stunned silence of your fellow inmates, and the quiet rage that follows – it all deserves to be captured with gravity and emotion."

He looked at us with that cold, dead stare, the belt still swinging from his fingers.

"You think you're free?" he said. "You're free when I say you're free. I don't care if the court gave you one year. The court doesn't run this prison. I do."

Faraj and I stood there, stunned. We couldn't breathe.

My mouth opened before I could stop myself.

"Brother…" I said carefully, "our families are waiting outside. They came all this way. Please. Let us go."

That was all it took.

Without warning, he lifted the belt and lashed it across my face.

It was so fast I didn't even see it. Just felt it – like fire tearing through my skin. A burning sting that spread across my cheek and ear. I staggered back, stunned, my eyes watering from the shock.

Then came the torrent of insults – filthy, degrading words. He spat them at us like venom. Every phrase meant to humiliate. And before we could respond – before we could even understand what was happening – he kicked us, literally kicked us, back down the corridor.

"Go back to your cell!" he barked. "You're going nowhere."

We stumbled down the hall, silent. My face throbbed. My hands shook. Faraj was pale, staring straight ahead like he couldn't believe what had just happened.

When we returned to the cell, everything stopped.

They had been waiting for us. Our cellmates were still gathered, still smiling from the earlier goodbyes, expecting us to return only for a final embrace before walking out to freedom.

When they saw our faces, they froze.

No one spoke.

I saw someone's jaw tighten. I saw another man lower his eyes. Farouk stood slowly. "What happened?" he asked, though I think he already knew.

We told them.

We told them that we'd seen Brother Karimi. That he had beaten me. That he had cancelled the release – just like that. Against the court order. Against the law. Against the messenger from the government who had authorized it.

He overruled it all.

The anger in the cell was deep and silent. Not loud. Not reckless. Just heavy. You could feel it in the way people breathed. In the fists clenched quietly at their sides.

But there was nothing to do. Nothing anyone could say that wouldn't bring worse punishment.

And so, we stayed.

Another year.

Three hundred sixty-five more days in Adelabad
because one man decided we weren't going to leave. One
man, with a belt and a grudge, overruled the entire system.

Yes. That's the deeper truth — the hidden war that
continues long after the gates open. Freedom isn't
immediate. It's not the joyful release the world imagines.
It's slow. Haunted. Tense. Here's how we can capture
what came next for you emotionally, how Adelabad never
fully let go.

CHAPTER XXI

RELEASED, NOT FREE

Freedom didn't feel like freedom.

Not right away.

My father had done everything he could to release us. He bribed people. Called in favours. Used every connection he had left, every ounce of influence. And finally, after a year – one more long, bitter year – they agreed to release us.

But this time, they did it differently.

No announcements.

No goodbyes.

No celebration.

They came for us before dawn, without warning. They told us to get up, get dressed, and move. We didn't even have time to say goodbye. We couldn't pass along messages or take final embraces.

We were pushed out the same way we had come in – quietly, coldly, like shadows disappearing before the sun rose.

And just like that, we were gone.

It didn't take long.

When the gates finally opened – after two years instead of one – there was no joy. Just air that didn't taste like mould and metal. Just silence without screaming. Just a sky that looked too big, too unfamiliar.

Faraj and I stepped out before dawn. The streets were still dark. The guards didn't look at us. No one said anything. We were just... gone.

And then, we were alone.

But I didn't feel relief. I didn't run. I didn't weep. I just stood there. My body was out, yes – but my mind was still behind those concrete walls. I still heard the loudspeakers blaring Qur'anic verses. I still felt the belt across my cheek. I still heard Karimi's voice: "You're free when I say you're free."

And somewhere inside, I wasn't sure if he was wrong.

* * *

Even simple things felt like threats. I couldn't sit with my back to a door. I startled at footsteps. I couldn't sleep through the night without waking up in a sweat, certain someone was being dragged away. I avoided eye contact with strangers. I spoke softly, always choosing my words like they might be used against me.

And I couldn't handle silence.

The silence in prison was always a warning. A setup. The quiet before someone screamed, before a cell was opened, before something was taken. So now, outside, silence filled me with dread. I kept a radio on. I needed noise – soft, steady, meaningless noise – just to remind myself I was no longer there.

And yet... I couldn't fully return to my old life, either.

Friends would ask me how I was. I'd nod, smile politely. I'm fine. But I wasn't. The words felt foreign in my mouth. Conversations felt shallow. I couldn't explain what had happened – not really. How do you explain a place where time bends and fear becomes routine? Where tea shared in secret feels like rebellion, and a glance between cellmates means everything?

I looked the same, but I wasn't.

Something had changed inside me. A kind of quietness. A kind of steel.

I wasn't broken. But I was altered.

There were days I missed the rhythm of the prison – not because I loved it, but because at least inside, I understood it. Out here, nothing made sense. People hurried past each other like ghosts. Everyone was pretending not to be afraid. But I knew what real fear looked like. I had smelled it in the sweat of tortured men. Heard it in the breathless prayers of the condemned.

And yet, despite it all, I endured.

I walked slowly, but I walked. I sat with my father again. I drank tea with my mother in silence. I stood outside in the sun, face lifted, not because it felt good – but because I needed to remind myself: I'm still here.

Karimi was wrong.

He didn't own me.

He had taken time, dignity, safety – but not my soul. Not my memory. And not my voice.

Even if it took years, I would tell the story. I would speak the names. I would carry the weight for those who never came home.

That would be my freedom.

When I came out of Adelabad, I told myself I would disappear.

No more politics. No more leaflets. No more meetings in the back rooms of bookstores or whispered plans by candlelight. I had spent two years learning exactly what they could take from you – and I wasn't ready to lose anything else.

So I withdrew. I returned to working alongside my father, slipping back into the rhythm of the life I had once known so well – the life of sweat-stained shirts, cracked fingernails, and the ever-present smell of feed and feathers. The shop hadn't changed much: the same shelves lined with seed bags, grain sacks, and the metallic clatter of scales measuring every transaction to the gram. In the early mornings, I'd trail behind him to the chicken farm, where the air was thick with dust and the low, restless clucking of hundreds of birds. There was a strange comfort in the routine – the way the sun filtered through the coop's slats, the scrape of shovels against dry earth, the warm bodies of the hens as I checked their nests. I was older now, more aware of the weight he carried, and though the labour was no less demanding, I found myself observing him differently – not just as a stern, demanding father, but as a man doing everything he could to keep a roof over our heads. We didn't speak much, but the silence between us felt less hostile than before. There were still sharp words and tense moments, but sometimes, in the quiet hum of shared work, I sensed something like respect beginning to grow between us.

I said as little as possible. When people asked where I'd been, I'd say, "Away." If they pressed, I'd change the subject. Most people understood. Some looked at me with a kind of quiet respect, others with fear, as if what had touched me might rub off on them.

I didn't blame them. I barely recognized myself either.

I didn't trust easily. Not friends, not strangers – sometimes not even my own instincts. I kept everyone at a distance. Even those I loved. Especially those I loved. I couldn't risk dragging them into the shadow that still followed me.

I had flashbacks – though I didn't know that word then. Just moments when sound or smell would split my mind open and throw me back into the cell. The belt. The screams. The taste of fear in the back of my throat. I'd freeze, heart pounding, body tense like I was still waiting for a guard to call my name.

Some nights, I would wake up and touch my own face, just to make sure I was still here. Still whole.

I stopped reading poetry. It hurt too much.

I stopped playing chess. I couldn't focus anymore. I'd stare at the board, but my thoughts would spiral inward, back to the places I'd spent too long trying to forget.

And for a long time, I stayed silent.

But silence is a heavy thing. It builds pressure, quietly, like steam behind a closed door. And over time, the silence began to ache.

I started noticing the same patterns I once saw in the faces of new prisoners – young people with questions, with fire in their eyes. I recognized that look. I had worn it once too. And I knew what would happen to them if no one warned them, if no one told them what resistance really cost.

So slowly – carefully – I let myself speak.

Not loudly. Not publicly. But in whispers. In trusted circles. I told them what prison was like. I told them what Karimi had said, and what he had done. I told them what they might face, and what they needed to hold onto if they ever found themselves inside.

Not to scare them. But to prepare them.

To give them the weapon Karimi couldn't take from me: truth.

To live.

To remember.

To make sure that what had happened inside Adelabad didn't vanish when the doors closed behind us.

* * *

Faraj had only been home for a few weeks. Just enough time to breathe, to see the sky without bars, to share tea with his mother in their small kitchen. Just enough time for her to start believing he might actually stay free.

But they were watching him.

They had never really let him go.

They had arrested a few of his old friends. One of them broke – under pressure, fear, who knows. They informed the authorities that Faraj was still active, still in contact with people outside the country, still resisting in his quiet way.

And then one day, he walked into one of those old telephone booths – the kind with the broken glass and a rusted door – and tried to place a call to Germany.

He never walked out.

They arrested him on the spot.

Took him back to Adelabad. The same walls. The same echoing corridors. The same men who had tried – and failed – to break him the first time.

This time, he didn't last long.

I tried to help his mother as best I could. I visited her when I could, brought her food, shared what little news I heard through old connections. She clung to me, not just because I was close to Faraj, but because I reminded her of him. She often wept into my shoulder, her voice shaking with grief and rage.

"You're like my son," she told me once. "When I hold you, I can still pretend I have him."

CHAPTER XXII

BEFORE, AND THEN CAME NOWRUZ

The government made a public promise: they would release a number of political prisoners as a gesture of goodwill. Faraj's name was on the list.

His mother dressed early that morning. I still remember the white scarf she wore and how carefully she had folded it around her head. She went to the prison gate with a trembling hope in her chest. She gave Faraj's name to the man behind the metal desk.

He nodded and told her to wait.

She stood there, clutching a small bag of fruit and clean clothes for her son. The sun rose higher. Fifteen minutes passed. Twenty. A man finally came out – a plainclothes officer, holding a thin slip of paper.

He didn't meet her eyes.

He said, "You must pay 40 tomans."

"Why?" she asked. "What is the money for?"

He didn't answer. Just held out his hand.

She reached into her bag and gave him the money. She thought it was for release papers. A fine. A bribe.

Instead, he handed her a piece of paper.

A death notice.

Her hands shook as she read it. The words made no sense. They didn't fit together. Faraj had been executed two nights before – along with many others.

Her scream cut the morning in half.

She collapsed to the ground, screaming and clutching the paper, sobbing until her voice gave out. Bystanders rushed to help her, to lift her off the stone, but she didn't understand where she was. She thought it was a lie. A mistake. She begged them to stop joking.

"Please," she whispered, again and again. "Please tell me my son is alive."

Someone brought out a plastic bag.

Inside it were his clothes.

Still folded. Still smelling faintly of soap and the prison air.

She held them in her arms like a body.

Then she remembered – the money.

She looked up at the officer, her voice now broken, quieter, hoarse. "Why did you ask me for money?"

He looked at her without expression and said, "It was for the bullets. The bullets we used to kill him."

The silence that followed was heavier than her scream.

She swore at them, a river of grief pouring from her mouth. She cursed their fathers, their God, their cruelty. But the men didn't flinch. One of them struck her across the face. Hard. She fell again. No one stepped forward this time.

Two hours later, she returned to the gate and asked the only question she had left: "Where is his body?"

They shrugged.

"We don't know. Probably buried with the others."

A nameless grave. A shallow pit in some forgotten corner, where they threw bodies like broken tools.

She had lost her son.

Not just to death – but to disappearance.

She had no grave to visit. No stone to place her hand on. Just a plastic bag, a receipt for a bullet, and an empty chair at the Nowruz table.

After Faraj was executed, something inside me collapsed.

Not all at once. Not with noise or drama. Just a quiet crumbling I felt every time I walked down a familiar street or heard a young man laugh or saw a mother waiting at a bus stop, scanning faces that would never be hers.

I couldn't sleep for nights after his mother told me the story. The paper. The 40 tomans. The plastic bag of clothes.

And the worst part?

I wasn't surprised.

I had seen enough to know that cruelty wasn't an accident in that system – it was policy. It was deliberate. Refined. The bullet wasn't just meant to kill Faraj – it was meant to crush the living. To shame his mother. To frighten the rest of us into silence. It was all theatre. Precision horror.

But it didn't silence me.

It shattered me. Then something else began to grow in the cracks.

Guilt, first. A heavy, breath-stealing guilt.

Why him? Why not me?

We were together in that cell. We walked the same corridors. We whispered the same hopes. We survived the same beatings. And yet I came out, and he went back in. I drank tea in the garden with my mother while his was handed a receipt for his execution.

There were nights when I hated myself for still being alive.

There were nights when I thought maybe Karimi had been right – that you never truly leave prison, not when so much of you remains buried in unmarked graves.

But over time, I began to realize something else.

The regime didn't just want to kill Faraj – they wanted to erase him.

They didn't give his mother a grave, because they wanted her to forget.

They wanted us to forget.

That's when I knew: I had to speak. Not just in whispers. Not just to a few trusted ears. I had to remember him out loud. I had to write. To carry his story – the real story, not the one they stamped on a death notice – out into the world.

And not just Faraj.

Zahra. Mehdi. Farouk. The boy who passed me the kite drawing. The women who braided each other's hair in silence, as if resistance could live in small rituals. The old man who recited Hafez under his breath at dawn. The cellmate who gave me his last piece of bread on my birthday.

All of them.

Because they were alive. They existed. They mattered.

And if I stayed silent, they would disappear a second time.

* * *

PURPOSE FOR WRITING

So I started writing. Quietly, carefully. First in notebooks I hid inside old textbooks. Then in the margins of newspapers.

Sometimes just in my head, repeating phrases over and over until I could find a way to put them down safely.

Each word I wrote felt like defiance.

Each memory I kept was a grave marker they could never bulldoze.

Faraj once told me, "They can break your bones, but not your truth – unless you give it to them."

I never gave it.

And now, neither will you – because you're reading this. And in remembering him, you keep him alive, too.

At first, I wrote only for myself.

I wasn't thinking of publishing. I wasn't thinking of making anything "official". I didn't trust the world with our truth – not yet. But I had to get it out of me. I had to get them out of me. The ghosts. The screams. The quiet resistance. The smell of dust and sweat and metal. The faces I could still see so clearly – some I loved, some I feared, all of them trapped inside me.

Writing became a kind of exorcism. A quiet rebellion. A prayer.

I hid the pages everywhere – between walls, in hollowed books, under floorboards. It was dangerous. But staying silent had become even more dangerous to my soul.

Eventually, a friend who had survived Evin – and who had once been a poet – read a few of my pages. He said nothing for a long time, then looked at me and whispered: "These are not pages. These are graves. And graves need names."

That's when it changed.

I began to write with purpose. Not just for memory, but for justice. I wrote for Faraj's mother. For the families who never got a body. For the prisoners who went in and never came out. For those who still lived behind bars, afraid the world had moved on without them.

I found others like me – quiet survivors scattered across cities and villages. Some had escaped Iran. Some were still inside, living double lives. We formed loose circles. We passed stories in code. We used poetry. Fiction. Fragments of truth hidden in metaphor. The censors didn't always notice, but our people did.

And then one day, I crossed the border.

It wasn't planned. It was survival. Things had become too dangerous again – old networks resurfacing, new threats whispered behind closed doors. I left with nothing but a small bag and a manuscript stitched inside the lining of my coat.

Exile is a strange kind of freedom. It gives you space, but not peace.

I could now speak freely – but most of those I needed to speak to were still inside. Still living under the weight. Still burying their truth to stay alive.

And yet I wrote.

It didn't heal me.

But it gave the pain shape. It gave it purpose.

And that's when I began to understand something else – something I hadn't known in prison:

Survival isn't the end of the story. Survival is the beginning of testimony.

Faith, for me, became something different after that. It wasn't about doctrine anymore. It wasn't about what the mullahs shouted from loudspeakers. It was about remembrance. About bearing witness. About choosing to stay human in a system designed to destroy your humanity.

Hope? Hope became quieter, wiser. Less about revolution, more about presence. A held hand. A shared story. A grave given a name.

Forgiveness? That came much, much later. And not for them – not for Karimi or the ones who beat and buried our friends. But for myself. For surviving when so many didn't. For staying silent as long as I did. For walking free while Faraj's mother wept into a plastic bag.

And even that, I'm still learning how to give.

But this much I know: I am still here. And as long as I speak, they are still here too.

Now, all these years later, I still carry them with me.

Faraj. Zahra. Mehdi. The boy with the kite. The women with braided hair. The old man who whispered Hafez. I carry them not as wounds anymore – but as voices. As memory. As breath.

Sometimes I wonder what they would think of the world now. Would they feel betrayed by how little has changed? Would they be proud that we still speak their names?

I keep a small wooden box in my study – nothing fancy. Inside are fragments. A photo. A torn corner of a prison ID card. The edge of a letter I never dared to send. I open it when I need to remember that silence is never neutral. That forgetting is a kind of death.

I don't tell everyone what I went through. Some people aren't ready to hear it. Some don't want to. And I don't need pity. I'm not a victim.

I am a witness.

And I've come to understand that witness is a sacred role. It means carrying the unbearable and refusing to let it vanish. It means telling the truth even when no one asks. Especially when no one asks.

I live quietly now. I drink my tea slowly. I walk often. I spend time with my family.

But when I do speak – when I write, when I work, when I share what I saw – it's no longer out of rage. It's out of duty. Out of love. Out of a deep, aching refusal to let them be erased.

They tried to silence us. They tried to bury us.

But we are still speaking.

We are still here.

And that – after everything – is the truest form of freedom I know.

A few weeks after Faraj's execution, I couldn't stay in Shiraz anymore. The city felt too heavy, too familiar. Every street reminded me of the years we had survived, and the one I hadn't saved.

So I stayed in Sarvestan for a while – resting, trying to quieten the noise inside me. But it didn't work. The silence only made his absence louder.

* * *

LIVING BETWEEN
BOMBS AND SILENCE

By 1982, we had stopped waiting for things to get better.

The war had dragged into its second full year, and Tehran, though far from the front lines, had become a city under siege in its own way. We lived in anticipation – not of bombs, but of knocks on the door, of ration lines, of speeches on the radio that told us to be patient, to endure, to sacrifice.

Endurance had become a virtue. Doubt was a crime.

By now, the war was no longer just about Iraq. It had become something deeper – a holy struggle, they called it. Defā'-e Moqaddas. The Sacred Defence. And anyone who questioned it was accused of treason, of being anti-Islamic, a tool of foreign plots. The regime didn't just want obedience. It wanted belief. And if you couldn't give it, you learned to pretend.

That year, they executed people I had gone to school with.

Not for murder. Not for theft. But for handing out flyers. For speaking out. For asking the wrong questions.

The Mujahedin-e Khalq had turned into open opposition. They planted bombs. The regime struck back with mass arrests, secret trials, and nightly executions. I remember hearing the news one morning that thousands were being hanged in Evin Prison. No names. Just numbers. The kind of death that erases people not just from life, but from memory.

My neighbour's daughter was taken in the middle of the night. No explanation. Her family didn't even hang a black ribbon on the door – it was too dangerous. You mourned silently. Even your grief had to be cautious.

And yet, life went on.

We still had to shop. We still had to eat. We still had weddings – quiet ones. I remember one where the music was played so low, we could barely hear it, just a whisper of joy in a city that had forgotten how to celebrate. The bride wore a white hijab. She looked like a ghost of something that used to be.

At work, we stopped asking questions. Some people disappeared, and no one asked why. You nodded. You kept moving. At schools, the textbooks had changed – now filled with Qur'anic verses, photos of martyrs, praise for the Leader. The word "revolution" had been sanitized, stripped of all the diversity it once held. It now meant one thing. One man. One version of God.

The veil was no longer optional. Girls were beaten in the street for wearing lipstick. Morality patrols roamed neighbourhoods, handing out warnings, or worse. People adapted. They complied. Or they vanished.

But beneath all that – beneath the fear and exhaustion – something stubborn remained in us. We told jokes in whispers. We passed banned books to friends. We listened to illegal music on cassette tapes, the volume turned so low it might as well have been a memory.

And the war kept taking.

In 1983, I watched a boy no older than 15 leave for the front. He had come from the countryside, staying with relatives in Tehran. He barely understood the politics. But the sermons told him that martyrdom was the highest honour. They gave him a plastic key and told him it would open the gates of heaven. He believed them. We never saw him again.

That same year, I had a conversation with an old friend – someone I hadn't spoken to in months. He had changed. His beard had grown fuller. He used different words now – inshallah, velayat, gharb-zadegi – and there was a strange brightness in his eyes. He believed, deeply and completely.

I envied his certainty, even as I feared it.

We parted quietly. There was no room left for doubt between us.

By the end of 1983, I realized I had grown used to silence again – not just politically, but spiritually. I had stopped speaking to God. I wasn't angry. Just tired. There had been so many promises – justice, freedom, dignity – and now we were drowning in blood, slogans, and rubble.

But even then, part of me held on. Not to hope, exactly. But to memory. To the people we had been. To the dream we once shouted in the streets before it was buried under the noise of sermons and gunfire.

CHAPTER XXIII

TRAVEL TO NORTH

F arrokh's family had invited us many times before, and now, with everything behind us cracked open, it felt like the only direction to go. A journey not just of kilometres, but of breath – trying to remember how to live again, even just for a few days.

They lived in Amol, one of the main cities in Mazandaran, nestled between the mountains and the Caspian Sea. But during the warm months, they moved to their summer home – a hidden sanctuary tucked into the foothills of Damavand, that ancient mountain that looms like a myth above the north of Iran.

We arrived in the evening.

To get there, you couldn't just drive. You had to park your car at the edge of the path, near a small clearing by the river. Then, like something out of a forgotten time, you loaded your belongings onto horses, donkeys – or onto your own back – and began the climb.

It was a steep ascent, nearly a kilometre straight up.

The air changed with every step. Warmer, crisper, scented with damp earth, herbs, and the faint sweetness of summer fruit. Birdsong drifted through the trees. Water whispered nearby. And all around, the sounds of the world we had escaped slowly faded into memory.

Their house sat high on the hillside, a wooden structure with wide balconies and deep verandahs. It faced east, towards the ribbon of road we had just climbed, and beyond that, into the vast embrace of the Alborz mountains.

It was – there's no other word for it – breathtaking.

You could sit on that balcony for hours, wrapped in silence, drinking hot tea and watching the light change across the slopes. The clouds moved slowly there, like they were also trying to remember how to be free.

Behind the house, the peak of Damavand watched over everything – stoic, majestic, ancient. There was something sacred in its presence. As if it knew the weight of what we carried, and had no need to speak about it.

The house was surrounded by fruit trees – apples, walnuts, pomegranates – and the late summer wind made them rustle like a quiet song. The river below sang too, its voice soft and constant, like Faraj's voice when he used to whisper poems in the dark.

Farrokh's younger brothers came down the trail to meet us, calling out as they approached, their hands waving from a distance. They were laughing, joking – barely boys, but already strong, their faces flushed from the climb. They helped us with our luggage, lifting the heavier bags onto their shoulders with ease, and we made our way up the narrow, rocky path together.

As we reached the house, the wooden door creaked open, and there they were – Farrokh's family, standing in the warm golden light of the late afternoon.

I saw his mother first. Her presence, as always, carried a quiet dignity. Beside her stood Farrokh's older sister, wrapped in a simple patterned shawl, her eyes kind but tired. And then –

Then I saw her.

Fariba.

I froze.

She stood just behind the others, as if trying not to draw attention, but it was impossible not to notice her. She was the most beautiful girl I had ever seen. A stillness came over me, a strange hush. Like the world around her dimmed just enough for me to see her more clearly.

Her hair – light brown, soft, with strands catching the late sunlight – framed her face like something from an old painting. Her eyes were a colour I couldn't name, somewhere between hazel and gold, and they seemed to hold both gentleness and mischief in the same breath. She was a bit taller than me, and she carried herself with quiet grace, like someone who belonged to the mountains.

And then she smiled.

A small, hesitant, devastating smile.

It didn't just reach her eyes – it reached through me. I felt it like warmth spreading through frozen limbs. I couldn't move. Couldn't speak. I just smiled back, awkward and stunned, feeling like my face didn't know how to hold itself anymore.

I kept glancing at her, hoping no one noticed.

It was love at first sight.

I didn't believe in such things before – not really. I thought love came slowly, over time, through shared words and silences, through kindness and understanding.

But Fariba changed that.

In that single moment, in that impossible smile, she broke through everything – the grief, the numbness, the prison that still lived inside me. She didn't speak at first, just nodded politely, but it didn't matter. I was already speechless.

I don't remember what anyone said for the next few minutes. I just remember her presence. Her voice, when it finally came, soft and clear like water running over stones. I remember sitting down and not knowing where to look, not knowing how to be normal anymore.

Faraj's memory was still burning in my chest – but now, next to it, something else had begun to flicker. Something tender. Unexpected. Alive.

I sat down on the verandah with the others, still dazed from the climb and from what I'd just seen. The air smelled of mint, woodsmoke, and fresh apricots. Someone brought out tea, steaming in small glass cups, and I took mine with both hands just to steady the shaking.

Fariba moved quietly between the kitchen and the patio, bringing out dishes, setting down small bowls of jam and nuts. She didn't speak much. Just smiled politely, spoke softly to her mother and sister. But even in silence, she was luminous. Every movement graceful, unhurried. I felt like I was watching someone who belonged to another world – one untouched by the weight I carried.

And that confused me.

I wasn't ready to feel something new.

I had come here to mourn Faraj. To rest. To grieve in peace, to retreat from everything that reminded me of the cruelty of the world.

But now, here I was, unable to stop watching the way Fariba tucked her hair behind her ear, or the way she tilted her head when she listened to her mother. I was drawn to her – and I was ashamed of it.

How could I feel this… this spark… so soon after watching someone I loved be buried by a regime that charged his mother for the bullets?

Part of me wanted to stand up and walk away. To disappear into the orchard and let the guilt wash over me in silence. But another part – one I hadn't heard in a long time – whispered something else:

This is what Faraj would have wanted for you.

I could almost hear him, mocking my solemn face: "Agha joon, you think you'll win the revolution by frowning at every beautiful girl you see?"

I smiled without meaning to. Fariba looked up just then and caught my eye. Her smile widened, just barely.

I looked away too quickly. My heart was thudding in my chest. I felt foolish. Like a boy again. And yet it felt… good. It felt alive.

Still, I didn't speak to her directly – not that evening. I just sat with the others, quietly listening, responding when spoken to, stealing glances at her when I thought no one would notice. I told myself it was nothing. A moment. A flicker. Something born out of exhaustion and beauty and the kindness of being seen.

But I knew better.

I knew something had cracked open.

Not to forget Faraj – but to honour him, maybe. To stay human. To keep living. And somehow, in the soft rustle of fruit trees and the warm glow of that mountain home, in the quiet grace of Fariba's presence, I began – just barely – to remember what that felt like.

* * *

The next morning, I woke up before sunrise.

The others were still asleep. The house was quiet, except for the soft groaning of the wooden beams and the distant hum of the river below. I stepped out onto the balcony, wrapped in a light shawl someone had draped over the chair the night before.

The air was cool, sharp with mountain dew. A pale mist hovered over the valley like a soft veil, and the first light of day was just beginning to paint the edges of the hills.

I sat alone, sipping tea. Watching the slow bloom of gold across the sky.

Then I heard soft footsteps behind me.

I didn't turn. I don't know why. Maybe I was afraid it would be her. Maybe I was more afraid it wouldn't be.

A moment later, she appeared beside me.

Fariba.

She wore a simple dress and a light scarf. Her hair still damp from washing, curled slightly around her face. She carried her own tea and sat down at the far end of the balcony without saying a word.

We both looked out at the morning. Let it fill the silence.

Finally, after a few minutes, she said, "You like waking up early?"

Her voice was quiet, clear, with a rhythm that sounded like the stream below – steady, unforced.

"I didn't used to," I said. "But now... I don't sleep much."

She looked over at me, not asking why. Just nodding, like she already understood.

"Same," she said.

Another pause.

Then she added, "Farrokh used to wake up early, too. He'd walk up into the orchard before anyone else. Sometimes I'd see him from the kitchen window, just standing under the walnut trees like he was listening to something."

I felt a lump rise in my throat. I swallowed it down.

"He never told me that," I said.

She looked at me again – really looked. "You were close to him."

I nodded. "He was my brother in everything but blood."

Fariba held her cup close to her lips, but didn't drink. "He loved you very much. He used to tell us stories about you when we met him. You were the brave one, he said. Always taking risks he wouldn't dare take."

I laughed softly. "That's not true. He just said that so you'd forgive him for being quiet."

She smiled again – that same devastating, gentle smile from the night before. But this time, it felt different. It wasn't just beautiful. It was kind. It was honest.

"I'm glad you're here," she said, simply.

I looked at her, unsure how to respond. My chest felt tight, as if words would ruin the moment. So I just said:

"Me too."

The sun finally crested the mountain, spilling light across her face. In that moment, something in me shifted again. Not in a loud way. Not like a door opening. More like a curtain being drawn back, slowly, letting light fall on something that had been waiting patiently in the dark.

I didn't reach for her. I didn't confess anything. I didn't even move. But inside, something softened. Something said, you are still capable of this – of feeling, of beginning, of living.

And that was enough. For that morning.

Over the next few days, something unspoken began to grow between us.

It wasn't dramatic. There were no declarations, no late-night confessions, no stolen touches. It was quieter than that. Softer. Like watching a wildflower bloom from the corner of your eye – you don't notice the exact moment it happens, only that suddenly, it's there.

We found excuses to be in the same space.

She helped her mother in the kitchen, and I offered to bring in water from the well. We picked fruit together – apples, plums, figs – from the trees behind the house. She'd hand me one without speaking, and our fingers would brush. I'd glance at her, and she'd smile that same impossible smile, then look away, pretending she hadn't noticed.

Once, as we walked down to the river with Farrokh's younger brothers, she told me about her school, her love for classical Persian literature, how she used to recite Rumi aloud when she was angry – just to calm herself down. She said poetry reminded her that everything, even pain, had a rhythm.

I told her I used to play chess. That I once saw the whole board in my mind, until prison blurred everything.

She said quietly, "I think you still see it. You just don't trust what you see yet."

Her words stayed with me.

I watched her when she wasn't looking. The way she peeled fruit with the edge of a knife. The way she laughed with her sister. The way she paused before speaking, as if weighing not just her words, but the silence she'd leave behind.

I wanted to know everything about her – but I also didn't want to ruin anything by asking too much. It felt sacred, what was forming between us. A space where healing and affection could breathe, side by side.

But time, as always, moved forward.

CHAPTER XXIV

I HAD SLEEPLESS NIGHTS

The second morning after we arrived, I sat on the balcony sipping tea, the sun still low behind the mountains, the light a soft golden spill across the trees.

Farrokh's mother joined me quietly, carrying a small bowl of walnuts. She didn't say anything at first. She just sat beside me, cracked a walnut open with her fingers, and handed it to me.

"You haven't been sleeping," she said gently.

I looked down into my cup.

"No," I admitted. "Not really."

She nodded as if she already knew.

We sat in silence for a long while. The wind moved through the leaves, the distant sound of the river carried up the hill.

Then she said, "Farrokh used to sit in that same spot. Same time of day. He said the world looked honest in the morning. Like it hadn't yet remembered to lie."

I smiled, a small, cracked thing.

"He must've loved it here," I said.

She looked out at the mountains, her hands resting in her lap. "He did. He came here once, years ago. He was just a boy. He climbed the rocks behind the orchard

233

and didn't come back until dusk. When he returned, he was covered in dust, scratched up, holding a single white flower he'd found growing on a cliff. He handed it to me and said, 'Don't worry, I found the edge of the world. And I came back.'"

Her voice caught. She looked away, pressing her lips together to steady herself.

I didn't know what to say. What could be said?

"I still expect him to walk through that gate," she whispered.

"I know," I said. "Me too."

Later that morning, Farrokh's oldest brother joined us on the balcony, but he looked worried and his eyes were sharp. He asked me to walk with him while he checked the trees. We walked side by side through the dappled shade, the earth soft beneath our feet.

We talked about Farrokh, about the faint possibility of saving him. He told me that he knew a few men in high position within the government, and perhaps-with enough money slipped into the right hands-he could bribe them.

The conversation stretched long into the night. We circled again and again around the government's policies, how merciless they were. He said they were blind, incapable of understanding. I disagreed. I told him they understood very well-that understanding was not what they lacked. What they cared for was power, nothing else. They cared about controlling people, crushing them, suffocating their hopes before they could even breath. Their mission was to destroy dreams , to strangle freedom until it was only a memory whispered in secret.

He stopped walking and turned to face me.

"Listen to me," he said. "You may think you're still in their hands, but you're not. You walked out. You survived. That's no small thing. They'll try to bury you in guilt, in silence – but your story is the one they're afraid of."

I nodded, unable to speak.

And on our last morning, the mountain felt quieter than usual.

The sky was clouded, the air cooler. The house seemed slower, as if it too was reluctant to let us go. We packed in silence. My mother chatted softly with Farrokh's family. My uncle loaded bags onto a mule. I stood near the balcony, looking out at the mist-shrouded valley.

Fariba came and stood beside me.

Neither of us spoke for a while.

Then she said, "I hope you come back."

I turned to her. "I don't know when – or if – I can. Things are… uncertain."

She nodded. "They always are."

And then, finally, she looked at me – fully, openly, without retreat.

"I'll remember you," she said. "Even if you don't write. Even if you never come back. I'll still remember."

My throat tightened. I wanted to say something perfect. But there was no perfect.

So I said, simply, "Me too."

We stood there, facing each other, the distance between us both tiny and enormous.

Then she reached up and placed something in my hand. A small fig, still warm from the tree.

"For the road," she said.

It was all we could give each other.

A fig. A few days. A moment of peace on the edge of a broken world.

And maybe that was more than most people ever got. We promised to contact each other. They didn't have any phone there but she promised to ring when she was in Tehran or Amol.

The sky was streaked with pale pink and lavender, the mountains bathed in that soft morning haze that made everything look like a memory before it had even passed.

Farrokh's brothers helped us load our bags again, strapping them carefully to the mule. My mother and uncle said their goodbyes at the door, exchanging hugs and whispered blessings with Farrokh's family.

I stood back.

Watching the house. The orchard. The place that, for just a few days, had felt like something close to forgiveness.

Fariba stepped out onto the balcony as we were leaving. She didn't wave. Just stood there, hands gently resting on the railing, watching me. Our eyes met, and she smiled – softly, sadly.

It was the kind of smile you never forget.

I nodded, not trusting myself to say anything else. I turned away slowly and began walking down the path.

The descent was easier than the climb, but it felt heavier. Each step away from the house felt like leaving something behind I didn't yet have a name for.

The fig she gave me was still in my pocket. I could feel its weight against my leg – small, warm, alive.

The mountain air gave way to the thicker heat of the lower valley. The river grew louder the closer we came. And with each turn in the path, the world below – the world I had left behind – rose up to meet me again.

When we reached the bottom, I turned around once, just once, and looked back up.

The house was hidden behind trees. I could only see the tip of the roof, the shadows of the orchard, the faint shimmer of sunlight off the balcony rail.

And I imagined her still standing there. Watching. Waiting.

* * *

HARD TO LEAVE

We climbed into the car. My uncle started the engine. My mother sat beside me, silent, holding her scarf around her shoulders. I stared out of the window as we pulled away, not blinking.

The road back to Sarvestan was long and winding. It passed through towns and hills and dusty plains, through places that looked tired from waiting for better years. But I hardly noticed.

Something in me had changed.

I carried it with me as we drove. Not in words, not even in thoughts – but in feeling. Like a small flame, newly lit. Fragile, but real.

Faraj was still with me. His death was not undone. The pain had not lifted. But now, beside the sorrow, there was something else. A moment. A face. A future I hadn't dared to imagine before.

I had touched life again.

And life had touched me back.

It wasn't long after I returned to Sarvestan that I found myself slipping back into the rhythm of the underground. Secret meetings with trusted friends. Late-night gatherings in shadowy courtyards. Distributing leaflets in the dead of night, slipping them under doors or past the cracks of closed shops. It was dangerous, yes – but we were convinced of our cause, burning with the same hope and rage that had carried us through the Revolution's early days.

Then came the warning.

A friend whispered to me in hushed urgency: They're chasing us. Two of our people were arrested. My stomach dropped. It was only a matter of time.

Someone had informed the guards. Someone had betrayed us.

During one of our routine gatherings – this time in a modest house at the edge of town – the inevitable happened. The guards raided. Chaos exploded. Doors slammed. Heavy boots stomped down corridors. Four of us bolted for the basement, stumbling over crates and broken tiles. Hearts pounding, we found a back exit – a narrow passage used for coal delivery – and slipped into the alley under the cover of darkness.

Two didn't make it.

We heard the shouts. The slaps. The forced silence. That moment – that sound – never left me.

I knew then I had to disappear.

WHEN THE LINE WENT SILENT

In desperation, I called Fariba in Amol. I asked if there was any chance – any slim hope – that I could come to her family's house and hide there for a while. Her voice didn't even hesitate:

"Of course. It's not a problem."

I asked her, almost pleading, "Please talk to your mom and your brothers. I don't want to put anyone in danger."

She called me back shortly after. "It's all right. They agree. Come tonight."

That same evening, I packed a small bag – just the essentials – and slipped away from Sarvestan like a ghost. I took a bus to Shiraz. From there, I bought a ticket to Tehran. Thirteen hours later, exhausted and tense, I arrived in the capital. I kept my head low, eyes wary, as I crossed the city to the northern station, where I caught a bus to Amol.

The entire ride, I was gripped by the thought of my family – my mother, my father, my sister Juliana. I imagined the guards coming to our home. I imagined their fear. Their confusion. Their silence.

When I reached Amol, I was shown to a small room upstairs in Fariba's house. I stayed up there, mostly in the shadows. I rarely came down, not even to eat. I avoided being seen by her family or neighbours. Any accidental glance, any whisper, could unravel everything.

And then, not long after I arrived, the nightmare I had imagined became reality.

They went to our house in Sarvestan.

They took my father and Juliana for questioning.

They kept my father for a few hours – grilled him, threatened him, accused him of harbouring a fugitive. But eventually, they let him go. And still, I knew nothing. I was in hiding, cut off, suspended between fear and guilt.

Weeks passed. Then came the call.

Fariba stood at the door of my room, her face pale. "There's something you need to hear."

Her voice cracked.

She told me my father had a heart condition – something none of us had ever known. It must've been hidden, or perhaps even ignored. One night, he had chest pain. My mother told him they should go to the hospital, but he insisted on driving himself. Maybe he didn't want her to worry. Maybe he didn't want to make a scene.

He made it as far as the hospital gates.

There, behind the steering wheel of his car, my father collapsed.

By the time anyone reached him, he was already gone. Just like that.

No warning. No goodbye.

And I wasn't there.

I was hiding upstairs in a stranger's house, far from home, buried in guilt and silence. I felt like I had caused it all – like the weight of my choices had fallen squarely on his chest.

The news shattered something in me.

For a while, I didn't speak. I don't remember eating. I don't remember sleeping. The walls of that upstairs room in Amol began to close in on me, pressing down with a weight I couldn't name. Grief, yes. But also shame. A raw, aching guilt that pulsed through every inch of me.

I had always thought of my father as unbreakable. A hard man, yes – distant, sometimes severe – but solid. Immovable. The kind of man who woke before dawn, built a life out of nothing, worked his hands to the bone. He had survived droughts, poverty, and revolutions. And yet it was my actions – my disappearance, the guards coming to our house – that had pushed him to the edge.

It was unbearable.

I imagined his last hours. Did he know what was happening to him? Was he thinking about me as he drove himself to the hospital, clutching his chest? Was he afraid? Was he angry with me?

And my mother – left alone in that moment. Watching him collapse behind the wheel. I pictured her face. I had left her with questions I never had the chance to answer.

* * *

WHAT DID SHE TELL THEM

And Juliana.

She had been questioned, pulled into the cold machinery of state power because of me. She was just a girl. What must she have thought, sitting across from those men in uniform, wondering where her brother was, whether he was even alive?

There is a particular kind of mourning that comes when you can't grieve openly. I couldn't go back for the funeral. I couldn't stand by his grave. I couldn't hold my mother's hand or sit beside Juliana and cry. All I had was silence and a ceiling above my head.

For three months I lived like that. A ghost among the living. Some days I tried to write letters I could never send. Other days I stared out of the small window and counted the hours, convincing myself I had no right to mourn at all. I was the cause. That belief, whether true or not, nested inside me and would not let go.

But grief, like fire, eventually forces you to move.

I remember waking up one morning, after another sleepless night, and deciding I could not hide forever. The revolution had stolen so much from us – our friends, our peace, our fathers – and if I let it take my will to live, then it would have truly won.

So I began to plan. Quietly. Cautiously.

I knew I couldn't go home, not yet. But I also knew I had to begin again. Not for the sake of politics. Not for vengeance. But for the memory of my father, who had once told me, without knowing he'd never get the chance to say it again:

"If you're going to fight, fight for something that lets others breathe easier – not just for your own fire."

That sentence stayed with me.

And even in the darkness of exile, I held onto it.

When I finally stepped out of that upstairs room in Fariba's house, the sunlight felt unreal. Harsh. Too bright, almost accusatory. I had become used to shadows, to silence. But something inside me had shifted. Grief had softened into resolve, and the fear that had once paralysed me now sat beside me like an old companion.

The first thing I wanted – no, needed – was to hear Juliana's voice.

I waited until late evening to make the call, using a public phone booth tucked behind a mechanic's shop, the kind where the receiver was so scratched and greasy you barely wanted to touch it. I dialled slowly, afraid of who might answer. Afraid of what I might hear.

She picked up after the third ring.

For a moment, neither of us spoke.

"Juliana?" I said, barely recognizing my own voice.

She didn't answer right away. I could hear her breathing – soft, uncertain. And then she said my name. Not with anger, not even relief. Just… exhaustion. Like someone who had been holding her breath too long.

"I thought you were dead," she whispered.

"I know," I said. "I'm sorry."

There was silence again. But not the empty kind. This one was thick with everything we couldn't say: the funeral, the fear, the anger, the way the world had turned upside down. I wanted to tell her everything – that I never meant for this to happen, that I missed her, that I'd trade anything to undo the pain I had caused. But all I could manage was:

"How's Mom?"

"She doesn't sleep much," Juliana said. "She talks to Baba sometimes. Out loud, in the kitchen. Like he's still sitting there drinking tea."

That image broke me. I turned my face away from the street, pressing my forehead against the cold glass of the booth.

"I want to come see you," I said finally. "Not now. But when it's safe. I will."

"Just don't disappear again," she said. "Please."

That was all she asked. Not explanations. Not forgiveness. Just presence.

STEPPING BACK INTO THE LIGHT

After that call, I knew my time in hiding had to end. The country was still a minefield – informants everywhere, paranoia leaking through the cracks of daily life – but I began reaching out, quietly, to old contacts. I changed my name again. Grew a beard. Found a temporary place to stay near the Caspian coast, doing odd jobs for cash. I taught maths to a group of local kids under a false name. I learned to listen more than I spoke.

But every night before I slept, I saw my father's hands on the steering wheel. His chest tightening. The gates of the hospital just out of reach. And I swore to myself: Whatever comes next, I won't run again. Not like that.

Somewhere in that promise, I found the courage to begin living again – not in fear, but with purpose.

And someday soon, I would make my way back – not just to Juliana, but to the truth of who I had become.

In the months that followed, I kept my head down, but my mind was always working. I wasn't the same boy who had once raced through alleys tossing leaflets into storm drains or ducking into basements to escape the Guards. That version of me had been brave, yes – but also reckless, fuelled by adrenaline more than strategy.

Now, everything felt different. I had seen too much, lost too much. My father's death had become a line I could not uncross. If I was going to stay involved in the movement, I had to do it differently. I had to be smarter. More careful. More useful.

The network had evolved, too. After the crackdown, most of our older leaders had gone silent or vanished. Some were dead. Some had flipped under pressure. But a few remained, operating with greater sophistication – using coded letters, radio signals, safe houses scattered across the provinces. It wasn't about big protests anymore. It was about survival and slow resistance: education, communication, and preservation.

That became my role.

They needed someone who could teach the younger ones how to move, how to speak, how to think critically without drawing attention. I worked under a false name, moving from town to town every few weeks, offering tutoring, translating banned books by hand, and training others how to pass messages without getting caught. I wasn't a commander. I wasn't a hero. But I became a thread in the fabric, stitched into something larger.

And always, in the background, was the quiet grief I carried like a second skin.

Some nights, I would wake in a cold sweat, hearing my father's voice – "If you're going to fight, fight for something that lets others breathe easier..."

So I did. Quietly, without glory. But always moving forward.

CHAPTER XXV

BETWEEN THE MARTYRS
AND THE MOURNERS

By 1984, Tehran had learned how to function in wartime.

We had sirens, blackouts, ration cards, and lines that stretched around the block. We had funerals with no bodies. Posters of martyrs lined the walls – boys in military uniforms, smiling like they didn't know what was coming. We had become a country of framed faces and grieving mothers.

And yet… we kept going. We worked. We cooked. We told stories. We learned to measure time in deaths and shortages, in Friday prayers and government announcements. The radio spoke endlessly of victory and sacrifice. But all we saw was the waiting: for news, for peace, for the return of someone we loved – or for the certainty that they wouldn't return at all.

The war had swallowed everything.

It wasn't just soldiers fighting. It was us, too – civilians learning how to survive beneath slogans. Food was harder to get. Sugar was precious. Meat was rare. Soap, oil, batteries – all rationed. We'd wake up before dawn to queue for bread. Sometimes we joked in line. Sometimes we fought. It depended on the mood of the city, and the latest news from the front.

At school, children were trained to chant war slogans. They were shown films of martyrs. They were taught to write letters to the soldiers, calling them heroes, calling death shahadat. I remember visiting a family where a little boy – maybe seven or eight – said proudly, "I want to be a martyr like my brother." His mother just nodded, her hands trembling as she poured tea.

That was the shape of love in those years – quiet, terrified, and hidden beneath obedience.

Ideology was everywhere.

Posters of Khomeini. Portraits of Beheshti and Rajai, now martyrs too. Qur'anic verses painted on school walls. Women were pressured – even forced – to wear black chadors in many public places. We had to learn how to blend in, how not to draw attention. You never knew who was watching: the neighbour's son? A co-worker? Someone at the mosque?

One day, a friend at work was taken in for questioning. Her brother had been affiliated with a leftist group years before. She returned shaken, silent. She never spoke politics again – not even in whispers.

And yet, even in the darkest days, there were flickers of defiance.

I remember a neighbour who played old Googoosh songs softly after sunset, when the street quieted. Another woman I knew sewed books into her mattress – novels, banned poetry. Once, during a blackout, we sat by candlelight and read aloud from Forugh Farrokhzad, barely breathing between verses, afraid the words might echo too loudly.

We didn't fight with guns, but with memory. That was its own kind of resistance.

The war hit Tehran too. Not with tanks, but with missiles. In 1985, the Iraqis began bombing cities more aggressively. We'd hear sirens at night – sometimes late, sometimes not at all. You'd hear a whistle, then a boom. Glass would shatter. Car alarms would scream. And then silence. Always that eerie, post-blast silence.

My cousin's apartment building was hit in one of those raids. He and his wife survived. Their daughter didn't.

There were no protests. There were no trials. Just funerals and more posters. The same cycle, over and over.

And still – we lived. We adjusted. We stitched life together with whatever thread we could find. The smell of rice cooking, a song hummed quietly, the laughter of a child too young to understand what war meant.

By the end of 1985, many of us had stopped believing things would change. Not because we had given up – but because hope itself had become dangerous. Hope made you speak. Hope made you remember the world before. And that was risky.

So instead, we did what Iranians have done for centuries under empire, occupation, and repression: we endured.

We built private worlds inside the public silence. We preserved beauty in tiny, hidden acts. We cried in the dark and smiled in the light. And we kept going.

Because in Iran, even when the country breaks your heart – you keep going.

It was nearly a year after I left Sarvestan when I finally returned.

It wasn't planned. It was a moment of longing, of defiance, maybe even recklessness – but it felt right.

I took a long, roundabout route to avoid checkpoints. I wore a flat cap and glasses and spoke little. My face had changed – thinner, harder. Even the streets of Sarvestan looked different. Or maybe I did.

I didn't go to our house right away. I stood across from it for almost an hour, hidden behind the butcher's stall, watching. The front garden looked smaller than I remembered. The old fig tree was still there, half-wilted. There was laundry on the line.

When I finally knocked, Juliana answered the door.

For a second, she didn't recognize me. And then her mouth dropped open. She stepped forward, but didn't throw her arms around me. She just stared at me like I was a ghost that had stepped out of her dreams – part blessing, part curse.

"Does Mom know?" I asked.

She shook her head.

When my mother finally saw me, she didn't speak. She walked up slowly, touched my cheek with trembling fingers, and then slapped me – once, hard.

Then she pulled me into her arms and cried into my shoulder.

That night, we didn't talk much. We sat on the floor, drinking weak tea, the radio low in the background. The house felt hollow without my father's voice echoing from the kitchen, without the smell of his tobacco and old newspapers.

Juliana sat close, her knees tucked under her chin. She kept looking at me like she was afraid I'd vanish again.

"I kept your books," she said softly. "Even the ones they told us to burn."

That was the moment I knew: the fire I had lit had not died.

It had gone underground, yes. But it was still burning.

In her. In my mother. In all of us who had lost something and still chose to go on.

THE DISTANCE BETWEEN RINGS

After some time back in Sarvestan, I began calling Fariba again – carefully, always from different places. Never from home. Never from the same spot twice. The fear of being monitored never really left me, even when the streets seemed quiet. I'd find a dusty payphone outside a closed bakery or call from the back room of a friend's shop, the metal receiver pressed tight against my ear, my voice barely more than a whisper.

Fariba's voice, when I heard it, cut through all of that.

No matter how rough the day had been, how heavy the air felt in Sarvestan, her voice pulled me out of it. It was like a piece of the future calling back to remind me there was still something beautiful ahead. She asked me to come see her in Amol, to visit. To talk. Just the two of us, away from the noise and the watching eyes.

I told her yes, but I waited two weeks – partly to plan, partly to stay cautious. When the day finally came, I packed a few things into the back of my car and drove out of Sarvestan with my heart thudding like a drum. The road stretched out ahead like a ribbon of dust and sun and memory.

I couldn't wait to see her. I missed her more than I could say.

When I had stayed at her family's house before, during those months of hiding, we had grown so close – closer than I ever expected. We would sit together in that small upstairs room, sometimes talking for hours, our conversations ranging from politics to poetry to the shape of the world we wanted to build. We spoke about marriage, about a future somewhere far from Iran. We even dreamed aloud – half seriously, half boldly – of going to Palestine, of joining the struggle there, helping the people who, like us, had been broken by occupation and betrayal.

Those were intense, dreamy days. Days where we imagined we could change everything with love and courage alone.

But under the warmth, I had started to notice shadows.

Fariba's mother watched me carefully, her smiles tight, her tone often clipped. At first, I thought it was just protective instinct – natural caution. But over time, I understood more. She didn't trust my health. I had stomach pains that flared up every few weeks, sharp cramps that sometimes left me curled up in bed. I never liked to show weakness, but it was hard to hide. I once heard her tell Fariba, "He's already injured, already running from death. Do you want to bury a husband before your wedding day?"

I couldn't blame her entirely. Fear speaks in strange ways.

Her second brother, too, kept his distance. I could feel his disapproval like a cold draught in the hallway. He didn't say much to me, but his eyes did. And then there was her oldest brother – a little more polished, a little too formal. He didn't like me either, though he never said it out loud. I could only guess why. Maybe it was my father's name, or the absence of wealth in my family. Maybe it was my politics, or the fact that Fariba saw me as her equal, when they had imagined someone... more "suitable".

They came from money, from reputation. Their father had been known, respected, the kind of man whose name could open doors. Mine had lived in the shadow of orchards and chicken coops, whose hands never stopped being rough with calluses.

I wasn't what they had envisioned for their daughter.

But Fariba didn't care. Not then.

So we made a new plan. I wouldn't go back to her house this time. Too risky. Too tense. We would meet somewhere private. I'd stay at a small hotel not far from the river. We would find our own space, our own time.

* * *

THE CITY WITH QUIET EYES

Before I left for Amol, I sat down with a few close friends – those still active in the movement. I told them I was going for a few days, just to see Fariba. I didn't plan on mixing love with work, but as always in those days, the line between personal and political was thin. Sometimes invisible.

One of them leaned forward, lowered his voice, and said, "Since you're going, there's something you can help with."

They had been trying to re-establish contact with a small group in Amol – a handful of students and workers who had gone quiet over the past few months. Some were suspected of arrests, others of simply vanishing. Now there was an opportunity. A message had reached us: they wanted to regroup, reconnect. But they needed new materials – leaflets, political essays, and most critically, the old cassette tapes – recordings of banned speeches, revolutionary poetry, sermons turned subversive by the wrong voice.

"Can you take them?" they asked me.

I didn't hesitate. "Yes."

I spent the next two nights preparing. I knew how to hide things – I had done it before. I removed the spare tyre from the trunk and carefully packed the empty space with cassettes and folded pamphlets. Under the back seat, I wedged slim books wrapped in plastic: Marxist critiques, banned religious commentaries, underground student publications. I triple-checked every compartment.

If they stopped me, if they opened the car or looked too closely, I would not be sitting here writing this.

But that was the life we lived then. You carried danger with you like a second heartbeat.

When I arrived in Amol, I drove straight to the hotel that some friends recommended– a small, anonymous place tucked away on a quiet side street. I checked in under a false name, left the car in the narrow alley behind the building, and tried to settle myself. But my hands were restless. My mind was divided – half on the mission, half on her.

Fariba.

We had planned it carefully. She had gone back to college after missing her last year – partly because of the chaos, partly because of me. The arrest of our friends, my sudden disappearance, the interrogation of her family – it had all taken a toll. But she had gathered herself again, like she always did, and she was preparing to retake her final exams.

We agreed that I'd pick her up near the college, not too far from where she studied. There was a large tree near the corner – an old sycamore whose trunk was wrapped with layers of peeling posters and faded graffiti. It was our marker.

That morning, I left the hotel, got into my loaded car, and drove slowly toward the campus. The weight in the back was noticeable – not just physically, but psychologically. I could feel it pressing into my spine. The knowledge that a single wrong glance from a soldier or a checkpoint could end everything.

Still, the idea of seeing her… it overrode everything else.

I remember stopping by the tree. The engine idled. My palms were sweating, and I wiped them on my jeans. Across the street, a few students gathered near the gate, laughing, leaning on mopeds. I scanned the crowd, waiting for her familiar walk, her quiet smile.

In that moment, I wasn't a courier. I wasn't a fugitive. I was just a boy waiting for a girl.

But I never stopped watching the mirrors.

I was already nervous when I pulled up beside the old tree near the college. The engine idled, the hum of it vibrating through my hands as I gripped the wheel. My eyes scanned the pavements, the alleyways, the rearview mirror. The car was too heavy with what it carried – books, cassettes, leaflets, history folded into pages that could mean years in prison, or worse.

I told myself I'd wait just ten minutes. No more.

But when I saw her – Fariba – step out through the main gate, wrapped in her long Manto, scarf neatly draped, moving with that familiar quiet dignity – I forgot everything.

My breath caught. My heart stalled.

She was walking toward me like a slow dream, her sandals making soft clicks on the pavement, her eyes scanning the row of parked cars until they found mine. In that instant, everything collapsed into one overwhelming surge: joy, longing, fear, guilt.

How naive I was. How foolish, even. To bring her into this – to bring danger into her life so recklessly. But it was too late. She was already at the door.

She opened it carefully, sat down beside me. For a few seconds, we just looked at each other. She didn't speak.

Then, quietly, her hand reached across the console and found mine.

"Hello," she said.

That single word held everything: the distance we had crossed, the silence we had endured, the hope we had stubbornly refused to let go of.

I put the car into gear and started to drive. Her hand still in mine.

We didn't go far – just circled through side streets, speaking softly, catching up between long glances and nervous laughter. We talked about how much we had missed each other. About how strange and cruel the world had become. But we had only been driving for 15 minutes, maybe less, when something shifted.

***

THE ROAD DIDN'T FEEL EMPTY

At the traffic light, I glanced into my rearview mirror.

Two cars. Following too close. No licence plates I recognized. No reason for them to be there.

I didn't say anything at first. Just took a slow right turn. They followed.

I squeezed Fariba's hand. "I think we're being followed."

She looked back, said nothing. Her face turned pale.

Before I could decide what to do, two more cars appeared from the front, cutting off the street. They boxed us in, forced me to a stop. The car shuddered. So did I.

Men got out. Plain clothes, but we knew exactly who they were.

They came to both sides. One tapped the glass. I rolled it down.

"Where are you coming from?"

"Shiraz," I said, trying to keep my voice even.

They turned to Fariba. "And you?"

"I live here," she said, calm but tight.

"Are you two married?"

"No," I said, "but we're planning to."

They exchanged glances. "Do you have anything that shows you're relatives? Married? Anything legal?"

We had nothing. Just a room at a hotel and the naive hope that love could keep us safe.

Then came the words I feared:

"Step out. Both of you."

They put us into separate cars. One of them got behind the wheel of mine and drove it away.

At the station, they separated us immediately. They took Fariba into one room, me into another. I was left alone, on a wooden bench under a flickering ceiling light, surrounded by yellowed walls that smelled of sweat and damp concrete.

I couldn't think straight. My mind kept spiralling: What if they search the car? What if they find the books? The tapes?

My own fate – I had already made peace with it. I'd had a sentence before. If they found the materials in my car, I would be looking at ten, maybe 20 years. Or they might not even bother with a trial.

But it wasn't myself I feared for.

It was her.

I didn't know what they were doing to Fariba. Whether they were questioning her gently, or shouting. Whether they believed her, or whether they already saw her as guilty by association.

I sat there like that for over an hour. The waiting was torture. The not knowing.

Then, finally, after what felt like an eternity, the door creaked open.

The door creaked open, and two men entered the room. Their clerical robes couldn't soften the hardness in their eyes.

They didn't waste time.

"We know everything," one of them said, his tone flat, almost bored. "We know who you are, where you've been. And we know what's in your car."

My mouth went dry. My hands clenched in my lap.

Then the hammer fell:

"Her brother – Fariba's second brother – he told us. Gave us everything."

I blinked. "What?"

They exchanged glances, then one of them continued. "He said you spent two years in prison. That you've been involved with political groups. He told us about your activities. In exchange for his sister's release."

I couldn't speak. My heart thudded in my throat, not from fear this time, but from something colder. Something deeper. Betrayal.

He knew what this meant for me. He knew. And still he chose to speak – for his sister's sake, or maybe to rid himself and his family of me once and for all. Perhaps both. He had always despised me – my background, my politics, my relationship with Fariba.

And now, he had likely signed my death sentence.

The Pasdars confirmed it: they had searched the car. They had found everything – books, leaflets, tapes. Evidence, more than enough.

"You're done," one of them said. "Finished."

And for a moment, I believed it.

But then the other Pasdar added, reluctantly, "You're very lucky. Because Fariba refuses to leave this station without you."

My breath caught. The floor seemed to tilt under me.

I learned later what had happened: during the hours they kept us apart, Fariba's oldest brother had arrived. She had told him, calmly and fiercely, that she would rather die – commit suicide – than walk out of that building while I was still inside.

"She said she would throw herself off the balcony," one of them told me, almost annoyed.

It shook them. Not because they cared – but because they didn't want the scandal.

Her brother – wealthy, connected, with ties to powerful clerics – saw how serious she was. He made himself vanish from the station and began working behind the scenes. He called in favours. He reached out to one of the most well-known mullahs in the region, someone respected and feared. A message was sent to the guards: "Let them go. Quietly."

But it wasn't that simple.

By now, too many people knew. Other branches of the security apparatus had heard about us. Different offices, different names, rivalries and whispers. They couldn't just erase it.

So they gave us a way out – a performance to justify their decision.

They brought me back into the room.

"You are going to be released," one of them said. "But not because we are fools."

He looked me dead in the eye.

"You have 48 hours. Go home. Bring your family. And get married. We want the certificate. Legal proof. Otherwise, you're finished. We'll keep the car. And we know where you live."

I looked at them, barely able to speak. I thought of Fariba on the other side of that wall. I thought of our whispered conversations in the upstairs room, dreaming of a future we didn't think we'd survive to see.

And now, here it was.

"Yes," I said. "I accept."

They spent the next half hour writing papers, having me sign every line. They took my shenasnameh – my identification card – as collateral. They said I'd get it back when I returned with proof of marriage. Only then.

CHAPTER XXVI

THE PAPER CAGE

A nd then – just like that – they opened the door. I was free.

I stepped outside into the dusk light, my legs trembling, my breath still shallow. But I didn't stop. I didn't wait. I headed straight for the bus station, my bag slung over one shoulder. I bought the next available ticket to Tehran. From there, I caught a bus to Shiraz. And then – finally – to Sarvestan.

The entire journey blurred past me in a haze of nerves and disbelief.

But my purpose was clear.

I had already spoken to my mother and Juliana before. I had told them about Fariba, about our decision, and what we had endured. Now I was asking more. I needed them to come with me, to stand beside me, and help us make it real. To help me marry the woman I loved – not in some romantic ceremony, but in defiance, in survival, in commitment carved out of the jaws of a system that wanted to crush us both.

I was tired. But I was alive.

And I was about to fight – not just for my cause – but for us.

When I arrived in Sarvestan, it was late. The bus wheezed to a stop like an old man sighing, and I stepped off with a body that felt held together only by nerves. I hadn't slept properly in days. My thoughts kept spiralling: What if Fariba changes her mind? What if her family blocks it? What if the guards go back on their word?

But as soon as I walked through our front door, my mother looked at me and said, "Tell me what you need."

That was all.

She didn't ask why everything had to happen so quickly. She didn't ask about the politics, the danger, the risks. She had lost a husband because of this life. And now her son stood before her, bruised by another close call, asking her to follow him again into uncertainty.

She only asked: what do you need?

Juliana helped pack. She folded a clean shirt for me, handed it over like a quiet blessing. "You'd better mean this," she said. "She's been through enough."

"I do," I said, with more conviction than I'd had in a long time.

Two days later, we were on the road – my mother, Juliana, and I – on a bus bound for Amol. We travelled through the night, the mountains looming like sleeping giants outside the window, the air thick with the scent of pine and diesel. None of us spoke much. Every mile felt like a countdown.

When we reached Amol, we didn't go to Fariba's house. I called from a nearby shop. She answered on the first ring.

"They're waiting," she said.

Her voice sounded calm, but I knew what that meant – tense negotiations behind the scenes, her brothers pacing, her mother in tears or silence, and her standing firm.

We arrived at the registry office later that afternoon.

Fariba was already there, wearing a simple beige scarf, her face calm but unreadable. Her oldest brother stood beside her, speaking with one of the Notary, papers in hand. Her second brother – the one who had betrayed me – wasn't there.

The two families barely greeted each other. My mother extended her hand politely. It was accepted, but without warmth. No words of blessing, no smiles. Just bureaucracy and silence.

It wasn't a wedding. It was a transaction, a ceasefire, a compromise pulled from the teeth of something darker.

We signed the documents in silence. No ceremony. No flowers. Just ink and paper and stolen time.

When it was done, the registrar said, "Congratulations." It sounded mechanical.

They gave us the certificate.

Fariba and I looked at each other. No kiss. No embrace. Just the knowledge that we had done something nearly impossible. We had survived another turn of the knife.

I handed the certificate to her oldest brother, who gave it to a courier. By that evening, it would be in the hands of the Pasdars.

They released my car the next day. Returned my identification card, still folded and stained with ink from their files. One of the Pasdars even nodded at me – not with approval, but with weary resignation. As if to say: You slipped through. This time.

Fariba and I spent that night sitting on the rooftop of her building. We didn't talk about what had just happened. We talked about small things – the sound of the wind, the mountains in the distance, a bird that landed near the water tank and hopped around like it owned the world.

That's what I remember most: not the fear, not the anger, not even the bitter tension between our families.

Just her beside me, her head leaning gently against my shoulder, both of us staring out at a future that still felt wildly uncertain – but, for the first time in a long while, ours.

* * *

A MARRIAGE IN THE SHADOW OF WATCHERS

Marriage didn't bring peace. It brought paperwork.

We were now legal in the eyes of the Islamic Republic – on paper. But we were never free. Not really. A marriage certificate didn't erase what I had done, what they had found in my car, what Fariba's family knew but dared not speak aloud.

They didn't kill me. But they watched me.

I felt it the moment we returned to daily life. The silence around us had teeth. There were faces I used to greet in the street who now crossed to the other side. The baker who once gave me an extra flatbread now looked straight through me. Neighbours who used to ask about my mother now closed their doors a little faster when I passed.

We lived in a small rented apartment in Sarvestan away from both families. It was supposed to be temporary – a quiet space, modest, tucked near the river where the reeds grew tall and the air felt just slightly freer. But even there, we felt them.

They never said they were watching. They didn't need to.

Once, I came home to find the edge of my bookshelf slightly off-centre – by less than an inch. Another time, Fariba swore her university notes had been touched. She had left them perfectly stacked. Now they leaned slightly, as if someone had skimmed the pages and put them back too quickly.

There were knocks at odd hours. A man asking if we had an extra room. A woman pretending to be looking for someone named "Hassan". The phone rang sometimes, and no one spoke on the other end. Just breathing.

And always, always, the quiet tension between us and her family.

Her second brother never forgave her for standing by me. He never said it openly, but the venom was in his absence, in the way his name stopped being mentioned at gatherings. Her mother visited once. She stayed exactly 15 minutes and left without touching the tea I had prepared.

Fariba pretended it didn't hurt.

But beneath all of that – beneath the surveillance, the distance, the stifled tension – there was something stronger.

Every night, when the curtains were drawn and the lights dimmed, we whispered to each other like children hiding from monsters. We told stories. We read poetry by candlelight – Forough, Shamlou, even banned translations of Neruda passed hand to hand. We made love with the desperation of people who didn't know how long they had.

Sometimes, I would look at her while she slept – her scarf long forgotten, hair sprawled across the pillow – and wonder how it was possible that two people could still find a pocket of tenderness in a world this cruel.

We kept up appearances. We smiled for those we had to. I got small tutoring jobs under a different name. Fariba studied like her life depended on it – maybe it did. She was determined to finish her exams, to reclaim the education they had stolen from her.

But all the while, I was counting shadows.

Once, a friend warned me in passing: "They won't arrest you again. Not yet. But they'll make sure you never breathe easy."

And that was exactly what it felt like.

Our marriage became a kind of resistance. Not just against the system, but against the fear it planted inside us. Every day we stayed together, laughed, planned, dreamed – we were defying what they wanted us to become: bitter, broken, alone.

I had to take Fariba away – from my family, from that suffocating environment. We moved to Shiraz and rented a small house. It was quiet. Too quiet. We were alone.

No one visited us. Not my mother. Not her family. Only her sister came once, despite her brothers' disapproval. That was the only gesture of warmth in a time when we desperately needed it.

THE DAYS WE LET OURSELVES PRETEND

Then, one morning, everything changed. Fariba woke up feeling unwell. She was nauseous, and soon she was vomiting. After a pause, pale and trembling, she looked at me and said she thought she might be pregnant.

I can still remember the shock that turned, almost instantly, into something else – something like joy. The thought of becoming a father lit something inside me. In that moment, despite the chaos of our lives, I was filled with hope. The dream of having a child, my own child, felt miraculous.

But of course, the joy came tangled in fear. It was the worst possible time – and somehow, also the best. We had no money, no security, no support system. We barely knew how to take care of ourselves, let alone a baby. And yet I couldn't help but dream. I pictured bringing up my child in a better world.

That child became my secret reason to hope, and also my reason to run. I couldn't imagine raising them in that place – under watchful eyes, under fear, where everything had to be hidden or pretended. I wanted a new country. A free place. Somewhere we could speak our minds without fear. Read what we wanted. Live without lying.

More than anything, I wanted my child to grow up in a world where they wouldn't have to unlearn how to be themselves.

Fariba's pregnancy changed everything. Suddenly, every decision had a weight it hadn't carried before. Even the smallest things – what we ate, how much rest she got, how much noise the neighbours made – felt like matters of life and death. I was both terrified and grateful. She was creating life in a place that felt lifeless.

The early months were hard. We had very little money, and I took whatever jobs I could find. Some days I translated letters, other days I moved furniture or helped in backrooms of small shops. I'd come home late, sore and exhausted, and find her lying on the worn-out mattress, one hand resting on her belly, her face lit up with a soft, unfamiliar peace. She would tell me how the baby had moved, or how she had dreamt of holding them in her arms. We didn't know if it would be a boy or a girl, but we already loved them. It was love we didn't have to hide.

But the loneliness persisted. Her family had effectively disowned her. Mine had long since gone silent. We were a family of two – and soon three – in exile, not across borders, but within our own country. We were ghosts to those who once claimed to care.

As Fariba's belly grew, so did the tension in the city. Shiraz had become a place of whispered fears and silent stares. I remember walking past a bookstore one day and seeing a pile of books being burned in the back alley. Someone must have reported them. I stood there for a few moments, watching the flames eat the pages. I thought of my unborn child and wondered what kind of world they'd enter. Would they have to live in fear for what they read, for what they said, for who they became?

It haunted me. I knew I had to leave. Not just for myself anymore – but for this new life, this fragile heartbeat growing inside Fariba. I couldn't raise a child in a place where truth could cost you your future. Where one wrong word could end everything.

So I began to plan. Quietly. Carefully. Every extra rial I earned went into a hidden envelope. I started asking questions in hushed tones. How to get a passport. Who might help. Where the safest route out was – if there even was one.

Fariba didn't always agree. Some nights, we argued. She was scared. She had just found a rhythm to her life again, a sense of home. But I couldn't shake the urgency. I would lie awake beside her, listening to the steady rhythm of her breathing and the wind scratching at our windows, and I'd picture the future. Not the ideal one – just one with air to breathe and the freedom to raise our child without shame or fear.

The baby gave us purpose. The baby made the risk feel worth it.

I didn't know then that hope, too, could be dangerous.

I thought I had time.

The plan was still in pieces – half-whispers, half-dreams. I hadn't told Fariba everything yet. I didn't want to scare her. I kept telling myself: just a little more time, a little more money, a little more clarity. Then we'll go. Then we'll be safe.

But life doesn't wait for plans.

One night, I came home late – dust on my clothes, my back aching from unloading crates in a storeroom. Fariba was sitting at the edge of the bed, pale, her eyes wide and unfocused. There was blood. Not much, but enough to send fear slicing through me.

We rushed to the hospital. The doctor was kind, but brisk – overworked, underpaid, and wary of giving false hope. He ordered her to bedrest immediately. "Too much stress," he said. "She must not be upset."

But how could I protect her from stress? From fear? From the walls closing in around us?

Every night, I sat beside her, holding her hand, speaking softly to her belly, trying to soothe two souls at once. I told her stories of the future – of parks and laughter, of books without censorship, of our child's first steps in a country where they could say their name aloud without shame.

She smiled, sometimes. But I could see how tired she was.
And then, it happened.

Just as I was getting close to finalizing our escape route
– through a friend of a friend in Bandar Abbas – there was
a knock at the door. Three sharp raps. Then silence.

I didn't open it right away. I moved quietly to the
window, pulled the curtain back just enough to see. Two
men in dark coats stood in the street. I didn't recognize
them. One held a folder in his hand.

I didn't wait to find out more. I told Fariba to get dressed,
quickly but calmly. We slipped out the back door and into
the alley, heart pounding, breath caught in our throats. We
walked fast, but not too fast. Always with our eyes down,
our steps measured.

That night, we didn't go back to the house.

We stayed with a distant cousin of mine, someone I
hadn't seen in years but who owed me a favour. It was a
single room, damp and cold, but it was shelter. It was safety
– for now.

I knew then: there was no more time. We had to leave.
Whatever risks lay ahead, whatever unknowns, they were
better than the slow suffocation we were living in.

Fariba cried that night – not out of fear, but something
deeper. A sadness for everything we were leaving
behind. Her sister. Her city. Her quiet dreams of giving
birth at home.

We held each other in the dark, surrounded by someone
else's worn-out furniture, and made the decision together.
No more waiting. No more pretending.

We would leave.

Everyone advised us to wait.

"Stay at least until the baby is born," they said.

"It's too dangerous to travel now."

And they were right. Fariba was nearly eight months pregnant. The journey we'd dreamed of – leaving it all behind – would have to wait.

We found a small house to rent in a quiet village outside Shiraz. It wasn't much, but it was safer. Hidden. Removed from watchful eyes. But Fariba was not well. The last month of her pregnancy, her body weakened. She was constantly sick – nausea, fatigue, the kind of quiet suffering that eats at you slowly. Food made her gag. Even sleep gave no relief.

I was terrified for her. And still, I had to leave her each morning to travel to Sarvestan for work – returning only at night, worn and worried. Friday was the only day I could stay with her fully, and on those days I did everything I could – cooking, cleaning, holding her through the waves of illness, speaking to our unborn child like they could hear me already.

WAITING FOR
SOMETHING TO BEGIN

Then, one morning, just as I was about to leave the house, she called out. Her voice was sharp, urgent – different. Her waters had broken. Time stopped.

I rushed her into the car and drove like a madman to the hospital in Shiraz. She was groaning in pain, clutching her belly, her face pale and shining with sweat. It all felt unreal. Two, maybe three hours later, it happened. A cry. A piercing, beautiful sound that tore through the sterile silence of the delivery room.

A little girl.

Our daughter.

Before she was born, we had chosen a name – Nina. It was from a book Fariba had once read in secret, a name that echoed something free, something gentle. But names were not simple things in that country. We couldn't register her with that name – it wasn't allowed. It wasn't Islamic enough. Not the name of a prophet or a martyr. So we found a small village office, far from the scrutiny of city officials, where the clerks were less rigid. We registered her there, quietly, and told almost no one.

We called her Nina only at home, only in hushed tones. In public, we avoided using her name. Even joy had to be whispered.

In the hospital, we were alone. No one came – not my mother, not Fariba's family. Only one of my aunts showed up to help for a few days, and I will always be grateful for that. Nina had a complication – some issue with oxygen at birth – and they kept her under observation for three days. Those days dragged on endlessly. My aunt stayed with us. But the silence from everyone else... it stung. A deep, familiar ache.

After a week, Fariba's sister finally visited. She stayed two days, then left. No phone call. No warmth. Just a gap where support should have been.

And still, I wanted to try. Maybe with a child in our arms, hearts would soften. I decided to take Fariba and Nina – just one week old – to see my mother in Sarvestan.

But it didn't go how I hoped. My mother greeted us coldly. She looked at Nina with a kind of distant curiosity, not joy. There was no warmth in her eyes. No congratulations.

Still bitter. Still silent. I didn't know if she blamed me, or Fariba, or simply couldn't accept how we had done things.

We stayed only two days. It was enough.

When we returned to our house, I sat quietly for a long time, watching Nina sleep on Fariba's chest. Her tiny fingers curled around the edge of a blanket. So fragile. So unaware of the world she'd been born into.

And I knew – I knew – this was not the place I wanted to raise her.

I was still in contact with the network, though less involved. Time was short. My focus had shifted. But now and again – two hours here, a few hours there – I still met with trusted comrades. Helped print leaflets. Folded them. Distributed them under cover of night.

The fight was still inside me. But now I had something more than ideology. I had a daughter. And I could no longer pretend that staying wouldn't cost her more than it cost me.

Those days with Nina were unlike anything I had ever known.

Our house was small – bare walls, second-hand furniture, the smell of dust never quite leaving the corners – but it pulsed with life. With her. That tiny girl, wrapped in mismatched blankets, filled the space with a presence far bigger than her fragile frame.

Fariba was exhausted, her body still recovering, her spirit bruised from all the loneliness and silence that surrounded her during the birth. But when she held Nina, something softened in her. She would sit by the window in the afternoons, Nina asleep on her shoulder, sunlight casting a golden glow over them both. In those moments, she looked like someone who had almost healed.

Almost.

We lived cautiously. Always looking over our shoulders. We kept the radio low and the curtains drawn. We didn't speak Nina's name out loud unless we were alone. I hated that. A child should never be born into secrecy. But that was the world we were in.

Our routine was fragile but precious. I'd rise early to prepare tea, sometimes boiling eggs if we had them. Fariba would nurse Nina, and I'd quietly watch them from the doorway, feeling something I didn't have a name for – something close to awe, mixed with helplessness. She would hum lullabies, half-remembered songs from her own childhood, while rocking Nina in her arms.

Sometimes, at night, I would lie awake beside them, watching their shadows on the wall. My girls. Mine to protect, and yet I felt powerless. The weight of our isolation crushed me in those quiet hours. I wanted to give them everything – freedom, joy, a future – but all I had were words, and even those had to be whispered.

On Fridays, when I didn't have to work, I cooked for them. I tried to make it feel like a home. I'd boil rice, stew lentils, slice onions so thin they were almost transparent. Fariba would smile faintly, tired but grateful. We'd eat quietly, often with Nina nestled in a shawl across her chest.

Occasionally, Fariba laughed. Not loudly – just small bursts of joy that escaped when Nina did something unexpected. A hiccup. A wide-eyed stare. Once, she peed while I was changing her, and Fariba laughed so hard she had to sit down. I laughed too. And for a moment, it felt like we were just a normal family. No fear. No secrets. Just parents, trying their best.

But the world never let us forget. Outside our windows, the air grew thicker by the day. There were more checkpoints on the road to Shiraz. Rumours spread of informants even in the villages. Leaflets I helped produce were being found in the wrong hands. I stopped staying long at meetings. Just in and out. No traces.

Fariba knew I was still involved, though I never gave her details. She didn't stop me. She just asked that I come home safe. Every time I closed the door behind me, I could feel her fear following me like a shadow.

Nina was growing fast. Her eyes began to focus. Her fingers reached out. Her cries turned from sharp gasps to full-throated demands. She was alive, truly alive, and it gave me both courage and dread. I didn't want her first memories to be of hushed voices and closed doors. I wanted her first steps to be on free ground.

One night, I stood by the window, holding her against my chest. The village was quiet, moonlight on the rooftops, only the soft rustle of wind in the trees. I whispered to her:

"We're going to leave, little one. I don't know how, or when, but I promise you – we will not stay here."

Her breath was warm against my neck. She made a tiny sigh and drifted off to sleep.

That was the night I stopped doubting myself. I began to prepare – not just in thought, but in action.

We didn't have time. We never really did.

But I was ready to risk everything.

For her.

Once I made the decision, everything took on a different weight.

Every purchase, every trip to the city, every whispered conversation felt loaded with meaning. The window of opportunity was small. We didn't know when it would close. Or how violently.

CHAPTER XXVII

NO ONE WAS SAFE ANYMORE

B y 1987, the war was a ghost that haunted every corner of Iran – visible in the ruins, in the empty chairs at family dinners, in the silence that followed every siren. But for many of us, it was no longer just the war outside that threatened to break us. It was the war within: the war against hope, against freedom, against the life we once dreamed of.

That year, I decided to leave.

It wasn't a sudden choice. It was a slow unravelling – a quiet, relentless tug at my heart, pulling me away from everything I had ever known.

The regime had tightened its grip like a noose. Friends disappeared overnight. Words became weapons. The streets were full of whispers, eyes turned away, hearts clenched tight. The universities I had once walked through with hope were now prisons of fear and silence. The schools had become machines to produce obedience. There was no future here, not the kind I wanted.

But leaving Iran was not simply walking out the door. It was a thousand small betrayals – selling possessions quietly, saying goodbye without crying, hiding your fears from your family. It was a secret prayer whispered on a packed bus to the airport: Please let me pass.

I remember the night before I left – my mother sat in the kitchen, tears streaming silently down her face, hands shaking as she folded a scarf she had embroidered for me. She didn't say goodbye. She couldn't. Instead, she pressed the scarf into my hands and looked away, as if by not seeing me leave, she could keep me safe.

Crossing the border was surreal. I felt like a ghost slipping between worlds – still Iranian, but not quite belonging anymore. The language, the smells, the way people moved – it was all both familiar and painfully distant.

I began reaching out, carefully, to contacts I trusted – men I had met through the underground, names passed between hands like contraband. One of them knew a smuggler who could get us out through the sea near Bandar Abbas. It would be long, dangerous, and expensive. And it would mean carrying an infant through cold and unfamiliar terrain. But it was a way.

I didn't tell Fariba everything right away. I didn't want to panic her. I started small: "We need to get Nina a warmer blanket. Start gathering only what we truly need."

She didn't ask why at first. Maybe she knew.

One evening, when Nina had finally fallen asleep after hours of fussing, I sat down across from her on the floor. She was folding one of Nina's undershirts, her hands moving slowly, deliberately. I told her we were leaving.

Not someday. Soon.

She didn't speak for a long time. Just kept folding. Then she said softly, "I had a dream last night. We were in a park. There were lights in the trees. Nina was running."

She looked up at me. "She wasn't hiding."

That was all. She didn't argue. She didn't cry. Just nodded and kept folding.

Every step of the preparation was like walking a tightrope between two cliffs – terror on one side, hope on the other.

The last visit I made was to say goodbye to my mother.

I didn't tell her we were leaving. I simply put Nina in her arms one final time, hoping that some part of her would feel what I felt. She looked down at her and said nothing. No blessing. No warmth. Just silence.

Maybe that made it easier.

We returned home in the dark. I held Nina the entire walk from the bus stop. Her small head pressed into my shoulder, her breathing light and rhythmic. Fariba walked beside me, arms crossed over her chest. Not from cold. From everything she carried inside her.

* * *

WALKING INTO THE DARK

Nina was just over a year old when we finally made the decision. No more waiting. No more weighing the risks. It was time to go – for her sake more than ours.

The smuggler said he would come and meet us in Dubai in three days. A truck. Covered. We were to meet it outside the village, by the old fig grove. He would take us part of the way, then hand us over to someone else for the next leg of the journey.

No promises. No guarantees. Just a possibility. That's all we had.

The night before, we barely slept. We lay side by side, Nina between us. Her tiny fingers reached out in her sleep and brushed my arm. I closed my eyes and memorized that moment. Just in case.

I whispered again, like I had done before:

"We're going to get you out. No matter what."

And this time, it wasn't just a wish. It was a promise.

The journey took three days, each step heavier than the last. We travelled in silence, through back roads and checkpoints, shifting between cars, trucks, even walking part of the way under the cover of night. Nina clung to Fariba's chest, wrapped tightly in a cloth sling. She didn't cry much – perhaps she could feel the urgency around her. Perhaps she had already learned to be quiet.

We had to leave behind nearly everything: no photos, no keepsakes. Just a bag for each of us. Nappies. Water. Dry bread. A flask of tea and Nina's cloths.

I had sold my car before leaving. I sold what little else we owned – my father's few remaining belongings, the last of what was passed down to me. Every rial counted. All of it went to the smuggler. He was the brother of a man I had met in prison years before, someone I had once trusted with my life. That trust now extended to his family. I didn't have a choice.

The plan was simple on paper: from Bandar Abbas, we would cross by boat into Dubai. Once there, the smuggler's contacts would take care of fake documents – passports, visas, tickets. Identities.

In reality, it was anything but simple.

We arrived in Bandar Abbas, the edge of the sea. The border before Dubai. The air was thick with salt and heat. Even the breeze felt like it was hiding something.

We arrived in Dubai at night, the boat creaking under us as we slipped across the water, unseen. I held Nina the entire time, her body warm and silent against mine. Fariba's hand didn't leave my arm for a second. We didn't speak. We didn't breathe. Not fully. Not until we stepped onto foreign soil.

In Dubai, they told us to wait – just three days. Enough time, they said, to arrange everything. We were taken to a small apartment on the edge of the city, windows covered, no names spoken. There were others there too – silent people with hollow eyes. All waiting for the same thing: escape.

It was there I met a young man named Ali. He had a long beard and the solemn face of someone much older. At first glance, I panicked. He looked like one of the regime's enforcers. One of the pious men who could ruin us with a single phone call. I pulled Fariba close. Kept Nina behind me.

But the man who had guided us from the coast leaned in and whispered, "Don't worry. He's one of us. You can trust him."

Later, Ali told us the truth. He was only 19. The beard was a disguise. His passport said he was 49, and he had grown that beard to match. He smiled when he told us, and for the first time in days, I felt something almost like relief. We weren't alone in this madness.

By the third day, they said everything was ready.

Fake names. Forged passports. Tourist visas. It was all just paper and ink – but it meant a second chance at life. The last night before our flight, we sat down to eat together. It was a simple meal – flatbread, tea, dates, and something resembling stew. We barely touched it. Our stomachs were too full of fear.

At the airport, every step felt like a lifetime.

We handed over our documents at the counter. Smiled like tourists. Tried to appear calm with a sleepy child in our arms and forged identities in our hands. The border officer looked at our passports for a long time. Too long. My heartbeat echoed in my throat. Fariba's grip on Nina tightened.

But then – stamp.

He nodded. Waved us through.

Only later we found out the truth: the policeman had been paid off. Bought by our smuggler. That's why he didn't ask questions. That's why we got through.

We walked towards the boarding gate like we were underwater. Weightless. Disbelieving. We sat in our seats on the plane and dared not look at each other until the wheels lifted off the ground.

And only then, when the land we had fled shrank beneath us, did we start to breathe again.

Not because we were safe yet.

But because – for the first time – we could imagine that one day, maybe, we would be.

We didn't even know where we were going until we got to Dubai. That's how desperate we were. That's how much we trusted strangers more than our own homeland.

The man who arranged everything met us on the second day. He looked at me, Fariba, and little Nina in my arms. Then he said quietly, "The only place I can send you now is Sweden."

Sweden. I didn't know much about it – only that it was far, cold, and somewhere people didn't disappear for speaking their mind. I had no idea what life would look like there. But I said yes. I would've said yes to the moon if it meant Nina could grow up safe.

The flight was quiet. We sat together, Fariba exhausted, Nina half-asleep on her chest. A flight attendant came over and smiled at us. "Do you need anything?" she asked in English, her eyes warm, not suspicious. She gave us extra juice for Nina. A blanket. Kindness. Real kindness – unexpected and unfamiliar.

Nina, our little angel, was the reason we were still standing. She gave us purpose when everything else had crumbled. Even the flight attendants seemed to soften when they saw her. It was like she carried a light with her.

IN A NEW COUNTRY

We landed in Paris.

Our connection to Sweden was just a few hours away. We thought we'd sit, wait, and board like anyone else. But France and Iran had friction at that time. Tensions were high. Even passengers in transit were being checked.

Then it happened.

A uniformed officer came up to us and asked for our passports. He didn't smile.

I handed him everything, trying not to show my fear. He flipped through the pages slowly, then looked at us again. "Please come with me."

He said it politely – but it wasn't a request.

They took us to a waiting room. It was small and cold, with metal chairs and fluorescent lights that buzzed faintly overhead. We sat there for over an hour, Nina asleep across our laps, our hearts pounding with every passing minute. We didn't speak. We couldn't.

And then they came back.

"Follow us," they said.

We were led outside, into the back of a van. No explanation. Just the quiet hum of the engine and the sound of my own thoughts racing:

If they send us back to Dubai, they'll deport us to Iran. And if we go back to Iran...

Dubai didn't want trouble. The Iran-Iraq War was still raging. The Gulf states were anxious, sensitive, watching every move. We were pawns in a game we didn't understand.

They took our passports. All of them. Without a word.

And then, the van stopped.

We were brought to a building – white, plain, quiet. Not a prison. But not a hotel either. A holding place for asylum seekers. There were guards at the entrance. One stood beside the door, arms crossed, eyes on everyone.

We were told we would stay for a day or two. For "investigation", they said. But no one told us what they were looking for. Or what they would decide.

We couldn't leave. We weren't free. The door stayed locked unless someone in uniform opened it. We didn't even have our names anymore – just strangers in a system that didn't know what to do with us.

Fariba was silent that first night. She held Nina and looked out the window, though there was nothing to see. Just another building. Another country we didn't belong to. I tried to tell her we were close. That Sweden was still waiting for us. But the words felt small.

That night, I lay awake on a hard mattress, holding Nina between us, listening to the soft click of the guard's boots in the hallway.

We had come so far. We had left everything. And now, it all hung in the balance – again.

They called us one by one, like suspects.

In a grey, windowless room at Charles de Gaulle airport, they sat us down separately. No warmth. No eye contact. Just questions.

"Where are you coming from?"

"Why are you here?"

"What are you running from?"

I told them we were from Iran. I told them we were political asylum seekers. I explained everything – how we had fled, why we couldn't go back, how we had only passed through Dubai. But they weren't interested in our truth. They were looking for excuses. And we had given them one: transit through Dubai. That was enough.

They had orders not to accept any new Iranian asylum seekers that day. I later learned it was about diplomacy – France didn't want more friction with the Islamic Republic. We were collateral damage in their politics.

I pleaded with them. I told them what would happen if we were sent back. I even lifted my shirt and showed them the scars on my stomach, the lines left by interrogators who didn't need a reason. I told them we had a child. That Fariba had suffered enough. That Nina didn't even know what safety meant.

They didn't care. Their faces didn't move. They wouldn't listen.

They didn't say what their final decision was. They simply gave us rooms for the night – one for me, Fariba, and Nina. Another for Ali. They kept us apart. They wouldn't allow us to speak.

CHAPTER XXVIII

A NEW PRISON

That night was the coldest night of my life.
Not because of the temperature – but because of what I knew was coming.

We couldn't sleep. Fariba stared at the ceiling. I held Nina in my arms, watching her chest rise and fall, trying to memorize her peaceful face before it all changed again. I didn't know if we'd be sent to prison, deported, separated. I just knew we were still in someone else's hands.

In the morning, two police officers arrived. Wordless. They gestured for us to follow. No smiles. No explanation.

They led us down a hallway, out the back of the building, into a waiting van. The same type of van that once took me to prison back home. I sat in the back seat, Fariba beside me, Nina on her lap. No one spoke. I looked at the road. I saw where we were headed even before it came into view.

The airport. Again.

And I knew.

They had denied our asylum. They were sending us back to Dubai.

I remember that moment clearly – how the pain didn't come with shouting, but with a quiet, helpless surrender. I thought: What difference is there between these uniforms and the ones we escaped from? We are still being escorted. Still under guard. Still under threat.

At the airport, we were led straight through security, straight past the lines of passengers. People stared at us like we were criminals. What did they see? A man, a woman, a baby... escorted by police. Maybe they thought we were smugglers. Maybe worse. I'll never know. But I could feel their judgment pressing into my skin.

Our passports were handed to the pilot – confiscated like contraband. We tried to resist. Fariba begged. I spoke louder, but they pushed us forward. Firm hands. Blank faces.

We were the first passengers to board the plane.

We sat down in silence, holding Nina tightly between us. We didn't know what was waiting for us on the other end. Dubai didn't tolerate uncertainty. Dubai deported people like us.

Then something unexpected happened.

The flight attendants came towards us. Not with suspicion, but with kindness. They looked at Nina, then at us, and their eyes softened. They knew. Maybe not all the details, but enough. Enough to understand that we were not criminals.

One of them knelt beside us and said gently, "Don't worry. We will try to help you. Please let us know if you need anything."

Then they brought food, drinks, a blanket. One gave Nina a soft toy from the galley, something small and colourful. Just something to hold.

For the first time in days, someone treated us like human beings.

We didn't know what would happen when we landed. We didn't know if we'd be held again, interrogated, deported further. But in that moment, thirty thousand feet in the air, we were given something precious:

Dignity.

Nina – our little saviour – had softened the eyes of strangers once again.

And it was her presence, her silent strength, that kept us believing we might still find a way.

The other passengers began to board. I sat still, Nina asleep against Fariba's chest, her breath warm and steady. My heart, on the other hand, was racing.

And yet – for some reason – I had this strange feeling as they passed by. It was in their glances, their soft expressions. Maybe they knew. Maybe the flight crew had said something. Maybe they could tell from our posture, from the presence of the guards earlier, from the weariness on our faces. I didn't know. But I felt seen. Not judged. Not pitied. Just known.

Then the pilot came down the aisle.

He stopped next to us, smiled gently, and took the empty seat beside mine. His presence alone was disarming – so different from every authority figure we had faced in weeks. His name was John.

"I just wanted to introduce myself," he said, his voice low and warm. "I heard about your situation. Let's get in the air first, and then we'll see how I can help."

I was stunned. No official had spoken to us like this. No one had offered help – only rules, silence, or threats.

He explained that our flight would stop in Saudi Arabia before continuing to Dubai. Then he asked me quietly, "What do you want to do?"

I didn't hesitate. "I don't want to go back to Dubai," I said. "They will send us back to Iran. I don't mind staying in Saudi Arabia if they can accept our asylum."

John nodded thoughtfully. "Leave it to me," he said. "I'll ask. From the air. I'll see what I can do."

Then, without any ceremony, he reached out and held my hand. "Whatever happens," he said, "be sure of this – I'll try to help you."

I felt something shift in me. After everything we had been through – the fear, the rejection, the shame – this gesture broke through. A simple human connection, from one stranger to another.

We took off.

About two hours into the flight, one of the crew – a kind, soft-spoken woman – approached me and said, "Please come with me."

I looked at Fariba, and she nodded slightly. I followed the flight attendant down the narrow aisle. To my surprise, she opened the cockpit door – something I never expected. It was against all rules, but somehow, in that suspended world between borders, she made space for me.

Inside, John greeted me again. "Wait here," he said. Then he stepped out with me to a quiet area near the lavatories. We sat on the small bench, away from the passengers, and spoke in hushed tones.

"I've asked Saudi Arabia," he said. "I told them about your case. But unfortunately... because of the war between Iran and Iraq, and tensions in the region, they've denied the request. They won't take more Iranian asylum seekers. Not now."

The words were like stones. I nodded, trying to keep calm.

"We'll land in Dubai," he continued, "but let's see what happens. You said you know someone there?"

I nodded. "Yes. A friend. He helped us before we left. He's still there."

"Good," John said. "That might help. Let me do the talking if I need to. We'll try to figure something out."

There wasn't much else to say. He placed a hand on my shoulder, gave a small smile, and told me to return to my seat.

Back with Fariba and Nina, I told her what had happened. She didn't speak, just pressed Nina closer and leaned her head against my shoulder.

We were in the sky, again suspended between decisions made in distant offices – still without a country, still not safe.

But there, at 30,000 feet, in that narrow seat on a crowded plane, I didn't feel entirely alone anymore.

There was still a stranger out there – John – who saw us not as a problem to be solved, but as a family worth helping.

BACK IN DUBAI

We landed in Dubai.

The flight crew had never stopped showing us kindness. They brought us food, juice, blankets – anything we needed. One of the stewardesses even took Nina in her arms for 15, maybe 20 minutes, so Fariba could close her eyes. I sat beside them and watched our daughter sleep in someone else's arms, safe for a moment. A moment that felt borrowed.

When the plane came to a full stop, the pilot – John – asked me to come forward again.

I followed him towards the front of the aircraft, heart pounding.

He looked me in the eye and said, "Stay here. Don't move. You're still on French soil as long as you're in this aircraft."

I nodded, speechless.

"I'm going to tell them you're refusing to disembark," he said, "and I won't force you off this plane."

One by one, the other passengers began to leave. By now, they all knew something was happening. They slowed as they passed us. Some offered kind words. Most said nothing, but many made eye contact – gentle, supportive, as if to say good luck. And several of them actually did say it: "Good luck."

As the cabin emptied, John called the airport from the cockpit. I watched him speaking calmly but firmly.

He told them we refused to leave the plane.

They replied that the airport was expecting us, that we couldn't stay onboard. That we had no legal right to remain.

John stood his ground.

"They are not criminals," he said. "They don't want to go back. I'm not putting them off this aircraft unless they agree to go."

Moments later, three men arrived from airport immigration. They weren't in uniform – plain clothes, clean shirts, no badges. Two of them came up the stairs and entered the aircraft.

They tried to reason with John. "Everyone knows they have no choice. They can't stay here. This isn't France."

But John didn't move. "I will not force them," he said.

Then he turned to me.

"Do you want to leave the plane?"

I looked at him and said what I had said before: "No."

They made another call – this time to the immigration department directly. Five minutes passed. The air in the plane felt heavy, as if the walls themselves were waiting for a decision.

Eventually, the officials came back and said, "You have to follow us. We'll try to help."

I didn't trust them. Not even a little.

They already had our passports. We were technically already in their hands. "Help" had become a word with too many meanings.

That's when John asked me, "Do you have a friend here? Someone who can help?"

"Yes," I said. "Akbar. He helped us before. He knows the situation."

"Give me his number."

I did.

He called right there, from the cockpit.

"Akbar? This is John, the pilot of the flight from Paris. I'm here with Hussain, Fariba, and Ali. They are still on my plane. Immigration wants to remove them. I need to know – can you guarantee their safety? Can you help them?"

Akbar answered calmly. "I'm at the airport. We're all aware of the situation. Even a reporter is here. People know. They're watching. Nothing will happen to them. I promise."

"Are you sure?" John asked again. "Because I won't leave them unless I believe that."

"I'm sure," Akbar said.

John turned back to me. "It's up to you now. You can stay, or you can go. I'll support you either way."

I looked at Fariba. At Nina, who was waking now, her little eyes blinking at the light.

And I said quietly, "We'll go. We don't want to put you in trouble. We have no choice."

He nodded and gently embraced me. One of the stewardesses brought us a bag of food and drinks. Others hugged Fariba and kissed Nina's hand. We were refugees – but in that moment, we were also just people. People someone had cared about.

* * *

NOWHERE IS SAFE

Outside, the heat hit us like a wall. It was summertime in Dubai, and we were wearing shorts. Our luggage was still missing – probably kept in France or lost in transit.

We were led into the terminal, not through the usual exit, but through a side passage. No crowds. No noise. Just another small waiting area.

They asked us to sit.

This time, there were no bars, but the door was watched. We were asked if we wanted food again. We said no.

We were tired. Uncertain. Stripped of our names, our documents, and our rights.

But we were still together.

And we still refused to go back to Iran.

I looked at Fariba. I looked at Ali. We were all exhausted, cold, and slowly breaking down. The air conditioning in that waiting area was like winter. We had no proper clothes. Our luggage had disappeared. No one offered it back. No fresh clothes, no blankets. Just fluorescent lights and concrete floors.

And still, they said nothing about our future.

"We should start a hunger strike," I said quietly. "Maybe that's the only way they'll listen."

So we did. We refused food and water – everything except a little milk and juice for Nina. She was just over a year old, still innocent to the horror we were living through. I watched her sleep curled against Fariba's side, her skin pale from the cold. That was the only exception we allowed ourselves. We would protect her, no matter what happened to us.

We got sick. Sneezing, coughing. Fariba was shaking. Ali sat silently with a scarf over his mouth. Eventually, they brought us thin blankets – only after we asked again and again.

We spent that first night curled on hard seats, trying to keep Nina warm. None of us slept.

The next day, three men from immigration came. They tried to speak gently, but the words were blunt.

"There is no other way," they said. "You have to go back to Iran."

We looked at them, hollow from hunger and rage.

"I would rather die," I told them, "than go back to that regime. We would rather kill ourselves."

They left without answering.

That afternoon, someone came for me. Told me I had a phone call. I followed him to a small side room and picked up the receiver.

It was Akbar.

His voice was low. Hesitant.

"I'm sorry," he said. "I can't help anymore. Even the head of immigration is involved now. The pressure is too much. The situation is too tense."

I couldn't believe what I was hearing. The man who had looked me in the eye on the phone with the pilot, who had promised we'd be safe – was now walking away.

If he had told me the truth earlier, I would never have left that plane.

I gave the phone back and walked in silence to where Fariba and Nina were waiting. I didn't have the courage to tell her what had just happened. Not yet. So I lied.

"They tried to help," I said. "They're still trying."

But I knew what was coming.

The third day, they tried to force us again. We refused. This time, we didn't do it quietly.

We screamed. Fariba cried out. I shouted in Farsi and broken English, yelling for help to anyone who could hear us. The guards froze. Around us, crowds of travellers began to gather, watching. Hundreds of them. People from all over the world, just trying to catch their flights – suddenly witnessing three desperate refugees refusing to be dragged onto a plane.

I shouted:

"They're sending us back to Iran! They're forcing us to die!"

One of the officials came over and hissed, "Be quiet, please. Not now. Be quiet."

But it was too late. The scene had unfolded in front of too many witnesses. There were even journalists in the terminal – watching. Writing.

We didn't eat for five days.

No food. No water, except for Nina.

I don't know how we survived it. I don't remember much of those final hours – only the pain in my stomach, the burning in my throat, and the growing fear that this was it. That this fight would end not in escape, but in silence. That they would simply wait for us to collapse.

And then – on the fifth morning – something changed. A new man came. Dressed differently. Calmer.

He called me aside.

"We've arranged something," he said. "We have a visa for you. You'll be going to Sweden."

I didn't believe him. I thought it was another trick, another way to corner us. I looked at him, eyes narrow, and said, "I don't believe you."

He swore. Then he pulled out a document. "Here is your visa. Here are your passports. We'll escort you to the gate. You're flying to Stockholm."

I was stunned. My legs gave out slightly. My hands started shaking. I was crying before I even realized it. I hugged him. I kissed his cheeks. I wept, not from weakness, but from release.

I ran back to Fariba.

"They gave us visas!" I said. "We're going to Sweden!"

She stared at me, trying to process it, then burst into tears. Nina, as if sensing something, began to clap her hands and smile.

Ali was speechless. For the first time in days, we were not shouting, not begging, not refusing. We were just laughing. Crying. Human again.

They escorted us to the gate. There was no more hostility – only quiet relief, even from the officials. They handed us food, drinks, even a few small items for Nina. They said goodbye, and no one tried to stop us.

We boarded the plane to Stockholm with nothing but the clothes on our backs and our daughter in our arms.

And this time, we weren't afraid of the sky.

This time, the sky meant something different.

It meant freedom.

The plane took off, and we held our passports tightly, almost afraid to believe it was real.

We were flying to Sweden. To safety.

Fariba clutched Nina against her chest, and I sat beside them, staring out of the window, my heart bursting with something I hadn't felt in so long – relief. Joy. A cautious kind of hope. We were still afraid, but for the first time, we were afraid of the unknown – not of what we already knew too well.

The flight took about five or six hours. We landed at Arlanda Airport, just outside Stockholm. The sky outside the windows was pale and wide. It didn't feel like we had arrived in a country – it felt like we had arrived on another planet. Quiet. Clean. Calm.

We stepped off the plane. And then, we made our final move.

* * *

HOPE FOR SAFETY

Before the police check, we found a bench near the toilet and sat down. Pretending. Waiting. Acting like we were just tired travellers. But we weren't.

We had already destroyed our passports on the plane – ripped them into pieces and flushed them down the toilet. We couldn't risk being sent back to Dubai. If they didn't know where we came from, they had no legal basis to deport us. It was a desperate act, but we were done taking chances.

After what felt like hours – though it was probably less – two policemen approached us. They looked curious, not hostile.

"Where are you coming from?" one asked. "Where are you going?"

I took a deep breath and said, "We are political asylum seekers. We are from Iran. We are in danger. We want to stay."

They looked at us carefully. Then nodded.

They didn't ask more right away. Instead, they called for backup – two more officers arrived shortly after. All of them were kind. Calm. Professional. No aggression. No threats.

They guided us gently to a private room. Offered us something to drink. Juice for Nina. Tea. A moment to sit and breathe.

About 20 minutes later – it felt like days – another officer came in. He asked for our story.

I told him everything – briefly at first. The arrests. The beatings. The underground work. The escape. I showed him the scars on my body. I didn't even need to go into deep detail. After just ten minutes, he said quietly, "That's enough. We believe you."

They called in Fariba. She told her side, holding Nina on her lap. She didn't cry. She just told the truth.

Ali too was questioned – and thanks to us, he was accepted as well. We were all linked now. Our fates had become one.

Later that day, they took us to a temporary accommodation – something like a small hotel. Just a bed. A door that locked. And no one chasing us.

We slept like we hadn't slept in months.

The next day, a car came and took us back to the airport, but this time to the immigration office. There, we had longer interviews. One by one. But it no longer felt like interrogation – it felt like people actually wanted to understand.

And once again, they believed us.

After that, we were transferred to a refugee camp.

They gave us a room in a shared apartment, food, and even a bit of money – just enough to buy a few groceries and necessities. We were surrounded by others – refugees from everywhere, but mostly Iran. It was a strange feeling. We were free, but still cautious. Still unsure. I wanted to trust these new faces, but part of me remained alert. In our world, not everyone who smiled could be trusted.

A week later, they announced we would be transferred to a small town in the north of Sweden.

It was summer. The weather was beautiful – light-filled days that never seemed to end. They put us on a bus with about 30 others, mostly families like ours. Ali came too.

After hours of travel, we arrived.

The town was small. A former mining town, now almost empty. Maybe two hundred people lived there. A few shops. A library. A swimming pool. Quiet streets and wide open space. It didn't feel like a place built for survival – it felt like a place built for healing.

They gave us a flat on the second floor. It was basic but clean. They gave us vouchers to buy food. Enough to live. Enough to breathe.

And for the first time in so long – we didn't feel hunted.

We were tired. Deeply tired. But we were happy. Really happy.

We were in a country that listened. That cared. That didn't ask us to hide who we were.

It wasn't paradise. But it was freedom.

And freedom was enough.

* * *

HOME, LOSING HOME

In exile, everything changed.

You think leaving will free you. It doesn't. It frees you from the prisons you see, but it traps you in new ones: loneliness, memory, and a fierce longing for a home that no longer exists – or worse, one that is changing too fast for you to recognise.

Letters came less and less often. News from Iran was filtered through whispers and shadows. Every phone call was a mixture of relief and fear: relief that your family was alive, fear that next time, the news wouldn't be the same.

I found myself caught between worlds – the life I had fled, and the uncertain life that awaited me. The culture shock was brutal. The freedom I longed for felt heavy and unfamiliar. I was both grateful and deeply sad.

Sometimes, I would sit in a café and listen to the language spoken around me, searching for the rhythm of Persian in foreign words. Sometimes, I would close my eyes and remember the dusty streets of Tehran, the smell of fresh bread in the morning, the quiet prayers before dawn.

Exile taught me that home is not just a place. It is a memory, a feeling, a wound that never fully heals.

And yet, in that painful space between loss and hope, I found a new strength – a stubborn refusal to forget who I was, and where I came from.

Because leaving Iran was not the end of my story. It was the beginning of another.

CHAPTER XXIX

ÉMIGRÉ

The first days in the small Swedish town felt like walking on clouds that hadn't quite solidified. We were safe – but not yet steady. Everything was unfamiliar. The silence. The clean air. The way people nodded politely and moved on. The absence of fear was disorienting.

We didn't know the language. We didn't know the customs. We didn't even know how to operate the stove in the small kitchen of the apartment they gave us. But there was something peaceful about that kind of ignorance. For the first time, not knowing didn't mean danger. It meant learning. It meant starting over.

The apartment was modest – second floor, two small bedrooms, a tiny balcony where Nina liked to stand and point at the trees. The mornings were crisp, even in summer. Birds were louder than cars. There were only a couple of shops, a library, and a swimming pool. No tension. No checkpoints. Just a quiet little town trying to keep living after its mines had closed.

The other refugees there were mostly Iranian. Some had stories like ours – others had spent years hiding or had lost family. But still, I found it hard to trust them fully. Old instincts die slowly. You learn not to speak too freely, not to share too much. You remember that betrayal often comes with a smile. I kept my past close to my chest.

Ali was with us. He had become part of our family in a way I hadn't expected. We had been through too much together to ever go back to being just acquaintances. In the quiet of our new home, we'd talk late into the night. Not about politics – just about what we missed, what we hoped for, what freedom might one day feel like when it wasn't so new and sharp.

Nina was the quickest to adapt. She was too young to remember fear. She played with pinecones in the park. She learned to say hej to the Swedish neighbours before any of us did. Her laughter filled the apartment and reminded us what all this struggle had been for.

The Swedish officials gave us small allowances – enough to shop for groceries, soap, some clothes. Fariba and I would walk to the store together, quietly pointing to labels we couldn't read, guessing what was milk, what was yogurt, what was bread. It became a routine. And a joy. To walk without looking over your shoulder. To be a couple, a family, just choosing apples.

Every week or so, they held orientation meetings. Translators helped. They explained how the asylum process worked. How long it might take. How to register for language classes. What rights we had. What rules.

And each time they spoke, I kept waiting for the "but". I kept expecting someone to say, "But you have to leave," or "But we've changed our minds". But the words never came.

They let us be.

We stayed in that town for several months. We began taking Swedish lessons. Slowly, awkwardly, I started learning how to speak again – not just the language, but how to speak without fear. It took time. The words came slower than they once did, but they came with less cost.

I started writing again too – letters, journal entries, even sketches of the events we'd lived through. I didn't know what I was writing it for. Maybe for myself. Maybe for Nina, when she grew up. Maybe for the parts of me I'd left behind along the way.

Sometimes I would walk to the library. There weren't many books in Farsi, but just being around the quiet, the shelves, the idea of knowledge without punishment – it was healing. I started to imagine a future that wasn't built on running.

We didn't know what would come next. We didn't know how long we would stay. But we knew this much:

We were alive. We were together. We were free.

And for now, that was everything.

Once we had a roof over our heads and the fear of deportation behind us, I knew I had no time to waste. Freedom was not a gift – it was a responsibility.

I began spending entire days at the local library. I asked the librarian for anything that could help me learn Swedish – books, audio cassettes, grammar guides, children's stories. I sat in the reading room with headphones on, repeating words out loud, over and over, filling notebooks with new vocabulary. I studied for ten hours a day, like it was a job. A mission. And slowly, the language began to take root in my mouth.

Life in the north was limited but peaceful. We began to know people – other refugees, some Swedes, a few kind neighbours who offered help or conversation. We even organized demonstrations in that little town, modest protests against the regime we had fled. Once, we travelled all the way to Stockholm to protest in front of the Iranian embassy. I held signs. I shouted. I gave speeches. I was interviewed twice by local newspapers. My name and face were printed, my voice carried.

We were settling in – but we were not settling down.

The longer we stayed, the clearer it became that we couldn't build a full life up north. There were no universities, few jobs, and the cold was relentless. Six months of sunlight, then six months of night. When we had first arrived in midsummer, the light never left. It was surreal, almost dreamlike. We couldn't sleep. Fariba would try to darken the windows, but the brightness still crept in.

Then winter came, and the light vanished.

Some days it dropped to minus 40 degrees. The darkness settled into our bones. It was beautiful in its own way – silent forests, snow like crushed glass – but it was not made for long-term living.

We requested a transffer to the south. Through friends, I was introduced to a man connected to a church group in Nyköping, a town about 80 kilometres south of Stockholm. They offered to help us relocate.

One week later, we moved.

Ali chose a different path – he went to Gothenburg. We hugged, promised to stay in touch. And we did. Over the years, we kept in contact, through all the changes in his life – two marriages, two divorces, and a permanent life in Sweden. A long story of his own.

In Nyköping, I enrolled in college. I studied Swedish formally, and began the difficult process of validating my education from Iran. Many of my subjects – physics, maths – were not recognized. I had to redo them, all in Swedish. It felt like learning to walk again with weights on your legs.

I worked nights in an elderly care home. Some days I worked in a nursery. I refused to live off social assistance. I wanted to earn, to contribute, to pay taxes. To rebuild myself from the ground up.

Fariba also started working, slowly. We placed Nina in nursery. She was adapting fast, her Swedish far better than ours within months. Children don't carry the same fear. They learn with joy.

After two years in Nyköping, I was accepted to university in Stockholm to study dentistry. It felt like the future was finally opening its door to me. Fariba began training to become a nurse. We packed our things and moved again, this time to the capital.

But even as our lives progressed outwards – studies, jobs, routines – something inside our marriage had begun to unravel.

Fariba's mental health had begun to decline. The weight of everything – the exile, the losses, the loneliness – caught up with her. Slowly, quietly, she began to sink. She lost her mother and then her two older brothers in Iran. Each death was a new silence between us. I didn't know how to help. I didn't even know how to reach her.

She was grieving. I was working constantly. We were both tired. Both trying to build something out of ashes. And slowly, without ever meaning to, we began to lose each other.

Our arguments became more frequent. Less about big things, more about everything and nothing. The distance grew. We were still in the same house, but we felt like strangers sometimes. As if the version of ourselves that had fled Iran – the young, desperate, hopeful couple clinging to a child and a dream – had stayed back there somewhere, and what remained were two people who no longer recognized the reflection.

We had come to Sweden to find a future.

But we had also come carrying pain. And that pain, no matter how quietly packed, finds its way to the surface.

Our relationship didn't end with a fight. It ended the way winter fades into spring – slowly, subtly, so gradually that by the time you realize the snow has melted, you're already standing in another season.

Fariba and I had survived war, betrayal, exile, and escape. We had shared nights on hard airport benches, whispered over a sleeping Nina in fear and determination. We had walked through fire together.

But freedom, I learned, brings its own kind of pressure.

In Iran, we were too busy surviving to see how far apart we were growing. In Sweden, with space to breathe, we began to realize we were not the same people we had once been.

She was grieving – deeply. She had lost her mother, then her two older brothers, one after the other. The grief didn't come with screaming or wailing. It came with silence. With long hours staring out of the window. With a certain absence in her eyes that I didn't know how to reach.

And I was busy – working at night, studying during the day, pushing my way through the Swedish education system, determined to succeed. Determined to give Nina the life I never had. But in that drive, I began to vanish from Fariba's world.

We stopped talking – not entirely, but meaningfully. Conversations became logistics: who would pick up Nina, what time the shift started, who would cook. The intimacy faded. The connection that once bound us so tightly – shared purpose, shared fear – began to dissolve.

Sometimes we argued. Sometimes we just sat in silence, pretending things were fine because neither of us had the energy to tear down what little we had built. I could see she was unhappy. I could feel the space between us widening like a fault line.

And I began to understand something quietly devastating: just because two people survive something together doesn't mean they're meant to build the rest of their lives in the same shape.

We had loved each other. We had leaned on each other through the darkest hours of our lives. But now we needed different things. She needed healing I couldn't offer. I needed energy she no longer had.

There were no betrayals. No shouting matches. Just two people, slipping past each other in the quiet hours between work, parenting, and trying to remember who they used to be.

We remained committed to Nina. Always. That part never changed. She was our anchor. Our miracle. Our constant reminder of what we had once risked everything to protect.

But Fariba and I had become something else – co-parents. Companions in memory. Not enemies, but no longer partners in the same way.

There was a moment – I remember it clearly. A quiet evening. We were cleaning up after dinner. Nina had already gone to bed. Fariba was stood by the sink, drying a plate, and I said, almost without thinking:

"Do you think we're still in love?"

She didn't turn around. Just stood there, towel in hand.

Then she said, "I think we used to be. I think we needed to be."

We never declared it out loud. But from that moment on, we both knew.

I had been accepted into university. Dentistry. It was a dream I had carried all the way from Iran – buried under prison memories, hunger strikes, lost friends, and the weight of starting over in a foreign land. And now, here it was.

But it didn't come easy.

Fariba had also begun studying – working towards becoming a nurse. Outwardly, it looked like we were moving forwards, building the new life we had once whispered about in hiding. But inside, we were collapsing.

Our relationship was brittle. Fragile. We had spent so long in survival mode, we didn't know how to be with each other in the quiet. I moved out for a few months – not in anger, but in confusion. I needed space to breathe, to think. We both did.

And at the same time, the pressure of university nearly crushed me.

The programme was entirely in Swedish. My Swedish was serviceable – but not fluent. I had learned it like a soldier learns the terrain, word by word, under fire. But dental school was different. Complex medical terms, dense lectures, fast-talking classmates.

I studied relentlessly. Nights, weekends. I memorized and memorized until my eyes burned and my brain rebelled.

While the younger, Swedish-born students skimmed and sailed through, I was drowning. They were confident. Casual. And much younger than me.

I carried textbooks with me to work, read anatomy charts on the bus, recited terms in front of the bathroom mirror. Every day was a battle between exhaustion and ambition.

And yet – despite everything – I had Nina.

She was my sanctuary. My rescue.

When I felt like giving up, she pulled me back. We rode bicycles through the parks together, her laughter like wind chimes behind me. I took her with me when I visited elderly homes, where I worked part-time. The residents adored her. She would toddle through the halls with her big eyes and her quiet presence, and something about her calmed everyone around her.

She followed me everywhere. She trusted me completely. And through her, I remembered what it meant to be loved without condition.

Fariba was struggling. She was still carrying the scars of everything that had happened – what her family had done, what mine hadn't done, what we had both lost. The silence between us grew heavier. We were talking more and more about separation, even divorce.

But we stayed together – for Nina. We tried to protect her from the cracks that had split us apart. We tried to pretend that the house was still whole.

But love and obligation are not the same.

And still – I pushed forward. I passed the exams. I stood in a room one day and was handed my dentistry degree. I held it in both hands and thought: this is for her – this is for Nina.

But dreams don't always lead to open doors.

In Sweden, finding work as a foreign-trained dentist was nearly impossible. Even with my degree, I was still "an immigrant". A political refugee. A name with an accent. My credentials didn't open the same doors.

* * *

It was the beginning of 1997 when Fariba told me she was pregnant again.

We hadn't planned it. Life was already difficult – uncertain finances, mounting pressures, our relationship hanging by threads we no longer knew how to repair. But sometimes life moves without permission.

She gave birth in the same hospital in Sweden where I had once studied dentistry. I still remember the moment I saw her – this new little being, impossibly small, impossibly perfect.

We named her Natalie.

She had thick dark hair, eyes that already seemed to hold a quiet knowing, and beautiful olive skin. She was like a spark in a cold room – sudden warmth in the middle of all that numbness. For a moment, she made me feel alive again.

But joy doesn't erase reality.

I still couldn't find work as a dentist in Sweden. My degree, though earned through blood, sweat, and sleepless nights, meant little without the right "background". I had no connections. No local name. And so, I made the decision: I would leave. Again.

This time, I would take Nina with me and move to the UK. The plan was for Fariba and Natalie to follow later.

Nina and I arrived in England and rented a small house – bare, modest, but ours. She was in Year 4 when we left Sweden, but because of her age, she had to enter Year 7 in the UK – a big jump. I worried it would be too much. But she managed. She always managed. I hired private tutors to help with English and maths. I watched her grow in resilience, just like I had seen her do so many times before.

After a few months, Fariba and Natalie joined us in England. We were a family again – but something in us had shifted too far to find its way back.

I began working as a dentist in a tough neighbourhood – Plumstead, southeast London. Some patients were rough, the hours long. I had no choice. I worked day and night. I handled emergencies, ran from one phone call to another, opened the clinic late at night, drove 20 minutes out and 20 back. Weekends were no different.

But I managed to buy the clinic – a long story, full of risks and stubborn belief. It became mine. My first real business. I had something to stand on.

But what I was building professionally came at a cost inside the home.

Fariba and I were already on fragile ground. The move to the UK didn't heal it. It magnified it. We argued constantly – resentment spilling into daily life. The silence between us turned to shouting. Often in front of the children.

There were moments when I would look at Nina or Natalie, and guilt would strike like lightning. I knew what we were doing to them. But I also knew that staying together under such tension was breaking us all.

By 2005, we separated. I moved out.

I didn't want to leave. I didn't want to hurt the children. But I had no choice. There was no peace left in the house. Fariba had changed – lost in her own confusion, disappearing for nights, talking about staying elsewhere, being somewhere else. She wasn't herself. And maybe, neither was I.

The separation wasn't peaceful. It didn't happen with calm voices and respectful understanding. We dragged pain through courtrooms and across kitchen floors. We involved the children in fights they should never have witnessed. It still haunts me.

But looking back – was it the right decision?

I believe it was. Not because it ended well, but because staying would have ended us all in other ways.

Sometimes survival isn't about staying together.

It's about knowing when to let go.

After I left, there was a silence. Not the kind I had known before – not the silence of fear, or hiding, or exile. This was the silence of a man who had finally run out of illusions.

I had imagined, at some point, that reaching safety would mean happiness. That building a career, owning a home, creating a life in a democratic country would somehow fill the holes left by everything I had lost.

But the wounds of the past follow you quietly.

The separation from Fariba was painful, not only for what it meant for the girls, but because of what it confirmed: we had made it out, but not together. After all we had endured, we couldn't endure each other. And maybe that was the most painful truth of all.

Still, life demanded movement.

I focused on my clinic. Worked hard. Tried to stay grounded. Patients came and went – some grateful, some difficult. But they kept coming. I built a small reputation, then a larger one. I learned how to run a business, to manage a staff, to speak in ways that earned trust even with my accent. Dentistry became more than a profession – it became my anchor.

But my greatest refuge was still Nina and Natalie.

They were my reason. My roots.

Nina was growing fast – curious, sensitive, bright. Despite everything she had seen, she had this unshakable calm inside her. We remained close. She trusted me. We still rode bikes when we could. We talked often – about school, about life, about things most kids her age probably didn't think about yet.

Natalie was younger, more playful, with a spark in her eyes that reminded me of the early days in Sweden. She had Fariba's stubbornness, but her own softness too. I made every effort to stay present in her life. I didn't want to be the kind of father who disappeared after a divorce.

The girls gave me a reason to stay human. When the weight of work became too much, when loneliness crept in, it was their voices, their drawings, their laughter on the weekends that pulled me back.

But I would be lying if I said it was easy.

There were dark days – nights when I came home and sat in silence, questioning everything. I missed Iran in strange ways – not the regime, not the repression – but the belonging. The familiarity. The language of my childhood. The smells of street bread and hot tea. The feeling that history was mine.

And underneath it all, there's a question none of us asks out loud: Was it worth it?

I may never see my brother again.

He lives somewhere in Shiraz, with his family. I don't know exactly where, and even if I did, I don't know if I could reach him – or if he would want me to. The years have put too much distance between us, not just in geography but in everything else too. Still, I think of him. I picture him walking down some quiet street, his shoulders older, his hair grey, than I remember of him when he was a kid. I wonder if he ever thinks of me.

I helped my sister and youngest brother come to Europe. That's something I carry with pride, even though I don't speak to my youngest brother anymore. There are reasons – too many, and too painful to unravel here – but the silence between us still hurts. Maybe it always will.

My sister lives in Sweden now, with her children. I don't know if she's happy. Sometimes I think she tries to convince me that she is, or maybe she's trying to convince herself. Maybe we all are. We don't talk about what we left behind. We talk about rent, school, work, the weather. Safe things. Things that don't hurt.

I still often look back – not to regret, but to remember. The prison cell. The protest. The hunger strike in the airport. The flight to Stockholm. The cold of northern Sweden. Nina's first words in English. Natalie's soft sleeping breath. The arguments. The court papers. The clinic. The quiet kitchen now.

There are mornings when I wake with the sound of Persian still on my tongue. I dream of Sarvestan sometimes – of its dry wind, the smell of sun-warmed earth, the cracked stone alleys I once ran through as a child. I see my father's hands, weathered from labour. I see Juliana's laughter, half-covered in shadow. I hear the distant call to prayer from the mosque, echoing not as religion but as a sound that stitched the day together.

But I remember the fear too.

The knock on the door. The scream in the night. The endless silences around dinner tables. The betrayal by those who smiled to your face. The feeling of your name being dangerous in someone else's mouth.

* * *

For a long time, I didn't believe peace was possible – not really.

I thought maybe some people were just meant to survive, not to be happy. That after everything I had seen and lost, contentment was something reserved for others.

But peace doesn't always arrive loudly. Sometimes it comes in quiet mornings, in long walks, in the way time softens the edges of old wounds. Sometimes it comes not as a single moment – but as a slow return to yourself.

I met someone – unexpectedly, gently. She wasn't from my past, and maybe that's why it worked. There were no old wounds between us, no shared traumas to relive. We met as two adults – two people shaped by very different lives, but both looking for quiet, for truth, for something real.

She listened when I spoke about Iran – not with pity, but with interest. She asked about Nina and Natalie, and never once made me feel like my history was a burden. She knew I came with scars. I knew she did too.

And slowly, companionship turned into something deeper.

Not the wild, desperate love of youth – but the kind that grows in the absence of noise. The kind that feels like sitting in a room without speaking and still feeling heard.

With her, I began to laugh again – not the polite laugh you give to strangers, but the full-bodied laugh that feels like it's coming from a place you forgot existed. We cooked meals together. We travelled. We talked about books. We talked about silence.

I found peace – not in forgetting the past, but in living alongside it.

The past no longer controlled me. It shaped me, yes – but it didn't define what I could feel or who I could become.

* * *

And now, I can see Iran not only as the land that hurt me, but also the land that shaped me.

I don't know if I'll ever go back. Maybe someday. Maybe only in ashes. But I no longer carry the same fire of anger toward it. Now it's more of a gentle ache, like remembering someone you once loved who never learned how to love you back.

Here in England, I've built a different life – on different soil, in a different tongue. I've watched my daughters grow up free to speak, to learn, to love whoever they want. They don't fear the knock on the door. They don't hide books beneath their beds. That was the point of everything. That was the dream that carried me through barbed wire, rejection, hunger, and divorce.

That they could live without fear.

And they do.

So, yes – I forgive, but I do not forget. I carry Iran with me, every day. In the way I speak to my daughters. In the way I pause before I answer authority. In the way I still keep certain things quiet, even when no one is listening.

And so, I end this story – not in the place I was born, but in the place I now live.

Home, for me, is not something I can walk into anymore. It exists somewhere between memory and loss – scattered across Sarvestan's fields, the courtyards of Shiraz, the prison walls that still echo inside me. Home is a language I still dream in, a mother's embrace I may never feel again.

The thought that I may never see my mother again – never hear her voice in person, never sit beside her – is a quiet sorrow I carry daily. It's a grief without ceremony. A farewell that never came. And I've learned to live with it, as one learns to live with a limp after a deep wound. You move forward, but never quite the same.

This was the choice I made. To leave. To survive. To protect my daughters. To start again.

And I accept it.

But I still have a dream – an unrealistic dream. It is so far from reality that I've never dared to share it with anyone, because I know the path to it is blocked, unreachable. Still, it lives inside me.

It was during long walks that the dream returned to me, like a forbidden whisper from the past. I never told anyone about it, not even those I trusted most, because the dream itself was dangerous. In Iran, even imagining such things could put you under suspicion. Back then, hope itself felt like a crime.

I had carried this secret vision all my life: a world without prisons, without firing squads, without the fear of a knock on the door in the middle of the night. A world where children weren't taught to march into war, where mothers didn't bury their sons with only a photograph left behind. I knew it was impossible, but still – it lived inside me, stubborn and radiant.

When I first heard Siavash Ghomeishi's song Tasavor Kon, it was as though someone had stolen the dream from my chest and given it voice. His words were my own unspoken longing, poured into melody. He spoke of imagining a world where everyone is happy and free, irrespective of where they were born, or where they grew up. I began listening to it during my walks, pressing repeat as if repetition could make the dream last a little longer. The music carried me back to Iran, to those years when we whispered in basements, when we passed leaflets under doors, when we imagined a different future even as our friends disappeared one by one.

As I walked, the past and present folded into each other. The cold wind on my face belonged both to the winters of exile and the desert nights of Shiraz. My tears blurred the path ahead, but I pretended it was nothing, just the sting of the air. Inside, I felt both comfort and sorrow. Comfort, because the song reminded me I was not alone in this impossible dream. Sorrow, because I knew – just as I knew the taste of betrayal, just as I knew the weight of war – that such a world would never come in my lifetime.

Yet I carried it with me. This fragile, untouchable dream, born in the shadows of my youth, hidden through the long years of silence, still beating softly inside me as I walked, step after step, with Ghomeishi's voice keeping me company.

Shiraz Nomad